International Political Economy Series

Series Editor
Timothy M. Shaw
Visiting Professor
University of Massachusetts
Boston, USA

Emeritus Professor, University of London, UK

The global political economy is in flux as a series of cumulative crises impacts its organization and governance. The IPE series has tracked its development in both analysis and structure over the last three decades. It has always had a concentration on the global South. Now the South increasingly challenges the North as the centre of development, also reflected in a growing number of submissions and publications on indebted Eurozone economies in Southern Europe. An indispensable resource for scholars and researchers, the series examines a variety of capitalisms and connections by focusing on emerging economies, companies and sectors, debates and policies. It informs diverse policy communities as the established trans-Atlantic North declines and 'the rest', especially the BRICS, rise.

More information about this series at
http://www.palgrave.com/gp/series/13996

John G. Glenn

Foucault and Post-Financial Crises

Governmentality, Discipline and Resistance

palgrave
macmillan

John G. Glenn
Politics and International Relations
University of Southampton
Southampton, UK

International Political Economy Series
ISBN 978-3-030-08393-9 ISBN 978-3-319-77188-5 (eBook)
https://doi.org/10.1007/978-3-319-77188-5

This Palgrave Macmillan imprint is published by the registered company Springer Nature Switzerland AG
The registered company address is: Gewerbestrasse 11, 6330 Cham, Switzerland

Contents

List of Abbreviations

ABS	Asset-Backed Security
CDO	Collateralized Debt Obligation
CRA	Credit Rating Agency
EC	European Commission
ECB	European Central Bank
EDP	Excessive Deficit Procedure
EMSA	European Markets and Securities Agency
ESA	European Supervisory Authorities
ESM	European Stability Mechanism
ESRB	European Systemic Risk Board
EU	European Union
EWE	Early Warning Exercise
FDI	Foreign Direct Investment
FSAP	Financial Sector Assessment Program
FSB	Financial Stability Board
FSOC	Financial Stability Oversight Council
G7	Group of Seven
G8	Group of Eight
G20	Group of Twenty
GDP	Gross Domestic Product
GSIB	Global Systemically Important Banks
IFI	International Financial Institutions
IMF	International Monetary Fund

IOSCO	International Organization of Securities Commissions
IPE	International Political Economy
ISD	Integrated Surveillance Decisions
MBS	Mortgage-Backed Security
OECD	Organization for Cooperation and Development
OMC	Open Method of Coordination
PCAOB	Public Company Accounting Oversight Board
RAM	Risk Assessment Matrix
SAP	Structural Adjustment Policy
SCAP	Supervisory Capital Assessment Program
SGP	Stability and Growth Pact
SOX	Sarbanes-Oxley Act
SPV	Special Purpose Vehicle
SSM	Single Supervisory Mechanism
TARP	Troubled Assets Relief Program
VEAEE	Vulnerability Exercises for Advanced and Emerging Economies

1

Introduction

The first signs that something was seriously wrong in the world of finance began in August 2007 with the French Bank, BNP Paribas, freezing several of its funds as it acknowledged that it was unable to accurately assess the collateralized debt obligations underpinning them. Further indication that this was not just a one off problem with one bank came just a month later with Northern Rock, a British bank, which was unable to sell its securitized mortgages on the markets. The resulting bank run involving vast lines of customers trying to withdraw their money was all too reminiscent of the Great Depression (indeed, the bank was only saved from collapse by its nationalization). In the spring of 2008, the full force of the crisis hit the shores of America with the buy-out of Bear Stearns by J. P. Morgan. But worse was to come in September with the collapse of Lehmann Brothers after it became clear that no bank was willing to take it over and the Federal Reserve refused to bail it out.[1]

The ensuing crisis led to $3 trillion worth of write-downs in the banking sector and a halving in value of the Dow Jones in just 18 months. With the possibility of meltdown staring them in the face, political leaders once again embraced Keynes (*The Economist* 16–22 May 2009, p. 13). Nationalization/bail-outs of financial institutions on both sides of the

J. G. Glenn, *Foucault and Post-Financial Crises*, International Political Economy Series, https://doi.org/10.1007/978-3-319-77188-5_1

Atlantic looked like a roll call of the great and the good: Freddie Mac and Fannie Mae, Citigroup, American International Group in the US; Northern Rock, Bradford and Bingley, Royal Bank of Scotland, Lloyds Banking Group in the UK; Hypo-Real Estate in Germany; Glitmir, Landsbanki, Kaupthing in Iceland; Dexia was rescued by Belgium, France and Luxembourg; and Ireland saved its banks by guaranteeing the payment of any banks' liabilities if need be. As the effects rippled throughout the global economy, the highly industrialized countries went into recession with the majority experiencing sustained negative economic growth. Indeed, most of Europe then experienced a double dip recession with dire consequences with regard to unemployment and welfare of their populations. Greece and Spain were the hardest hit with total unemployment levels reaching 25% and youth unemployment totalling a previously inconceivable level of 50%.

At the heart of the crisis was the drive for ever-increasing profits via various financial innovations that facilitated vast increases in financial leverage. The challenge was how to increase the amount of credit available to consumers within the parameters of the regulatory framework that was supposed to limit the risk of financial collapse while at the same time ensuring a level playing field for competition within the financial world. The solution to this conundrum came in several forms, but the result was essentially the same—the displacement of risk away from the banks' balance sheets to other investors and 'off-book' accounts in special purpose vehicles (SPVs) which were all too often located offshore.

Asset-backed securities (ABSs) (and especially the sub-category mortgage-backed securities [MBS]) appeared to provide the ideal answer to the problem of having to maintain certain capital adequacy ratios by facilitating a move away from the 'originate and hold' model that pertained to loans towards an 'originate and distribute model' (Augar 2009, p. 12). Financial institutions were able to create a package of claims giving the right to 'the lender to receive regular interest and capital from their borrowers' on the open market (Arnold 1998, pp. 484–5). The future repayment of debt became a commodity in its own right, bought and sold in the open market converting '*expected cash flow*, wherever and whenever it might occur, into instant spending power' producing liquidity from what would otherwise be 'a relatively illiquid asset' (Hoogvelt

2001, p. 82; Best 2010, p. 34). Essentially, this enabled financial institutions to receive income immediately, allowing them either to lend to an even greater number of clients or to diversify and invest the money in other financial instruments.

These securities became valid commodities precisely because it was believed that by their very nature the risk-spread was such that even in the direst of economic circumstances they would remain relatively stable forms of investment. However, these claims began to be sliced up into tranches according to their risk ratings. The claims on securities were split into three tranches or notes (senior, mezzanine and junior) with a different level of risk pertaining to each note. In the case that some borrowers in a security defaulted, then the losses would be borne, in the first instance, by those holding junior notes, then mezzanine and finally, in the unlikely event (at least at that time it was deemed improbable) that an unprecedented number defaulted, the holders of senior notes would incur losses. Of course, the tranches with the highest risk also attracted the highest returns.

At the same time, the development of the credit default swap enabled actual loans and the risk of the borrower defaulting on that loan to be separated. When making a loan, financial institutions covered themselves by paying an annual fee to another company insuring itself against the risk of default, thus keeping the claim but transferring the risk associated with such credit lines. In other words, 'credit-default swaps enabled them to convert risky assets, which demand a lot of capital, into supposedly safe ones, which do not' (*The Economist* 11–17 October 2008, p. 10). Moreover, they bundled these credit default swaps together thus reducing the risk for the insurers because it was believed that the likelihood of a string of borrowers defaulting was less probable. Despite initial reticence, regulators agreed that the capital reserves for this type of loan could be reduced.[2] They thus hit upon the financial world's equivalent of El Dorado, 'releasing banks from age-old constraints and freeing up vast amounts of capital, turbocharging not only banking but the whole economy' (Tett 2009, p. 36). As one J. P. Morgan employee who attended the 1994 away day from which the widespread use of this innovation arose commented, 'I've known people who worked on the Manhattan Project—for those of us on that trip, there was the same kind of feeling of being present at the creation of something incredibly important' (Tett 2009,

p. 24 and pp. 159–60).[3] Little did he realize how accurate his description would turn out to be.

Connected to these innovations was the development of bank subsidiaries or SPVs which were often set up in offshore jurisdictions by these financial institutions (Tett 2009, p. 63). These SPVs enabled the financial institutions to offload their loans which the offshore entities would structure into 'plain vanilla' MBS, collateralized debt obligations or more complex derivatives and then sell them on to investors. The benefits of establishing this shadow banking system were obvious, it took many of the loans off the books and these subsidiaries were offshore in tax havens. Moreover, the parent bank lent money to these SPVs on a short-term basis (364 days or less). This meant that such loans would not affect the amount of capital reserves they held because the Basel Accord did not require such reserves for short-term lending (Tett 2009, p. 114).

Such activities made for a perfect storm. Although the banks were formally complying with the capital adequacy requirements of the Basle Accords, the low risk ratings of certain CDO tranches alongside the extensive use of offshore SPVs meant that in reality the banks were dangerously over-leveraged. As interest rates began to rise, so did delinquency and default rates on mortgages and loans to the extent that investors lost faith in the new financial alchemy of collateralized debt obligations, credit default swaps, CDOs squared and so on. It was also patently clear from BNP Paribas' freezing of certain funds that the complexity inherent within such financial instruments had also produced a high degree of uncertainty with regard to risk exposure. Suddenly, the market's appetite for ABSs disappeared. Banks found themselves facing the possibility of not having enough reserves to cover non-performing loans. This situation was greatly exacerbated by the fact that the offshore SPVs that the banks set up were financing much of their long-term loans through the issuance of short-term asset-backed commercial paper—but they found themselves unable to refinance their operations in the repo market as trust in ABSs dwindled. The resulting 'Great Freeze' where banks struggled to even obtain overnight lending at reasonable rates and the unwillingness to buy out collapsing banks for fear of the unknown almost led to the collapse of the financial system (Germain 2010).

What followed was a series of regulatory reforms aimed at shoring up confidence in the banking system and endeavouring to ensure that another crisis of this magnitude would not occur. Yet, even as these reforms were still being debated, another crisis hit Europe. The decline in GDP alongside burgeoning state debt (in most cases as a result of trying to jump-start economies through government spending) led to a loss in confidence in the government bonds of the sovereign periphery of Europe. As a result, the yields that these governments had to offer began to rocket and, in several cases, the risk of default was so great that the market demanded unsustainable returns. As a result, bail-outs by the European Commission, European Central Bank and IMF (the so-called Troika) became necessary. In response to this crisis, the European Union embarked upon a series of economic reforms that have led to a further intensification of neo-liberal policies with unprecedented limits imposed upon national government spending. Concomitant with this deepening of neo-liberal economic policies, a relatively new discourse emphasizing the need for citizens to become resilient subjects arose emphasizing various qualities that help individuals overcome adverse conditions such as those that we have witnessed in the post-crisis environment. As the next section explains, it is these three elements (regulatory reform, the imposition of neo-liberal policies via the European Union and the emergence of the resilient subject) that are the subject of this book.

A Foucauldian Analysis of the Aftermath of the Financial Crises

There is now a burgeoning literature on the emerging post-crises international economic landscape. Much of the literature provides a detailed analysis of the crises (Tett 2009; Augur 2009) or provides a detailed analysis of the post-financial crises reforms (Acharya et al. 2010; Porter 2014). Some take a traditional state-centric view of the process, arguing that such international agreements reflect the relative economic capabilities of the states involved, the most powerful establishing exclusive 'clubs' thus ensuring regulatory outcomes that they favour (Drezner 2007). Moreover, given the growth of emerging economies, the effectiveness of the reform process will be highly dependent on these countries reaching accord amongst themselves and the more established economic powers. From this perspective, the question of the longer-term stability of the international economic system arises as issues surrounding credit supply, interest rates, exchange rates and trade imbalances continue.[4] Others look to the domestic arena in an attempt to answer why states are at times proponents of international regulation, yet at other times seek other alternatives. David Singer, for example, examines the tendency of regulators to attempt to resolve issues through domestic legislation, arguing that their 'penchant for international standard-setting emerges only when they are unable to fulfill their domestic mandates with unilateral regulation' (Singer 2007, p. 4).[5] Layna Mosely, on the other hand, adopts a top-down approach and examines how 'domestic political institutions, as well as interests, often will lead to the failure of governments to implement global codes and standards in middle to low income countries' (2010, p. 724).[6]

Many authors raise the issue of diminishing government autonomy with the state increasingly finding itself at a 'crossroads position in a complex *network* of actors, institutions, and processes—nodes of power and authority—from the local to the global' having to 'share and coordinate more and more of its regulatory power with those other nodes' (Cerny 2010, p. 269). Others have applied previously established concepts to the post-financial crisis economic landscape, such as regulatory capture and the relative absence of a global financial public sphere (Germain 2010; Baker 2010). Specifically in finance, the last few decades have witnessed both a sharp increase in the numbers of self-regulatory bodies and an increase in the frequency of regulatory capture. This has given rise to several studies on the fusion of public/private authority and the input and output legitimacy of actual decisions concluded at the national and international level, that is, 'policy capture on the input side, and how this might skew substantive outcomes on the output side' (Underhill et al. 2010, p. 6).[7]

Specifically, with regard to Foucauldian analyses of the financial system, some have viewed the New International Financial Architecture initially established after the Asian financial crisis through the lens of Foucault's disciplinary mechanisms (Vestergaard 2009; Deuchars 2004). William

Vlcek (2017) and Anthony Amicelle (2011) have been central in bringing to our attention the increasing levels of financial surveillance as a result of the 'war on terror' and the 'war on drugs'. Others have viewed finance as 'a classic biopolitical strategy which capitalises "life" by translating contingency into risk and risk into a tradeable asset' (Dillon 2008, p. 268). Indeed, Paul Langley has applied all three modalities of power (Sovereign power, disciplinary and biopolitical) specifically to the workings of the recent Troubled Assets Relief Program (TARP) (2010).

This book adds to these works by placing the global financial crisis and the European crisis alongside the attendant reforms of the financial system within a Foucauldian theoretical framework. In so doing, it provides a contemporary analysis of the two financial crises that have recently beset the global economy. But, it does so by providing an understanding of these events within an overarching Foucauldian framework; applying his insights into governmentality, biopolitics and discipline to the reforms that have been implemented in the aftermath of these crises.

The main body of the book begins with a theoretical chapter that sets out some of the main approaches established by Foucault, namely, governmentality, biopolitics and disciplinary mechanisms and explains how these analytical frameworks will be applied to the post-crises economic landscape. The first substantive chapter (Chap. 3) takes as its starting point the economic downturn of the 1970s and compares the transformation in economic policies that occurred after that crisis to the changes that we are currently witnessing. The solution to the 1970s crisis of capitalism was a re-scaling of production to the global level alongside a shift towards financialization. But to understand how this was managed we need to employ Foucault's analysis of governmentality to the neo-liberal rationalities that emerged and the interpellative process that led to the emergence of a new mode of subjectification—the neo-liberal entrepreneurial subject.

The new competitive landscape for labour led to lower wage demands within the core industrialized countries, but this created a contradiction for capitalism as aggregate consumer demand was also weakened. The solution was a shift towards financialization and a large increase in credit availability—the so-called rise of privatized Keynesianism (Crouch 2011). Inextricably tied to these reforms were fundamental changes in governmentality giving rise to neo-liberalism. This involved an interpellative process where the very identities of the population underwent radical transformation. Enterprise and entrepreneurship became the new watchwords with the worker 'no longer construed as a social creature seeking satisfaction of his or her need for security, solidarity and welfare, but as an individual actively seeking to shape and manage his or her own life in order to maximize its returns in terms of success and achievement' (Miller and Rose 1990, p. 9). A palpable shift occurred away from the self-disciplines of prudence and thrift towards 'new moral and calculative self-disciplines of responsibly and entrepreneurially meeting, managing, and manipulating the outstanding obligations that arise from extended borrowing' (Langley 2008, p. 186).

Chapter 4 of the book speaks to recent debates on the rise of the resilient subject and whether this truly represents a shift away from neo-liberalism. Some have argued that we are entering a post-modern phase after the financial crisis in which the limits of knowledge and agency are more fully appreciated (Chandler 2014). It is argued that the new emphasis on resilience reflects the radical uncertainty that confronts us in both the natural and social worlds. Others have argued that the rise of the resilient subject is simply a new phase in the ongoing project of neo-liberalism (Joseph 2013). The chapter concludes that the sedimentation of resilience thinking has much to do with its resonance with neo-liberalism and indeed reflects the uncertainty induced by neo-liberal economic policies.

The next chapter of the book (Chap. 5) examines the continuing policy of minimal intervention by the state in the financial sphere. After the crisis of the 1970s, states adopted a policy of minimal regulation with regard to finance, but this should not be taken to imply complete absence of governance, rather governance became more concerned with ensuring that financial behaviour was delimited within certain parameters. What has emerged over decades, therefore, is a regulatory (modulatory) form of regulation which seeks to modulate financial behaviour within certain given risk parameters that are supposed to prevent financial meltdowns while allowing the freest possible movement for financial institutions (Foucault 2007, p. 93). Moreover, this regulatory mechanism relies on the self-correcting mechanisms of the market with credit rating agencies and auditors providing market-based incentives for financial entities to act within an acceptable set of risk parameters.

In so doing, it treats risk analysis as a core constitutive element of the financial system. From this perspective, risk is viewed as 'a way—or rather, a set of different ways—of ordering reality, of rendering it into a calculable form' (Dean 1999, p. 131). Yet, as the recent financial crisis has demonstrated, the multitude of micro-calculations of risk associated with the vast array of financial activities that occurs today produces a macro-risk at the level of the system itself. The task of governance is therefore to balance the ostensible benefits of finance (efficient intermediation) with the security and smooth operation of the economy itself. This chapter therefore analyses the reformed security *dispositif* that operates at the heart of financial governance.

The book argues that despite the dangers to the security of populations, fundamental reforms have failed to take place in the financial sphere. Instead, the market-led regulatory and self-corrective mechanisms have been reinforced. This has involved the tightening of risk parameters, but also an attempt to improve the performance of credit rating agencies and auditors that serve as critical nodal points in what is supposed to be a homeostatic system. However, a stronger emphasis on pre-emptive surveillance has emerged—which may partly compensate for the lack of radical reforms in other areas. Although some of these surveillance practices were in place before the crisis, the intensity of such practices and degree of coordination between various supervisory bodies since the crisis is such that we can speak of the emergence of a pan-optic pre-emptive regime.

In the sovereign periphery of Europe, the second leg of the dual financial crisis brought with it a reconfiguration of relations between sovereign European states and the Troika (the IMF, World Bank and the European Central Bank). Chapter 6 argues that the post-financial crisis Eurozone is experiencing a transformation away from the more consensual and indirect methods of inculcating neo-liberal norms towards a regime based on surveillance, discipline and punishment. In other words, since the financial crisis, the more consensual subjectification process involving self-identification with the European Union and its economic regime has moved to the background. At the same time, the process of 'othering' through scientific classification and dividing practices (financially delinquent indebted states versus the rectitude of financially prudent states) has come to the fore, identifying certain countries as profligate and in need of reform—a process that requires discipline and punishment to ensure compliance with neo-liberal practices. The chapter therefore examines the mechanisms employed and the attempts to limit the sovereign economic autonomy of European member states.

The book concludes by arguing that a more fruitful avenue is to examine the current period in terms of power and resistance, rather than resilience (although one must be resilient in order to survive crises and resist). It is abundantly clear that those who have suffered most from the crises are those least responsible for creating this state of affairs. Resilience thinking tends to mask the fact that the economic system works overwhelmingly for the few and it also diverts attention away from an analysis of who is most responsible for our current plight. It also ignores the structurally inscribed biases within institutions that favour certain dominant social forces over others. However, we can see hope in the resistance to both the activities of financiers by the occupy movement and the resistance to various austerity policies in the sovereign periphery of Europe. The book contends that we should thus shift our focus towards resistance and the overcoming of both the dominance of certain classes within society and the institutions that tend to support the maintenance of this domination.

Notes

1. For an excellent summary, refer to Kingsley (2012).
2. For example, in August 1996 the Federal Reserve agreed that financial institutions could reduce their capital reserves with regard to this type of loan. Refer to Tett (2009, p. 57).
3. Although the Bankers Trust was the actual initial source of this innovation.
4. For the implications of the changing monetary landscape, refer to Cohen (1998). On the decline of the US and the significance for the international organization of credit, refer to Germain (1997). For earlier work on the differential power approach, refer to Gilpin (2000, 2001).

5. Singer also examines the plurality of regulatory agencies in the US arguing that this decreases the likelihood of assertive action on the international stage (Singer 2010, pp. 93–106).
6. See also her joint work with Singer which examines the influence of large financial firms on the domestic process in Mosely and Singer (2009).
7. See also, Porter (2005) and Porter and Ronit (2006). With regard to possible policies to address these issues, refer to Pagliari (June 2012) and Helleiner et al. (2010).

References

Acharya, V., T. Cooley, M. Richardson, and I. Walter, eds. 2010. *Regulating Wall Street: the Dodd-Frank Act and the New Architecture of Global Finance.* Hoboken: Wiley.

Amicelle, A. 2011. Towards a "New" Political Anatomy of Financial Surveillance. *Security Dialogue* 42 (2): 161–178.

Arnold, G. 1998. *Corporate Financial Management.* Harlow: Prentice Hall.

Augar, P. 2009. *Chasing Alpha: How Reckless Growth and Unchecked Ambition Ruined the City's Golden Decade*. London: Bodley Head.

Baker, A. 2010. Restraining Regulatory Capture? Anglo-America, Crisis Politics and Trajectories of Change in Global Financial Governance. *International Affairs* 86 (3): 647–663.

Best, J. 2010. The Limits of Financial Risk Management: Or What We Didn't Learn from the Asian Crisis. *New Political Economy* 15 (1): 29–49.

Cerny, P. 2010. *Rethinking World Politics: A Theory of Transnational Neopluralism.* New York: Oxford University Press.

Chandler, D. 2014. *Resilience: The Governance of Complexity*. London: Routledge.

Cohen, B. 1998. *The Geography of Money*. Ithaca: Cornell University Press.

Crouch, C. 2011. *The Strange Non-Death of Neo-Liberalism.* Cambridge: Polity Press.

Dean, M. 1999. Risk, Calculable and Incalculable. In *Risk and Sociocultural Theory: New Directions and Perspectives*, ed. D. Lupton, 131–59. Cambridge: Cambridge University Press.

Deuchars, R. 2004. *The International Political Economy of Risk: Rationalism, Calculation and Power*. Aldershot: Ashgate.

Dillon, M. 2008. Biopolitics of Security in the 21rst Century: An Introduction. *Review of International Studies* 34 (2): 265–292.

Drezner, D. 2007. *All Politics Is Global: Explaining International Regulatory Regimes*. Princeton: Princeton University Press.

Foucault, M. 2007. *Security, Territory, Population: Lectures at the College de France 1977–78*. Basingstoke: Palgrave Macmillan.

Germain, R. 1997. *The International Organization of Credit*. Cambridge: Cambridge University Press.

———. 2010. *Global Politics and Financial Governance*. Basingstoke: Palgrave Macmillan.

Gilpin, R. 2000. *The Challenge of Global Capitalism: The World Economy in the 21st Century*. Princeton: Princeton University Press.

———. 2001. *Global Political Economy: Understanding the International Economic Order*. Princeton: Princeton University Press.

Helleiner, E., S. Pagliari, and H. Zimmermann, eds. 2010. *Global Finance in Crisis: The Politics of International Regulatory Change*. London: Routledge.

Hoogvelt, A. 2001. *Globalization and the Postcolonial World*. 2nd ed. Basingstoke: Palgrave.

Joseph, J. 2013. Resilience as Embedded Neoliberalism: A Governmentality Approach. *Resilience: International Policies, Practices and Discourses* 1 (1): 38–52.

Kingsley, P. 2012. Financial Crisis: Timeline: The Financial Crisis, Five Years On: How the World Economy Plunged into Recession. *The Guardian*, August 7. http://www.theguardian.com/business/2012/aug/07/credit-crunch-boom-bust-timeline

Langley, P. 2008. *The Everyday Life of Global Finance: Saving and Borrowing in Anglo-America*. Oxford: Oxford University Press.

———. 2010. Liquidity Lost*: Sovereignty, Security and the Subprime Mortgage Crisis*. Stockholm: ECPR Standing Group on International Relations. http://stockholm.sgir.eu/uploads/Liquidity%20Lost%20SGIR%20Version%20Langley.pdf

Miller, P., and N. Rose. 1990. Governing Economic Life. *Economy and Society* 19 (1): 1–31.

Mosely, L. 2010. Regulating Globally, Implementing Locally: The Financial Codes and Standards Effort. *Review of International Political Economy* 17 (4): 724–761.

Mosely, L., and D. Singer. 2009. The Global Financial Crisis: Lessons and Opportunities for International Political Economy. *International Interactions: Empirical and Theoretical Research in International Relations* 35 (4): 420–429.

Pagliari, S., ed. 2012. *The Making of Good Financial Regulation Towards a Policy Response to Regulatory Capture*, June. http://www.icffr.org/assets/pdfs/June-2012/ICFR-Regulatory-Capture-Book-25-June---The-Making-.aspx

Porter, T. 2005. *Globalization and Finance*. Cambridge: Polity Press.

———. 2014. *Transnational Financial Regulation After the Global Financial Crisis*. New York: Routledge.

Porter, T., and K. Ronit. 2006. Self-Regulation as Policy Process: The Multiple and Criss-Crossing Stages of Private Rule-Making. *Policy Sciences* 39: 41–72.

Singer, D. 2007. *Regulating Capital: Setting Standards for the International Financial System*. Ithaca, Cornell University Press.

———. 2010. Uncertain Leadership: The US Regulatory Response to the Global Financial Crisis. In *Global Finance in Crisis: The Politics of International Regulatory Change*, ed. Eric Helleiner, Stefano Pagliari, and Hubert Zimmermann, 93–106. London: Routledge.

Underhill, G., J. Blom, and D. Mügge. 2010. *Global Financial Integration Thirty Years On: From Reform to Crisis*. New York: Cambridge University Press.

Tett, G. 2009. *Fool's Gold: How Unrestrained Greed Corrupted a Dream, Shattered Global Markets and Unleashed a Catastrophe*. London: Little Brown.

The Economist. 2008. Taming the Beast: How Far Should Finance Be Re-Regulated? *The Economist: A Special Report on the World Economy*, October 11–17, p. 10.

———. 2009. Three Trillion Dollars Later, May 16–22, p. 73.

Vestergaard, J. 2009. *Discipline in the Global Economy?: International Finance and the End of Liberalism New Political Economy*. New York: Routledge.

Vlcek, W. 2007. Surveillance to Combat Terrorist Financing in Europe: Whose Liberty, Whose Security? *European Security* 16 (1): 99–119.

2

Governmentality, Biopolitics and Disciplinary Mechanisms

Introduction

This chapter sets out the theoretical framework that will inform the substantive chapters that follow. In so doing, the chapter examines three key aspects of Foucault's later works: governmentality, biopolitics and disciplinary mechanisms. Although biopolitics and disciplinary mechanisms (as well as sovereign power) were, of course, studied in their own right, it is possible to understand these concepts under the wider umbrella of governmentality.

The chapter argues that Foucault's concept of governmentality should not be elided with a statist understanding of government. Rather, it has a far broader meaning and is concerned with both the government of others and government of oneself. As such, it examines regimes of practices, that is, institutionalized practices involving 'routinized and ritualized' ways of doing things and this includes the way in which these institutional practices 'can be thought, made into objects of knowledge, and made subject to problematizations' (Dean 2010, p. 31). Analysis of such regimes of practices therefore involves the way in which problems are enframed—

J. G. Glenn, *Foucault and Post-Financial Crises*, International Political Economy Series, https://doi.org/10.1007/978-3-319-77188-5_2

ways of thinking about issues and a subjectification process involving the formation of identities and inculcation of values which can involve discipline and punishment at one end of the spectrum and non-coercive recommendation, encouragement and felicitation at the other end.

The chapter concludes with the key focus for the rest of the book—explaining how we can further our understanding of international political economy (IPE) by using a Foucauldian analytics of government to political, social and economic transformations in prevailing neo-liberal regimes of practice that tend to emerge during and after major historical moments/conjunctures. The recent global financial crisis and the European crisis that followed is one such historical moment. During such periods, a questioning of rationalities of government and associated subjectivities tend to occur whereby sedimented practices are re-examined, questioned, reformed and possibly replaced (Dean 2010, p. 38). The rest of the book therefore investigates the degree to which these crises have challenged or altered the dominant rationalities and subjectivities associated with neo-liberalism.

In addition, the chapter also argues that it is not simply enough to examine the 'how' questions that Foucault so ably presents, but to also ask why. What causes/series of events led to a particular historical conjuncture? (Marsden 1999, p. 135). An analytics of government examining how we are governed and how we govern ourselves and how such regimes of practices are transformed during historical conjunctures is, of course, essential. But equally, we must examine why such historical moments arose in the first place. The chapter therefore leads into and informs the subsequent chapters that examine the preceding crisis in 1971 and the more recent crises and the neo-liberal practices that have emerged from these historical moments.

Disciplinary Mechanisms

Foucault published *Discipline and Punish* in 1975. This work contrasts disciplinary power to the more traditional notion of sovereign power. Sovereign power, argues Foucault, is 'exercised mainly as a means of deduction (*prélèvement*), a subtraction mechanism, a right to appropriate a portion of the wealth, a tax of products, goods and services, labor and blood, levied on the subjects. Power in this instance was essentially a right of seizure: of things, time, bodies, and ultimately life itself; it culminated in the privilege to seize hold of life in order to suppress it' (1978, p. 136). Sovereign power is said to operate through 'a binary division between the permitted and the prohibited, and a coupling, comprising the code, between a type of prohibited action and a type of punishment' (Foucault 2007, p. 20). This form of power is most clearly seen in what Foucault terms the 'spectacle of the scaffold'—the public display of torture and death—which was 'not an economy of example', but a 'policy of terror' in order to make 'everyone aware, through the body of the criminal, of the unrestrained presence of the sovereign' (Foucault 1995, p. 49). The objective of such rituals was not simply to punish transgressions, but to reassert the power of the sovereign 'the punishment is carried out in such a way as to give a spectacle not of measure, but of imbalance and excess … by breaking the law, the offender has touched the very person of the prince; and it is the prince—or at least those to whom he has delegated his force—who seizes upon the body of the condemned man and displays it marked, beaten, broken' (Foucault 1995, p. 49).

The method and telos of punishment undergo a transformation with the emergence of disciplinary power (Dean 1994, p. 161). Now the punishment 'will not just be the spectacular, definitive moment of the hanging, fine, or banishment, but a practice like incarceration with a series of exercises and a work of transformation on the guilty person in the form of what we call penitentiary techniques: obligatory work, moralization, correction, and so forth' (Foucault 2007, p. 19). In contrast to sovereign power, disciplinary power involves a 'series of adjacent, detective, medical, and psychological techniques … which fall within the domain of surveillance, diagnosis, and the possible transformation of individuals' (Foucault 2007, p. 20). Disciplinary power asserts control over the individual, identifying aberrant behaviour and adopting the most appropriate techniques to ensure such behaviour is corrected. Of course, disciplinary mechanisms were in existence before the seventeenth/eighteenth century, but Foucault argues that it is at this time that the mechanisms associated with this 'new micro-physics of power' start to become 'general formulas of domination' (Foucault 2007, pp. 137–8).

Disciplinary mechanisms entail a 'policy of coercions that act upon the body ... The human body was entering a machinery of power that explores it, breaks it down and rearranges it' (Foucault 2007, p. 138). The objective of discipline was not merely one of subjection, but also of utility—to 'have a hold over others' bodies, not only so that they may do what one wishes, but so that they may operate as one wishes, with the techniques, the speed and the efficiency that one determines. Discipline increases the forces of the body (in economic terms of utility) and diminishes these same forces (in political terms of obedience)' (Foucault 2007, p. 138). Discipline's objective is to increase the utility of the individual in the most efficacious manner; it is 'the unitary technique by which the body is reduced as a "political" force at the least cost and maximized as a useful force' (Foucault 2007, p. 221).

Foucault connects this emergence to population and economy—to the increase in population and the increase in the 'apparatus of production' ('not only "production" in the strict sense, but also the production of knowledge and skills in the school, the production of health in the hospitals, the production of destructive force in the army') which he asserts was becoming more costly (Foucault 1995, pp. 218–9). But, interestingly, he also relates the disciplinary technique and its objective of obtaining 'the exercise of power at the lowest possible cost' to the emergence of capitalism—'it would not have been possible to solve the problem of the accumulation of men without the growth of an apparatus of production capable of both sustaining them and using them; conversely, the techniques that made the cumulative multiplicity of men useful accelerated the accumulation of capital' (Foucault 1995, pp. 218 & 221).

We thus witness a transformation in the objective of the actual penalty itself. Rather than simply seeking to punish, the new disciplinary mechanisms also sought, to supervise the individual, to neutralise the dangers he or she presents, to normalise him or her in the ultimate hope of altering his or her criminal tendencies' (Dean 1994, p. 161). In order to render the individual compliant, discipline focuses on the character of the individual, seeking to place the aberrant individual within a classificatory grid, to engage in corrective training depending on this classification in order to normalize the subject under consideration. As Mitchell Dean points out, 'scientific' technical knowledge of human behaviour is applied to pinpoint the form of aberrant behaviour of the individual concerned and the reasons behind such actions, 'individualising knowledges' are 'brought to bear upon him or her through experts of various sorts: of psychologists, counsellors, social workers, members of the prison service, educators, and so on' (Dean 1994, p. 161).

Foucault argues that this objectification of the individual is carried out through three inter-related instruments: hierarchical observation, normalizing judgement and their 'combination in a procedure that is specific to it, the examination' (Foucault 1995, p. 170). Central to producing a field of visibility over subjects is hierarchical observation, indeed discipline 'presupposes a mechanism that coerces by means of observation; an apparatus in which the techniques that make it possible to see induce effects of power' (Foucault 1995, p. 170). For Foucault, Jeremy Bentham's model of the panoptican represents the archetypal form of this hierarchical surveillance, in which the supervisor is placed in a tower in the centre of a ring whose outer periphery is populated by back-lighted prison cells rendering inmates constantly visible. The panoptican represents the 'perfect disciplinary apparatus' because it makes it 'possible for a single gaze to see everything constantly' (Foucault 1995, p. 173). Ideal forms of hierarchical observation may be capable of inducing the effects of power even in the absence of a supervisor. If the supervisor can see without being seen, individuals will conform at all times because they will never know when they are being watched and when they are not. An individual 'subjected to a field of visibility, and who knows it, assumes responsibility for the constraints of power; he makes them play spontaneously upon himself; he inscribes in himself the power relation in which he simultaneously plays both roles; he becomes the principle of his own subjection' (Foucault 1995, pp. 201–2).

Normalizing judgement, Foucault argues, is both individualizing and homogenizing at one and the same time. It does so by establishing classificatory grids that are distributive in nature. Unlike the binary division between conformity and transgression apparent under sovereign power, normalizing judgement establishes 'a distribution between a positive pole and a negative pole; all behaviour falls in the field between good and bad marks, good and bad point' (Foucault 1995, p. 180). This classification of behaviour not only produces a ranking but also establishes the gaps between individuals enabling micro-punishments to be implemented—thus establishing a 'classificatory, penal distribution' (Foucault 1995, p. 181).

The normalizing judgement therefore individualizes by placing the individual within a distributive classification, but it also homogenizes by applying micro-punishments that increase in severity according to the degree of transgression from the norm. It thus ensures that 'the whole indefinite domain of the non-conforming is punishable' (Foucault 1995, p. 178). These micro-penalties are applied to a whole series of minor transgressions, such as, 'time (latenesses, absences, interruptions of tasks), of activity (inattention, negligence, lack of zeal), of behaviour (impoliteness, disobedience), of speech (idle chatter, insolence), of the body ("incorrect" attitudes, irregular gestures, lack of cleanliness), of sexuality (impurity, indecency)' (Foucault 1995, p. 178). The penalties applied depend on the degree of deviance and are of similar intricacy—'from light physical punishment to minor deprivations and petty humiliations' (Foucault 1995, p. 178). The normalizing judgement thus introduces the 'perpetual penalty that traverses all points and supervises every instant in the disciplinary institutions compares, differentiates, hierarchizes, homogenizes, excludes. In short, it *normalizes*' (Foucault 1995, p. 182). This normalizing judgement has 'the function of reducing gaps. It must therefore be essentially corrective' (Foucault 1995, p. 179).

The examination is said to combine the 'techniques of an observing hierarchy and those of a normalizing judgement' (Foucault 1995, p. 184). As such, it is what Foucault calls 'a normalizing gaze, a surveillance that makes it possible to qualify, to classify and to punish. It establishes over individuals a visibility through which one differentiates them and judges them' (Foucault 1995, p. 184). The examination is a procedure that precisely locates and objectifies the individual within the various classificatory grids (level of criminality, insanity, sexual 'deviance', etc.) and enables a normalizing judgement to be made according to the extremity of the transgression under examination. The examination is thus the technique 'by which power, instead of emitting the signs of its potency, instead of imposing its mark on its subjects, holds them in a mechanism of objectification. In this space of domination, disciplinary power manifests its potency, essentially, by arranging objects' (Foucault 1995, p. 187).

Foucault's Later Works

In Foucault's later works, his attention turned towards a genealogical analysis of governing. In so doing, he argued that a shift in political reasoning could be identified in the sixteenth century away from the divine rule of sovereigns and obedience of subjects through overt violence. Foucault concentrates on Machiavelli's *The Prince* and the *raison d'état* of the sixteenth century with its emphasis on securing the principality both from external threats and threats from within. Machiavelli's work was significant for its re-orientation away from the divine right of sovereigns to rule, Foucault argues that Machiavelli presents sovereign rule as 'a purely synthetic link; there is no fundamental, essential, natural, and juridical connection between the Prince and his principality' (Foucault 2007, p. 130). Yet, despite this radical rupture, his political treatise does not break with the circularity of reasoning apparent in traditional notions of sovereign power, that is, 'the end of sovereignty is circular; it refers back to the exercise of sovereignty. The good is obedience to the law, so that the good proposed by sovereignty is that people obey it' (Foucault 2007, p. 136). With Machiavelli, the good becomes the survival of the principality, but the same circularity of political reason is apparent with justification for a prince's actions referred constantly back on to itself, that is, the survival of the principality.

A more radical break appears in reaction to Machiavelli's work with Guillaume de La Perrière's *Le Miroir Politique* and its emphasis on the art of government. Whereas sovereign power operated under the condition of inseparability of the sovereign and law and the imposition of law to ensure the obedience of subjects, the art of government was said to be concerned with the 'disposition of things, that is to say, of employing tactics rather than laws, or, of as far as possible employing laws as tactics; arranging things so that this or that end may be achieved through a certain number of means' (Foucault 2007, pp. 136–7). The art of government is thus understood to involve the objective of specific ends, for example, ensuring 'that the greatest possible amount of wealth is produced, that the people are provided with sufficient means of subsistence, and that the population can increase' (Foucault 2007, pp. 136–7). For Foucault this marks a significant departure from earlier thought, because the art of government is not viewed as being 'related to the territory, but to a sort of complex of men and things. The things government must be concerned about, La Perrière says, are men in their relationships, bonds, and complex involvements with things like wealth, resources, means of subsistence, and, of course, the territory with its borders, qualities, climate, dryness, fertility, and so on. "Things" are men in their relationships with things like customs, habits, ways of acting and thinking. Finally, they are men in their relationships with things like accidents, misfortunes, famine, epidemics, and death' (Foucault 2007, p. 134).

As Vestergaard points out, this rupture that is identifiable in the sixteenth century actually took significant time to fully develop and government as a 'new modality of the exercise of political power only fully matures in the late eighteenth and nineteenth century' (Vestergaard 2009, p. 195). This evolution involves a shift away from *raison d'etat* and its 'obsessive fantasy of a totally administered society' towards liberal government that 'confronts itself with realities ... that have their own internal logics and densities, their own intrinsic mechanisms of self-regulation' (Rose 1996, p. 43).[1] The tactics of government are understood to be limited by the naturalistic laws of economy and population, viewed by states as external realities which placed 'constraints upon political governance by means of an arena of naturalistically conceived laws, including those of capital, population and subsistence that would be foolish for the state to ignore' (Dean 1994, p. 190). From this emerge two key inextricably related issues that become the focus of Foucault's later work: governmentality and biopolitics.

Biopolitics

In volume one of *History of Sexuality* (Foucault 1978) published originally in 1976 and the lecture series *Society Must Be Defended* (Foucault 2003) given between 1976 and 1979, Foucault turns his attention towards the emergence of population as a field of interest from the eighteenth century onwards (Foucault 1978, p. 139). In so doing, he argues that the power over life actually encompasses two developments linked together by 'a whole intermediary cluster of relations' (Foucault 1978, p. 139). The first of these developments, anatomo politics of the body, was previously covered in his 1975 work, *Discipline and Punishment* detailing the various disciplinary mechanisms centred on the body. Whereas in his slightly later work his attention shifts somewhat towards biopolitics focused on regulation at the aggregate macro-level of the population as a whole.

Anatomo politics is said to be 'centered on the body as a machine: its disciplining, the optimization of its capabilities, the extortion of its forces, the parallel increase of its usefulness and its docility, its integration into systems of efficient and economic controls' (Foucault 1978, p. 139). Whereas biopolitics focuses on the 'species body, the body imbued with the mechanics of life and serving as the basis of the biological processes: propagation, births and mortality, the level of health, life expectancy and longevity, with all the conditions that can cause these to vary'. (Foucault 1978, p. 139). Foucault points out that the regulatory 'technique does not simply do away with the disciplinary technique, … because it has a different bearing area, and makes use of very different instruments' (Foucault 2003, p. 242). 'In reality you have a series of complex edifices in which, of course, the techniques themselves change and are perfected, or anyway become more complicated' (Foucault 2007, p. 22).

In fact, these two techniques combine to produce what Foucault terms a 'normalizing society'—'a sort of generalized disciplinary society whose disciplinary institutions have swarmed and finally taken over everything—that, I think, is no more than a first and inadequate interpretation of a normalizing society. The normalizing society is a society in which the norm of discipline and the norm of regulation intersect along an orthogonal articulation' (Foucault 2003, p. 253).

This interest in population, we are told, is related to 'the demographic expansion of the eighteenth century, which was linked to the abundance of money, which was itself linked in turn to the expansion of agricultural production through circular processes' (Foucault 2007, p. 140). The art of government is now occupied with how best to understand and deal with both the economy and population. This emergence of economy and population as fields of reality and foci of intervention are, for Foucault, inextricably intertwined—'It is through the development of the science of government that the economy could be re-focused on a level of reality that we now describe as the economic; and it is again through the science of government that the specific problem of population could be identified' (Foucault 2007, p. 140).

As a result of these developments, population now becomes the object of government. As Zebrowski points out, population is a 'particular framing of life…it is one which emphasizes the species-existence of humans understood in the aggregate' (2016, p. 11). What emerges is a focus on improving 'the condition of the population, to increase its wealth, its longevity, and its health' (Foucault 2007, p. 141). As such, biopolitics treats the population as a set of 'coexisting living beings with particular biological and pathological features, and which as such falls under specific forms of knowledge and technique' (Foucault 2007, p. 474). Government becomes focused on the natural processes associated with living beings, such as, 'the ratio of births to deaths, the rate of reproduction, the fertility of a population, and so on. It is these processes-the birth rate, the mortality rate, longevity and so on-together with a whole series of related economic and political problems ... which, in the second half of the eighteenth century, become biopolitics' (Foucault 2003, p. 243).

Foucault makes an important distinction when introducing biopolitics—a distinction that is important for this study. As Foucault points out, although biological processes such as morbidity, mortality, fertility, longevity and so on are unpredictable and aleatory at the individual level, they do exhibit regularities when analysed at a macro-level. If you like, they are 'known unknowns'—we may not be able to know at the individual level when such life events will occur, but we are able to know that, on average, a certain percentage of a given population will suffer from 'X' with a probability of 'Y' in any given year. In other words, 'at the collective level', these phenomena 'display constants that are easy, or at least possible, to establish. And they are, finally, phenomena that occur over a period of time, which have to be studied over a certain period of time; they are serial phenomena' (Foucault 2003, p. 246). Thus, biopolitical techniques 'sought to secure populations by regulating the "general" rates of incidence of contingencies correlated with biological and environmental factors. Security technologies aimed to tame the milieu in which the species-life operated' (Zebrowski 2016, p. 12).

When compared to the disciplinary mechanisms, biopolitics differs both in its mechanisms and mode of intervention. Biopolitics is said to utilize 'forecasts, statistical estimates, and overall measures' (Foucault 2003, p. 246). And the purpose is 'to intervene at the level at which these general phenomena are determined, to intervene at the level of their generality. The mortality rate has to be modified or lowered; life expectancy has to be increased; the birth rate has to be stimulated' (Foucault 2003, p. 246). In order to do this, 'regulatory mechanisms must be established to establish an equilibrium, maintain an average, establish a sort of homeostasis, and compensate for variations within this general population and its aleatory field. In a word, security mechanisms have to be installed around the random element inherent in a population of living beings so as to optimize a state of life' (Foucault 2003, p. 246). Security or regulatory mechanisms must act in such that they 'achieve overall states of equilibration or regularity; it is, in a word, a matter of taking control of life and the biological processes of man-as-species (sic) and of ensuring that they are not disciplined but regularized' (Foucault 2003, pp. 246–7).

These new security mechanisms are thus said to operate through the 'delimitation of phenomena within acceptable limits' (Foucault 2007, p. 93). As a result, risk calculus becomes a key function, fixing the range of phenomena that are possible in any given field and calculating the risks associated with given segments of the population or a given range of behaviour—'There are therefore differential risks that reveal, as it were, zones of higher risk and, on the other hand, zones of less or lower risk. This means that one can thus identify what is dangerous' (Foucault 2007, p. 89). What emerges is not a binary division of the permitted and prohibited, but 'an average considered as optimal on the one hand, and, on the other, a bandwidth of the acceptable that must not be exceeded. In this way a completely different distribution of things and mechanisms takes shape' (Foucault 2007, p. 20).

Governmentality

Foucault terms his studies on the question of governing, 'governmentality' which he initially defines in his fourth lecture (1 February 1978) on Security, Territory, Population, as 'the ensemble formed by institutions, procedures, analyses and reflections, calculations, and tactics that allow the exercise of this very specific, albeit very complex, power that has the population as its target, political economy as its major form of knowledge, and apparatuses of security as its essential technical instrument'. He continues, it is the 'type of power that we can call "government" and which has led to the development of a series of specific governmental apparatuses (*appareils*) on the one hand, [and, on the other] to the development of a series of knowledges (*savoirs*)' (Foucault 2007, p. 144).[2] Throughout this lecture series, Foucault is also occupied by the notion of government in a much broader sense as concerned with the 'conduct of conduct'. In his lecture on 1 March 1978, he makes clear that he is employing this in two senses—conducting others '(*conduire*) and conducting oneself (se *conduire*)' (Foucault 2007, p. 472). Foucault is using a much older idea of government that goes beyond the statist notion used today to include the governance of others and the governance of oneself. This broader sense of governing thus encompasses 'all those ways of reflecting and acting that have aimed to shape, guide, manage or regulate the conduct of persons—not only other persons but also oneself—in the light of certain principles or goals' (Rose 1996, p. 41).

Foucault's concept of governmentality thus covers several aspects of governance. The first concerns itself with the genealogy of political thought and rationalities of government. As Foucault pointed out at the time, the 'government of men by men (sic)—whether they form small or large groups, whether it is power exerted by men over women, or by adults over children, or by one class over another, or by a bureaucracy over a population—involves a certain type of rationality' (1979, p. 254). Governing involves particular ways of enframing problems that make them understandable and amenable to a certain degree of control. These rationalities of government involve 'styles of thinking, ways of rendering reality thinkable in such a way that it' is 'amenable to calculation and programming' (Miller and Rose 2008, p. 16). Foucault therefore seeks to examine the 'vocabulary of the state', which 'functions as an historically variable linguistic device for conceptualizing and articulating rule … Hence political discourse is more than ideology or rhetoric. It should be seen, rather, as a kind of intellectual machinery or apparatus for rendering reality thinkable in such a way that it is amenable to political deliberations' (Rose 1993, p. 289).

This notion of government, thus 'addresses itself specifically to the domain of the political, not as a domain of State or a set of institutions and actors but in terms of the varieties of political reason' (Gordon 1991, p. 42). Governmentality can thus be understood as the 'reflexive rationalisation of governmental practice that provides a discursive field of power/knowledge through which governmental problems are articulated and techniques of governance are rendered "thinkable and practicable both to its practitioners and those upon whom [they are] practiced"' (Zebrowski 2009, p. 11).[3] Governing thus involves defining a 'discursive field in which exercising power is "rationalized". This occurs, among other things, by the delineation of concepts, the specification of objects and borders, the provision of arguments and justifications, etc. In this manner, government enables a problem to be addressed and offers certain strategies for solving/handling the problem' (Lemke 2001, p. 191).

As outlined in the next section, this concern with the rationalities of government is most clearly seen in Foucault's lecture series entitled the 'Birth of Biopolitics' (despite focusing primarily on governmentality) where he dissects two main forms of neo-liberalism, German ordo-liberalism and American neo-liberalism, and their divergent views on the market, the individual and the resulting divergent understandings of how best to govern. The former argues for regulatory intervention in the market to ensure its effective functioning. In direct contrast, the Chicago School emphasizes the 'consistent expansion of the economic form to apply to the social sphere, thus eliding any difference between the economy and the social' (Lemke 2001, p. 197).

The second aspect of governmentality addresses the issue of what forms of subjectivity issue from these rationalities of government and what forms of socialization are employed in attempts to regulate the conduct of the individual. For example, for liberal forms of governmentality under which subjects exercise 'free' choice, a general problematique arose—how best to govern 'a population that were independent realities with inherent processes and forces' (Miller and Rose 1990, p. 9). As Dean has pointed out, liberal regimes of government come 'to operate on the conduct of the governed. It seeks a direction of conduct rather than a violent or gross form of corporeal domination. In this sense, the microphysics of power may have been overstated if it gave the impression of a determinism of power operating upon the body. Here, governmental power assumes a "free subject", not an individual existing in an essential space of freedom, but one whose subjection is consistent with forms of choice' (Dean 1994, p. 178). Liberal regimes of government 'do not *determine* forms of subjectivity. They elicit, promote, facilitate, foster and attribute various capacities, qualities and statuses to particular agents' (Dean 2010, pp. 43–44). Rather than direct control of the population, a shift of emphasis occurred towards the inculcation of certain norms, beliefs, forms of behaviour—'The external constraint of police was to be translated into an internal constraint upon the conduct of the self, the formation of subjects who were prepared to take responsibility for their actions and for whom the ethic of discipline was part of their very mental fabric' (Rose 1999, p. 227). Thus, to analyse government is 'to analyse those mechanisms that try to shape, sculpt, mobilise and work through the choices, desires, aspirations, needs, wants and lifestyles of individuals and groups' (Dean 2010, p. 20). As such, governmentality 'has entailed a range of attempts to shape and modulate the relations that individuals have with society's productive apparatus', 'reshaping persons at the level of their subjectivity, so that they exercise their newfound capacities and attributes freely' (Miller and Rose 1990, p. 19; 2008, p. 147).

Agencies thus engage in programmes to 'shape, guide, channel, direct, control—events and persons distant from it. Persons and activities were to be governed through society, that is to say, through acting upon them in relation to a social norm, and constituting their experiences and evaluations in a social form' (Rose 1996, p. 40). This is what Miller and Rose refer to as the technologies/techniques of government—the manner in which certain ideas, values, identities and so on are inculcated. These technologies/techniques of government are the 'actual mechanisms through which authorities of various sorts have sought to shape, normalize and instrumentalize the conduct, thought, decisions and aspirations of others in order to achieve the objectives they consider desirable' (Miller and Rose 2008, p. 32). As they point out, if 'political rationalities render reality into the domain of thought, these "technologies of government" seek to translate thought into the domain of reality, and to establish "in the world of persons and things" spaces and devices for acting upon those entities of which they dream and scheme' (Miller and Rose 1990, p. 8).

As mentioned previously, the concept of governmentality should not be completely elided with a statist understanding of government. This is most clearly seen with regard to self-governance where technologies/techniques of government by the state become imbricated with technologies/techniques residing within capitalist society and the choice of individuals. For example, health programmes seek to inculcate certain values like non-smoking, reduction in alcohol consumption and weight reduction—this is reinforced by the promotion of health foods and exercise via the media by the fitness and food industries. Inculcation of these values will vary on an individual basis depending upon the general disposition of the individual and which values they are subjected to.

It is also important to point out that Foucault later interpreted his earlier notions of sovereign and disciplinary power within the wider framework of governmentality and biopolitics. Anatomo politics, as he called it, was now viewed as just one of several modalities of power. However, this did not imply that such mechanisms became less important, rather, for biopolitics, 'discipline was never more important or more valued than when the attempt was made to manage the population: managing the population does not mean just managing the collective mass of phenomena or managing them simply at the level of their overall results' (Foucault 2007, p. 143). Similarly, he emphasized the continuing salience of both sovereign and disciplinary power within a governmental framework—'we should not see things as the replacement of a society of sovereignty by a society of discipline, and then of a society of discipline by a society, say, of government. In fact we have a triangle: sovereignty, discipline, and governmental management' (Foucault 2007, p. 143). As Dean points out, rather than replacing these forms of power, 'the modern art of government recasts them within this concern for the population and its optimization…and the forms of knowledge and technical means appropriate to it' (2010, p. 3). The subjectification process involving the formation of identities and inculcation of values can involve discipline and punishment at one end of the spectrum and non-coercive recommendation, encouragement and felicitation at the other end.

Foucault's analysis of modern society can therefore be seen as encompassing sovereign power, disciplinary power, biopower and technologies/techniques of liberal government. Where disciplinary mechanisms can be understood as a subset of the technologies/techniques of government that have as their object normalization, but that these 'disciplinary practices—the panoply of the political technology of the body—is displaced, and somewhat subsumed, under a more general concern for governmental practices seeking the direction of conduct' (Dean 1994, p. 179). Liberal government can thus be understood as including disciplinary mechanisms where necessary, while at the same time seeking 'a direction of conduct rather than a violent or gross form of corporeal domination' (Dean 1994, p. 178). Although this 'non-coercive' socialization process is the dominant *modus operandi*, as others have pointed out, disciplinary mechanisms are subsumed within liberal regimes of government and may come to the fore when less direct attempts at inculcating certain norms, values, forms of behaviour and so on fail (Merlingen 2003).

An analytics of government in this wider sense therefore involves an analysis of the emergence, maintenance and transformation of these regimes of practices (Dean 2010, p. 31). Where regimes of practices are institutionalized practices involving 'routinized and ritualized' ways of doing things and this includes the way in which these institutional practices 'can be thought, made into objects of knowledge, and made subject to problematizations' (Ibid., p. 31). According to Dean, such an analytics of government has four associated dimensions.

1. Characteristic forms of visibility, ways of seeing and perceiving
2. Distinctive ways of thinking and questioning, relying on definite vocabulary and procedures for the production of truth (e.g. those derived from the social, human and behavioural sciences)
3. Specific ways of acting, intervening and directing, made up of particular types of practical rationality ('expertise' and 'know-how'), and relying upon definite mechanisms, techniques and technologies
4. Characteristic ways of forming subjects, selves, persons, actors or agents (2010, p. 33).

As Graham Burchell neatly sums up, in examining governmentality in this manner, we are asking 'through the operation of what practices of government and by reference to what kind of political reasoning, have we been led to recognize our self-identity' (Burchell 1991, p. 121). From a Foucauldian perspective, we can thus define the wider concept of government as, 'any more or less calculated and rational activity, undertaken by a multiplicity of authorities and agencies, employing a variety of techniques and forms of knowledge, that seeks to shape conduct by working through the desires, aspirations, interests and beliefs of various actors for definite but shifting ends and with a diverse set of relatively unpredictable consequences, effects and outcomes' (Dean 1999, p. 18).

A Foucauldian Approach to IPE

This book sets itself apart by placing the global financial crisis and the European crisis alongside the attendant reforms of the financial system within a Foucauldian theoretical framework. The book therefore provides a contemporary analysis of the two financial crises that have recently beset the global economy—the global financial crisis and the regional European crisis. It is the contention of this book that we can further our understanding of IPE by using a Foucauldian analytics of government to political, social and economic transformations in prevailing liberal regimes of practice that tend to emerge during and after major historical moments/conjunctures. By historical conjuncture we have in mind 'a space of time within which a particular combination (or conjunction) of causes exercises a predominant (causal and imaginative) influence over the course of events and the production of ideas' (Rosenberg 2005, p. 29). During such periods, problematizations of government tend to occur whereby sedimented practices are re-examined, questioned, reformed and possibly replaced (Dean 2010, p. 38).

In other words, certain crises are of sufficient severity to prompt a change in ideas and behaviour with regard to established social, political and economic practices. But it is the contention of this book that it is not simply enough to examine the 'how' questions that Foucault so ably presents, but to also ask why. What causes/series of events led to a particular historical conjuncture (Marsden 1999, p. 135). An analytics of government examining how we are governed and how we govern ourselves and how such regimes of practices are transformed during historical conjunctures is, of course, essential. But equally, we must examine why such historical moments arose in the first place. Indeed, Foucault was not adverse to such an approach pointing out that there are not only intra-discursive and inter-discursive dependencies but also '*extradiscursive* dependencies (between discursive transformations and transformations outside of discourse)' (Foucault 1991, p. 58).

The book also diverges from Foucault by arguing that, in practice, the economic policies/financial regulation that have emerged at the global and European level have been predominantly neo-liberal in nature. Foucault, alongside other writers, distinguished German ordo-liberalism, with its emphasis on the importance of the state in establishing the 'institutional parameters for economic competition in order to serve the larger interests of society', from the Anglo-American version of neo-liberalism that emphasizes the rolling back of the state, self-regulation of the market and the marketization of hitherto de-commodified spheres of activity (Young 2015, p. 11). Although ordo-liberalism initially emerged in the late 1920s within the Freiburg School, its influence as the guiding economic philosophy of the German state only began after the Second World War. Rather than viewing the market as some naturally occurring phenomenon, they argued that the economic 'must be considered as a set of regulated activities from the very beginning: it is a set of regulated activities with rules of completely different levels, forms, origins, dates, and chronologies', in other words 'economic processes only really exist, in history, insofar as an institutional framework and positive rules have provided them with their conditions of possibility' (Foucault 2008, p. 163).

As a result, instead of 'distinguishing between an economic belonging to the infrastructure and a juridical-political belonging to the superstructure', the two are viewed as inextricably intertwined within an economic-juridical order so that 'one mutually presumes the existence of the other' (Foucault 2008, p. 163; Lemke 2001, p. 193). From an ordo-liberal perspective, intervention is not only possible but actually fundamentally necessary 'enabling the formal mechanisms of competition to function' (Foucault 2008, p. 160). In contrast to the Chicago School of neo-liberalism, economic governance is not viewed as unwarranted, producing aberrations and inefficiencies; it is argued that the market is 'constituted and kept alive only by dint of political interventions' (Lemke 2001, p. 163). Yet, this intervention was supposed to be limited to setting the 'institutional parameters for economic competition in order to serve the larger interests of society' (Young 2015, p. 11). Because ordo-liberals 'believe markets left to their own devices are prone to systemic anti-competitive cartelisation and rent-seeking by capitalists, labour unions and bureaucrats', the state is required to establish a pro-competitive rule based order regulating the market (Cerny 2016, p. 78).

On the other hand, the Chicago School of neo-liberalism promotes economic rationalism throughout the social body, such that 'the object of economic analysis should be identified with any purposeful conduct which involves, broadly speaking, a strategic choice of means, ways, and instruments, in short, the identification of the object of economic analysis with any rational conduct' (Foucault 2008, p. 269). The contrast with ordo-liberalism could not be more stark. As Thomas Lemke points out, whereas 'the *Ordo*-liberals in West Germany pursued the idea of governing society in the name of the economy, the US neo-liberals attempt to re-define the social sphere as a form of the economic domain' (2001, p. 197). Neo-liberalism turns ordo-liberalism on its head, arguing that 'the state does not define and monitor market freedom, for the market is itself the organizing and regulative principle underlying the state. From this angle, it is more the case of the state being controlled by the market than of the market being supervised by the state' (Lemke 2001, p. 200).

However, in practice, these dominant forms were never as neatly divided in practice as their conceptual approaches would suggest and may even be co-evolving towards what one author has called post-ordo-liberalism (Cerny 2016). Neo-liberalism has always required regulatory reform that strengthens the state in some areas (e.g. trade union laws) and rolls it back in other areas (e.g. business deregulation) (Cerny 1997). Equally, in practice, Germany has engaged in Keynesian economics, monetarism and, very recently, agreed to the direct intervention in markets through the European Stability Mechanism (Young 2015). Both tendencies have always sought to promote efficient market competition and recently, at the European level, there has been little to distinguish the two in terms of pursuing the re-regulation of the financial spheres, reductions in welfare provision, the further marketization of hitherto de-commodified spheres, labour market deregulation and attendant wage reductions, and wholesale privatizations.[4] For this book, it is argued that, the policies promulgated by the European Union (often at Germany's behest) and the policies agreed upon at the global level have been, by and large, neo-liberal in nature.[5]

Although the main focus of this book is on the more recent dual crisis from 2007/2008 onwards, the next chapter contends that many of the reasons for these recent events can be found in the changes ushered in at the end of the seventies/beginning of the eighties as a result of the previous economic crisis of the early seventies. In order to understand the emergence of neo-liberalism, the discourse dominating how we now govern ourselves and are governed, we need to understand the causes of the economic crisis of the seventies. Equally, to understand the current problematization of practices associated with neo-liberalism, we need to understand the causes of the global financial crisis in 2007/2008.

This book therefore examines the changing regimes of practice at the state, regional and global level in relation to the economic crisis of the seventies and then again with regard to the dual crisis (2007/2008 and the Euro Crisis). In so doing, it examines both the change in governmental rationalities and the reconstitution of subjects during these periods. However, it does not divorce these transformations from the underlying economic tendencies that are so apparent in the various circuits of capital. The crisis of the seventies heralded the advent of neo-liberal governmentality: the marketization of extra-economic spheres, deepening commodification and deregulation and the rise of the entrepreneurial self. But the unpredictability of this transformation has become all too apparent—with the shift away from Keynesian fiscal stimulus towards massive private borrowing as an alternative economic stimulus came the danger of financial instability.

Since the dual crisis, we have witnessed the emergence of resilience as a new object of interest. Although some have interpreted this as heralding a break from neo-liberalism and a reaction to the 'unknown unknowns' of the financial world, this book questions such assertions contending that there are sound reasons for considering the emergence of the resilient subject as a deepening of neo-liberal governmentality. For sure, the global financial crisis initially unsettled the sedimented practices associated with neo-liberalism, but rather than supplanting such practices, resilience thinking has tended to be reform orientated in practice and has therefore supplemented rather than supplanted neo-liberalism. The absence of such a challenge not only points to the abiding strength of the neo-liberal social imaginary and the ideational bankruptcy of those who govern, but also points to the power and entrenched interests of political and economic elites. In addition, it is difficult to see how the economy can undergo a similar restructuring to that of the 1970s. The reconfiguration of production from a national to a global scale involved a historic shift towards employment in services for the highly industrialized countries. The slower growth in wages was partly compensated for by increased access to credit. Yet, if a similar change occurs in services through either shifting jobs to cheaper sites or the utilization of new technologies, it will simply increase unemployment and pressure on wages as well as increase the reliance on credit in the core industrialized countries.

The next chapter examines the change in governmentality prompted by the economic stagnation in the seventies of the highly industrialized countries. In so doing, it examines the transformation of liberal rationalities away from Keynesian demand management towards neo-liberal forms of governmentalities. The latter obviously differs across states, but the dominant Anglo-American version places special emphasis on the further marketization of the social sphere. This includes at a minimum: 'deregulation, privatisation, internationalisation and devolving state activities to market forces' (Joseph 2012, p. 8). For this book, deregulation covers a plethora of regulatory policies covering issues from labour, the environment, corporate activities and finance.

At the same time, there was a wholesale reconstitution of subjectivities associated with the emergence of this neo-liberal rationality. The seventies and eighties therefore witnessed a shift away from the notion of citizenship 'construed in terms of solidarity, contentment, welfare and a sense of security established through the bonds of organizational and social life' (Miller and Rose 1990, p. 24). Enterprise and entrepreneurship became the new watchwords with the worker 'no longer construed as a social creature seeking satisfaction of his or her need for security, solidarity and welfare, but as an individual actively seeking to shape and manage his or her own life in order to maximize its returns in terms of success and achievement' (Miller and Rose 1990, p. 9).

Some have argued that, just as the economic crisis of the seventies prompted a reconstitution of subjectivities, so too has the dual financial crisis with the emergence of the resilient subject. Given the uncertainties of our natural and social worlds resilience emphasizes 'a systematic, widespread, organizational, structural and personal strengthening of subjective and material arrangements so as to be better able to anticipate and tolerate disturbances in complex worlds without collapse, to withstand shocks, and to rebuild as necessary' (Lenztos and Rose 2009, p. 243). However, much that is emphasized in the resilience literature chimes with an earlier emphasis upon responsibilization, self-reliance, self-management and so on. Following Joseph, Chap. 4 therefore argues that this 'recent enthusiasm for the concept of resilience across a range of policy literature is the consequence of its fit with neoliberal discourse', rather than signalling a radical divergence from it (2013, p. 38).

Chapter 5 argues that we can best understand the reforms of the financial system as aimed at securing a smooth functioning of this circuit of capital and reducing the risk of it endangering the economy as a whole. The task of financial governance is to balance the ostensible benefits of finance with the security and smooth operation of the economy itself. In attempting to achieve this outcome, neo-liberal governmentality adopts policies that are analogous to biopolitical strategies. The enframing of the financial system is centred on a 'naturalistic fallacy' that treats the financial system as something akin to naturally occurring homeostatic systems. Although Foucault applied the biopolitical approach to the well-being of the population, it is argued that current reforms continue to treat the financial system in a naturalistic manner viewing it as a homeostatic system that will self-correct itself as long as appropriate limits to risk-laden behaviour are established and complied with.

Financial security is thus said to operate through the 'delimitation of phenomena within acceptable limits' (Foucault 2007, p. 93). At the heart of this financial security apparatus lies a security *dispositive*. Just as with the biopolitics of the population, for the financial system there are 'differential risks that reveal, as it were, zones of higher risk and, on the other hand, zones of less or lower risk. This means that one can thus identify what is dangerous' (Foucault 2007, p. 89). The reforms have thus focused on establishing and maintaining acceptable levels of risk within the financial system in order that it can return to its homeostatic mode of functioning. The emphasis has thus been less on radical reform and more on establishing more restrictive risk parameters and strengthening the nodal points of the system in order that it can withstand economic shocks and the homeostatic 'norm' can be reinstated.

In addition, the perceived unpredictability of the financial system has led to a stronger emphasis on pre-emption, surveillance and resilience (O'Malley 2010, 2013). Of course, pre-emptive policies were present previously. For example, in the mid-nineties the Federal Reserve attempted to pre-empt financial bubbles by announcing possible shifts in policy in advance (Krippner 2011, p. 127). Similarly, stress tests and early warning exercises had been used prior to the crisis (Berg et al. 2000, 2004). However, the intensity of such practices and degree of coordination between various supervisory bodies since the crisis is such that we can speak of the emergence of pre-emptive governance.

The book then moves on to Chap. 6 which examines recent events in the Eurozone, particularly the strengthening of neo-liberal policies for the peripheral sovereigns and the reforms aimed at greater fiscal rectitude of Eurozone members. The chapter argues that these recent reforms within the European Union mark a shift from a consensual economic regime to one in which the emphasis has been on disciplinary mechanisms. As Joseph has detailed, governmentality in the European Union tended to emphasize an intergovernmental approach that worked through consensus building (Joseph 2012, p. 202). Of course, the governmental regime employed scientific technical apparatuses in assessing whether countries were being fiscally prudent or not—but the assessments were frequently ignored even when (or because) the country was France or Germany. There were of course associated surveillance techniques, such as, the submission of detailed economic and social data to Eurostats. Just how loosely these techniques of control were employed became rather obvious when, in October 2009, the new Greek Prime Minister George Papandreou announced that the budget deficit had been under recorded for over a decade (Djankov 2014, p. 63).

The book argues that the level of surveillance and nature of disciplinary mechanisms was to change radically as the Euro crisis took hold. Eurozone states are now subjected to hierarchical observation, examination and normalizing judgements and, of course, punitive mechanisms in the form of market reactions and fines meted out by the European

Union. The chapter focuses particularly on the Troika and their continual monitoring and examination of the periphery's performance with regard to the neo-liberal conditions set out as part of the bail-out agreements. The chapter highlights the manner in which compliance to neo-liberal norms was encouraged using typical carrot and stick policies of rewarding those that followed the 'correct' course of economic reforms, whereas those that failed were confronted with the threat of double punishment: having bail-out funds withheld and an ensuing negative market reaction leading to a downgrading of their bonds and skyrocketing borrowing costs.

Finally, the conclusion argues for shifting our emphasis towards resistance rather than resilience. The emphasis on resilience is in danger of shifting attention towards *ex-post* policies of survival and recovery rather than challenging the current economic order and resisting the further imposition of neo-liberal policies on already beleaguered populations. Indeed, the concept of resistant subjects is notable by its absence in the academic literature that has emerged since the financial crisis. The chapter rectifies this lacuna by examining Foucault's work on resistance and his insights into the micro-physics of both power and resistance. From a Foucauldian perspective, power and resistance are inextricably intertwined so that 'Where there is power, there is resistance' (Foucault 1978, p. 95). For Foucault, these relations are best understood as agonistic in nature, which are 'at the same time reciprocal incitation and struggle, less of a face-to-face confrontation which paralyzes both sides than a permanent provocation' (Foucault 1982, p. 791).

The book therefore concludes that we are likely to see an evolution in resistance movements in reaction to the various austerity measures foisted on populations since the financial crises. These movements are unlikely to simply focus on the economic measures associated with austerity, but will become articulated with other struggles against social and economic inequalities and their lack of voice. Because of the complex interactions that such articulations take, we are as yet unable to divine the overall strategy. What will eventually emerge will depend on how these various struggles become articulated with other protests and the manner in which those in power react.

Notes

1. Quoted in Vestergaard (2009, p. 196).
2. Words in brackets added.
3. The embedded quote is from Burchell et al. (1991, p. 3).
4. This is very clear from the various memoranda of understanding that the Troika have signed with various national governments setting out bailout conditions. For example, refer to Greek MOU (11 August 2015) and Portugual MOU (17 May 2011). For an overview of the various policies, refer to Pisani-Ferry, Sapir and Wolff (2013).
5. Of course, it can be argued that the re-regulation is more Oro-liberal in nature, but much of this regulation seeks to ensure the free play of financial markets once again (within stricter risk parameters) and, as we shall see, European reforms have promoted further privatization and commodification of the public realm.

References

Berg, A., E. Borensztein, G. Milesi-Ferretti, and C. Pattillo. 2000. Anticipating Balance of Payments Crises—The Role of Early Warning Systems, IMF Occasional Paper No. 186. https://www.imf.org/external/pubs/nft/op/186/index.htm

Berg, A., E. Borensztein, and C. Patillo. 2004. Assessing Early Warning Systems: How Have They Worked in Practice? IMF Working Paper, WP/04/52.

Burchell, G. 1991. Peculiar Interests: Civil Society and Governing "The System of Natural Liberty". In *The Foucault Effect: Studies in Governmentality*, ed. G. Burchell, C. Gordon and P. Miller, 119–150. Chicago: Chicago University Press.

Burchell, G., C. Gordon, and P. Miller, eds. 1991. *The Foucault Effect: Studies in Governmentality*. Chicago: Chicago University Press.

Cerny, P. 1997. Paradoxes of the Competition State: The Dynamics of Political Globalization. *Government and Opposition* 32 (2): 251–274.

———. 2016. In the Shadow of Ordoliberalism: The Paradox of Neoliberalism in the 21st Century. *European Review of International Studies* 2 (3): 78–91.

Dean, M. 1994. *Critical and Effective Histories: Foucault's Methods and Historical Sociology*. London: Routledge.

———. 1999. 'Risk, calculable and incalculable', in D. Lupton, (ed.) 1999, *Risk and sociocultural theory: new directions and perspectives*. Cambridge: Cambridge University Press, pp. 131–159.

———. 2010. *Governmentality: Power and Rule in Modern Society*. Los Angeles: Sage.

Djankov, S. 2014. *Inside the Euro Crisis: An Eyewitness Account*. Washington, DC: Institute for International Economics.

Foucault, M. 1978. *History of Sexuality Vol. 1: Translated by Robert Hurley*. New York: Pantheon Books.

———. 1979. Omnes et Singulatim: Towards a Criticism of 'Political Reason', Tanner Lectures on Human Values. http://tannerlectures.utah.edu/_documents/a-to-z/f/foucault81.pdf

———. 1982. The Subject and Power. *Critical Inquiry* 8 (4): 777–795.

———. 1991. Politics and the Study of Discourse. In *The Foucault Effect: Studies in Governmentality*, ed. G. Burchell, C. Gordon and P. Miller, 53–72. Chicago: Chicago University Press.

———. 1995. *Discipline and Punish: the Birth of the Prison*. 2nd ed. New York: Vintage Books.

———. 2003. *Society Must Be Defended: Lectures at the College de France, 1975–6*. New York: Picador.

———. 2007. *Security, Territory, Population: Lectures at the College de France 1977–78*. Basingstoke: Palgrave Macmillan.

———. 2008. *The Birth of Biopolitics: Lectures at the College de France, 1978–79*. Basingstoke: Palgrave Macmillan.

Gordon, C. 1980. *Power/Knowledge: Selected Interviews and Other Writings 1972–1977*. New York: Pantheon Books.

———. 1991. Governmental Rationality: An Introduction. In ed. Burchell, Gordon and Miller, 1–52.

Joseph, J. 2012. *The Social in the Global: Social Theory, Governmentality and Global Politics*. Cambridge: Cambridge University Press.

———. 2013. Resilience as Embedded Neoliberalism: A Governmentality Approach. *Resilience: International Policies, Practices and Discourses* 1 (1): 38–52.

Krippner, G. 2011. *Capitalizing on Crisis: The Political Origins of the Rise of Finance*. Harvard: Harvard University Press.

Lemke, T. 2001. The Birth of Bio-Politics': Michel Foucault's Lecture at the Collège de France on Neo-Liberal Governmentality. *Economy and Society* 30 (2): 190–207.

Lenztos, F., and N. Rose. 2009. Governing Insecurity: Contingency Planning, Protection, Resistance. *Economy and Society* 38 (2): 230–254.

Lupton, D., ed. 1999. *Risk and Sociocultural Theory: New Directions and Perspectives*. Cambridge: Cambridge University Press.

Marsden, R. 1999. *The Nature of Capital: Marx After Foucault*. London: Routledge.

Merlingen, M. 2003. Governmentality Towards a Foucauldian Framework for the Study of IGOs. *Cooperation and Conflict* 38 (4): 361–384.

Miller, P., and N. Rose. 1990. Governing Economic Life. *Economy and Society* 19 (1): 1–31.

———. 2008. *Governing the Present: Administering Economic, Social and Personal Life*. Cambridge: Polity Press.

O'Malley, P. 2010. Resilient Subjects: Uncertainty, Warfare and Liberalism. *Economy and Society* 39 (4): 488–509.

———. 2013. Uncertain Governance and Resilient Subjects in the Risk Society. *Oñati Socio-legal Series* 3 (2): 180–195.

Pisani-Ferry, J., A. Sapir, and G. Wolff. 2013. *EU-IMF Assistance to Euro-Area Countries: An Early Assessment*. Belgium: Bruegel Blueprint Series.

Rose, N. 1993. Government, Authority and Expertise in Advanced Liberalism. *Economy and Society* 22 (3): 283–299.

———. 1996. Governing "Advanced" Liberal Democracies. In *Foucault And Political Reason,* ed. A. Barry, T. Osborne, and N. Rose, 37–64. London: UCL Press.

———. 1999. *Governing the Soul: The Shaping of the Private Self*. 2nd ed. London: Free Association Books.

Rosenberg, J. 2005. Globalization Theory: A Post Mortem. *International Politics* 42 (1): 2–74.

Vestergaard, J. 2009. *Discipline in the Global Economy?: International Finance and the End of Liberalism New Political Economy*. New York: Routledge.

Young, B. 2015. Introduction: The Hijacking of German Ordoliberalism. *European Review of International Studies* 2 (3): 7–15.

Zebrowski, C. 2009. Governing the Network Society: A Bio-political Critique of Resilience. *Political Perspectives* 3 (1): 1–36.

———. 2016. *The Value of Resilience: Securing Life in the Twenty-First Century*. London: Routledge.

3

The Rise of Neo-Liberal Governmentality

Introduction

This chapter focuses on two historic moments through the Foucauldian framework of governmentality: the recent financial crises and the collapse of the Bretton Woods system in 1971. In so doing, it argues that the core policies adopted since 2008 are marked more by continuance than change. Neo-liberalism still dominates, and the further retrenchment of the state and marketization of the social sphere is readily apparent. There is a greater emphasis on resilience both with regard to the financial system and with regard to the human subject. However, this chapter argues that the emphasis on an emergent resilient subject fits within the dominant form of governmentality—neo-liberalism. Indeed, as Jonathan Joseph has argued, 'the recent enthusiasm for the concept of resilience across a range of policy literature is the consequence of its fit with neoliberal discourse' (2013, p. 38). As will be discussed in Chap. 5, with regard to system resilience, this has been combined with a greater emphasis on surveillance and pre-emption.

The 1971 crisis heralded enormous changes in the modes of governmentality in the highly industrialized countries, both in terms of

J. G. Glenn, *Foucault and Post-Financial Crises*, International Political Economy Series, https://doi.org/10.1007/978-3-319-77188-5_3

governing rationalities (an intensification in the marketization of the social sphere) and the reconstitution of subjectivities. At the regulatory level, rather than adopting the interventionary measures of previous decades a much more hands-off approach was introduced that relied upon the power of the market rather than the state per se. These changes coincided with the shift towards financialization and the rise of global production chains as a result of the restructuring of national economies.[1] However, the second major economic crisis (actualized as a series of crises) in the core industrialized countries has not led to another innovatory restructuring in the actual economy. Instead, we have witnessed the continuing retrenchment of the state and further marketization of the social sphere. With regard to finance, the reforms continue to enframe the financial system in a naturalistic manner applying policies that are very much akin to those applied in the sphere of biopolitics. However, in order to prevent another meltdown, there has been an increase in the regulatory and surveillance powers of the state as well as the introduction of pre-emptive policies aimed at nipping problems in the bud before they can ramify throughout the system. Similarly, continuity and change are apparent with regard to citizens qua economic subjects. A new discourse has emerged around resilience thinking with an emphasis on the inculcation of certain dispositions that enable citizens to adapt and survive when confronted with crises. Although this discourse is relatively new (at least in the economic sphere), this chapter argues that it coheres with neo-liberalism and has, by and large, become integrated into the dominant discourse of the latter.

This chapter therefore argues that the fundamental principles of neo-liberal governmentality regimes remain unchanged: the basic principles of neo-liberalism remain in place and an emphasis on market-led solutions as opposed to Keynesian demand management or another alternative approach continues. However, the reasons for this continuation do not only rest with the dominance of multinational corporations as Colin Crouch avers. The explanation is also to be found in the problems of over-capacity which first appeared in the late sixties and early seventies which have been greatly exacerbated with the economic rise of China. Indeed, the solutions to the earlier crisis sowed the seeds for many of the problems that have confronted the highly industrialized states in recent times. The highly industrialized states are now confronted with a tripartite dependence on the financialization of the economy that has occurred over the last few decades. The individual qua enterprising entrepreneur seeks to supplement wages (which since the seventies have received a decreasing proportion of the overall profit generated by companies) through high levels of debt and asset accumulation. The corporate and financial sectors, on the other hand, are highly dependent on the shift from the socialization of risk towards entrepreneurship and self-management involving a 'societal inculcation of a particular understanding of risk and uncertainty'.[2] Finally, governments find themselves trapped within this financial web because of the tax revenue the financial sector generates and the wage supplement cheap credit provides.[3]

Explaining the Shift to Neo-Liberal Governmentalities

The shift to neo-liberal forms of governmentality was preceded by an over-capacity crisis of the late 1960s and early 1970s which witnessed a rapid decline in the rate of return on investment in industry within the highly industrialized countries (Brenner 2006, pp. 143–229; Callinicos 2003; Harvey 2003, 2006). The crisis was not just one of US hegemony (i.e. the double deficit and Triffin's dilemma), but of capitalism in general with industrial over-capacity in combination with commodity-based cost-push inflation leading to the worst possible outcome—stagflation—low growth alongside high inflation (Glenn 2016). Some have argued that the decline in the rate of return on investment failed to recover in the core highly industrialized countries evolving into a 'long downturn' (Brenner 2006). Others, like David McNally, agree that this period experienced a rapid decline in the rate of return on investment, but argue that this recovered in the eighties and nineties, yet started to decline once again in the late nineties (McNally 2011, p. 49; Mohun 2006). But all agree that the seventies was a period of 'excess capacity galore and declining profits, the world economy had entered a new period of global turbulence' (McNally 2011, pp. 29–30).

As a result of the 1970s crisis, fundamental transformations in the social, technical and spatial organization of capitalist production were inaugurated. This is not to imply that some unifying blueprint emerged that was simply pursued unproblematically (Joseph 2012). Rather many discourses and solutions to the crisis were proposed at the time, but those that became sedimented were those that ensured the continuing reproduction of capitalism and, much of the time, reflected the dominant interests within society. It is useful here to employ Bob Jessop's notion of strategic selectivity. Although there was no unified blueprint at the beginning of the crisis, the various solutions, arguments and assumptions that underpinned the dominant neo-liberal discourse arose from 'specific strategies pursued by specific forces (or specific sets of such forces) with specific identities in order to advance specific interests over specific spatial and temporal horizons relative to specific other forces, each advancing their own interests through their own strategies' (Jessop 1999, p. 54). These discourses and their solutions to the crisis were subject to the biases within various institutions favouring the dominant social forces at the time. Such structurally inscribed biases are most pronounced in the state (as an ensemble of institutions) where there is an in-built 'bias that makes it more open to capitalist influences and readily mobilized for capitalist policies' (Jessop 1990, pp. 147–8). The discourses and strategies pursued by the dominant industrial and financial classes therefore found a receptive audience in the various circles of state elites.

The various policies that emerged had as their object a temporary resolution to capitalism's contradictions. These changes included extracting greater profit from cost cutting with regard to circulating capital: increases in labour productivity, wage reductions, cheaper raw materials and intermediate goods. But it also involved spatio-temporal displacements that facilitated the reproduction and expansion of capitalism. This spatio-temporal fix was in response to excess capital arising from the paucity of lucrative investments and was targeted at 'opening up new markets, new production capacities, and new resource, social, and labour possibilities elsewhere' (Harvey 2003, p. 109). This is not to say, that this spatio-temporal fix involved the shift of capital to the periphery to the extent that it constituted the main site of capital investment. As Ray Kiely points out, the empirical evidence for such a reorientation of investment is highly questionable and it certainly was not the case in the seventies (Kiely 2007, p. 78; 2010, p. 59). Yet, contra Kiely, an intensification of investment in other countries of the core does not preclude an intensification of investment in the periphery at the same time.[4] Solutions to the problems of the seventies were found in both the core and periphery, involving fundamental transformations in the social, technical and spatial organization of capitalist production. Solutions to the problems of the seventies thus involved fundamental transformations in the social, technical and spatial organization of capitalist production both in the highly industrialized core and in the relatively less industrialized periphery/semi-periphery.

This spatio-temporal fix had a multifaceted character (Harvey 2003). First, neo-liberalism in the core created a much-improved environment for capital investment through tax reductions, labour deregulation and mass privatization. Second, a major restructuring of capital on a global scale took place. The objective was to break down spatial barriers to the restructuring of capital by demanding the removal of barriers to trade and investment in other countries while programmes of mass privatization and land reform provided new opportunities for manufacturing, services and agribusiness through the 'appropriation and marketization of hitherto uncommodified realms'.[5]

Production was reconfigured on a global scale with much of the labour-intensive industry relocated to the periphery, thus lowering costs of production and providing a strong negotiating position for pressuring labour in the core. In order to counter the downturn, companies engaged in restructuring, new ventures, mergers and acquisitions as well as outright buyouts of competitors. The subsequent reforms in the work place have meant 'lay-offs and systematic pressure to worsen collective bargaining and weaken union power' with a subsequent downward pressure on wages and greater dependency upon casual labour (Peters 2010, p. 12). Combined with the high unemployment which already existed as a result of the economic downturn that began in the seventies, it had the adverse effect of worsening the economic conditions within the core industrialized countries, real wage increases and wage share dramatically declined and consumer confidence nosedived (OECD 2004, p. 136; Mohun 2006, pp. 347–370). During the seventies 'Growth in real hourly compensation slowed from 4%…to just over 1% annually since 1990' (OECD 2004, p. 136). This was despite the continuing productivity gains made in the workplace during these decades—in fact, during the eighties 'the growth rate of the real wage per efficiency unit of labour was actually negative…and has been approximately zero since' (OECD 2004, p. 136). Indeed, in the US, Canada, Australia and New Zealand, real wages actually declined for the period 1983–1992 (Western and Mealy 1999, pp. 233–249).

Many companies began to engage in vertical rather than horizontal foreign direct investment, with companies slicing up the production chain locating the different stages of manufacturing wherever they were cheapest. Improvements in technology facilitating improved coordination and reductions in transport costs enabled them to divide the production process across countries and even continents. At the same time, there was a sharp increase in the practice of 'out-sourcing'. Establishing factories in other countries implies that the suppliers of the component parts of a product continue to be at least partly owned and managed by the company in question. But, rather than investing in setting up their own service or production plant and directly managing the business, many corporations sought to procure the required components or services from independent sources.

As a result of these transformations, greater emphasis is now placed on the core functions of managing the supply chain and final assembly rather than concentrating on 'in-house' manufacturing of a product from start to finish. As Fareed Zakaria put it, for the highly industrialized countries, this is the happy face mode of production:

> At the top left of the curve one starts with the idea and high-level industrial design—how the product will look and work. Lower down on the curve comes the detailed engineering plan. At the bottom of the U is the actual manufacturing, assembly, and shipping. Then rising up on the right of the curve are distribution, marketing, retail sales, service contracts, and sales of parts and accessories. (Zakaria 2011, p. 186)

The reason that the name given to this process is so apposite for multinational companies is that the 'real money is in the brand name, plus retail'.[6] For example, although Nike is regarded as an example par excellence of a large multinational company, it actually employs only '9000 people, while nearly 75,000 people are employed by its independent sub-contractors' (Hoogvelt 2001, p. 127). In a similar fashion to that of 'vertical' FDI, the growth of 'out-sourcing' heralds a new form of business structure, one in which the upstream linkages of suppliers and the downstream linkages to the final customer have become stretched across continents (Christopher 1992, p. 15).

As long as multinational companies can protect the patents arising from their research and development (and that is a big if) and the distribution of the product, that is, the retail side, then (from their perspective) it matters little if the actual manufacturing is done overseas at some low-cost location, because the main value added is at the beginning and end of the chain. Indeed, this has fundamentally altered the economic structure of the highly industrialized countries with most of the annual economic activity being generated by the service sector.

This restructuring of capital on a global scale was greatly expedited by two roughly simultaneous events.

First, as a result of the oil price hikes that followed the reduction in supply of the commodity by Arab petroleum exporting countries in protest at US involvement in the Yom-Kippur War of 1973, oil-exporting countries became awash with petro-dollars. Much of this was recycled as loans to developing countries at relatively low interest rates. Inevitably, many countries over borrowed and when US interest rates rose with the Volcker Shock of 1979, global interest rates rose to the extent that developing countries struggled to repay their debts. The IMF and World Bank stepped in to help, but the loans came with conditionalities entailing a series of economic reforms, or so-called structural adjustment policies (SAPs), thus ensuring the adoption of neo-liberalism by the majority of less developed states. So, unlike the industrialized countries that had adopted such policies, the South was given little choice as to whether or not to accept. Refusal of the recommended economic reforms could result in a full-blown financial crisis and as a result most leaders reluctantly implemented such policies, often without the requisite political mandate from their populations. Such reforms included several discrete stages associated with this process: stabilization, structural adjustment and export-led growth (Thomas 2000, pp. 328–9). Reducing inflation was regarded as the top priority, often resulting in lower government spending (which would also lower budget deficits) and high interest rates.[7] The second phase involved structural adjustment proper, including the selling to private interests of previously nationalized industries and the closure of inefficient enterprises; the cancelling/reduction of subsidies to both private and nationalized industries; abstention of price intervention by the government. The final stage had the objective of promoting export-led growth by liberalizing trade (reduction of tariffs), eliminating non-tariff barriers to trade, removal of restrictions on finance and investment from abroad thereby providing an investor-friendly environment for those seeking a low-cost base from which to produce and export from (Thomas 2000, pp. 328–9).

As argued by Peter Gowan, using loan conditionality as political leverage, the IMF and World Bank essentially carried out a revolution of the world economic system based on the free movement of goods, services and capital, coercing indebted governments to adopt

> domestic deflation, currency devaluation and an export drive along with measures to ease budget deficits and earn foreign currency on the capital account by privatising with the help of foreign capital and attracting inward flows of hard-currency funds through liberalising the capital account. Thus did US rentiers get their debts paid, US industry got cheaper imports of the inputs needed for production, US companies could buy up assets including privatised utilities in the country concerned, and the capital account would be liberalised so that local stock markets could be played. (Gowan 1999, p. 42)

The debt crisis of the early 1980s was therefore essentially used to 'organize the internal relations of production in each country where they occurred in such a way as to favour the further penetration of external capitals', particularly through the imposition of structural adjustment by the IMF and World Bank (Harvey 2003, p. 42). The objective was to break down spatial barriers to this restructuring of capital by demanding the removal of barriers to trade and investment while programmes of mass privatization and land reform provided new opportunities for business.

Second, Deng Xiaoping's announcement of an open door policy in 1978 opening China up to overseas investors represents a largely serendipitous moment in this globalization process. Given its almost inexhaustible supply of labour and land at the time, foreign direct investment poured in from both the West and the East shifting their labour-intensive processing and assembly plants to the country (Lardy 2002, p. 56). This led to a massive decline in employment in certain industrial sectors in the highly industrialized states as production shifted to China. For example, for Hong Kong's toy manufacturing, employment fell from '56,400 in 1981 to only 2000 in 1999' and for textile and apparel it fell from '382,000 in 1981 to only 75,000 in 1999' (Ibid., p. 56). Moreover, following the reforms of 1992 which permitted wholly owned foreign enterprises into the domestic market of China, a significant increase in investment occurred once again. Indeed, foreign funded enterprises and joint ventures now 'employ 15.9% of the urban workforce' of China (Morrison 2013, p. 10).

China has become the second largest recipient of FDI inflows after the US.[8] This boom in global investment has altered the pattern of FDI coming into the country. In 1992 'FDI from Hong Kong and Taiwan constituted 80% of total FDI flows into China', but once China's boom was well under way investors across the globe became interested and now 'about 400 of the Fortune 500 firms have invested in over two thousand projects' (Zhang 2002, p. 26). At a global level, we have thus seen a dramatic shift of industrial production to regions of the world that offer stable environments and cheap factors of production—primarily Mexico and East Asia, particularly China. This has provided the world with incredibly low prices for consumer goods and helped tame inflation, but it has also led to a global reconfiguration of industry to the extent that, for most of the highly industrialized countries, the service sector now constitutes between 70% and 80% of GDP and employment.

Major restructuring also occurred in other spheres. With the relinquishing of capital controls by the US in 1974, other countries found it increasingly difficult to maintain their capital controls. The pressure for change arose from two main sources.[9] First, from corporations seeking to establish a presence abroad—particularly in light of the ongoing industrial restructuring. Second, the increasing internationalization of finance meant that there were ever greater opportunities to evade domestic restrictions anyway, yet the remaining capital controls were preventing legitimate 'domestic agents from participating fully in international activities' (Quirk and Evans 1995, p. 11). The economic environment therefore evolved into a liberal financial order allowing money to flow around the global system relatively unfettered by state control. New York bankers, who had been vociferous opponents of capital controls from the outset, finally achieved their aim in the 1980s of a financial regime in which investment and speculation could be conducted on a global scale with New York at the centre of such operations (Helleiner 1996, pp. 8–9). As Gowan points out, this involved a qualitative shift away from the Bretton Woods system because 'the new arrangements brought international private finance into the very centre of the workings of the new international monetary system and enabled this force to operate on a scale qualitatively different from that under the old regime' (Gowan 1999, p. 22).

The abandonment of US capital controls alongside the deregulation of the New York securities market and the advent of market-based trading fees gave the US a competitive advantage in the financial services sector over its rivals. If others failed to follow suit, they would find that international investors would simply use New York as the main base for their financial operations. Britain thus followed in 1979 with a full relaxation of capital controls and with the 'Big Bang' in 1986 whereby overseas financial firms were given untrammelled access to the London Stock Exchange. Japan followed suit with revision of its exchange controls in 1980 and, after US pressure to open its financial markets to international investors, an accord was reached in 1984 between the two countries to that effect. Germany likewise fully liberalized its capital account in 1981 (although many controls had been eased some years before this), followed belatedly by France from 1986 to 1990.[10] Across the rest of Europe, with the future of a single market planned for the European Community in 1992, the Council of Ministers passed a directive in 1988 providing for the free movement of capital throughout the EC by the mid-nineties (Helleiner 1996, Chapter 7).

Concomitant with these transformations, in all three traditional areas of intervention: regulatory, distributive and redistributive, states' activities became highly circumscribed. In terms of taxing, regulating and establishing the macroeconomic conditions for the country, governments now concerned themselves with ensuring non-inflationary growth and a business-friendly regulatory framework (Cerny 1990, 1997, p. 260). As Philip Cerny has recently pointed out, this was not so much complete deregulation but rather a form of re-regulation, that is, 'not the removal of rules, but a form of re-regulation, with the promulgating of even more complex pro-market forms of regulation' (Cerny 2009, p. 378). Instead of output-orientated interventionism by the state that had occurred previously, the state saw its role as an 'arms-length' regulator establishing and enforcing 'general rules applicable to a particular sector, industry or service in order to make it work more efficiently in the economic sense of the word' rather than state qua provider state (Cerny 2008, p. 24). In terms of production (i.e. control of the production and distribution of goods), states relinquished direct ownership of production, concentrating instead on improving infrastructure, thus providing the private sector with an abundance of lucrative investment opportunities (Cerny 1995, p. 611).

The highly industrialized states essentially reconstituted themselves as providers of business-friendly environments by promoting 'enterprise, innovation and profitability in both private and public sectors' (Cerny 1997, p. 260). The state as business facilitator is said to involve providing a highly skilled, well-educated workforce (human capital); high-quality reliable infrastructure such as roads, fibre-optic networks, mobile communications; research and development sites (e.g. universities); and a favourable investment climate (Cerny 1995, p. 611). In order for corporate profitability to be restored, states had to create the right conditions for the internationalization of capital. However, this radically altered the balance between risk and opportunity. The new economic environment certainly improved the opportunities for capital investors but it also increased the level of economic risk that the general population was exposed to. The new level of trade openness combined with capital account liberalization increased the degree of economic dislocation experienced. Less competitive industries lost their markets to their foreign counterparts and at the same time companies now had the opportunity to relocate to countries where the factors of production were cheaper.

Financialization and the Emergence of Privatized Keynesianism

With this global restructuring of production, populations were caught in a pincer movement. Those that were employed received a smaller proportion of the gains from industry (and in some cases experienced a decline in real wages) whilst those on benefits found themselves in a much harsher environment. The economic paradox that Keynesianism sought to ameliorate now hit the highly industrialized countries with full force, namely capitalism which

> needs on the one hand, consumers on whose confidence firms can depend when planning their production, and on the other, a capacity to respond to periods of declining demand by reducing the quantity and wages of labour, which in turn undermines consumer confidence. (Crouch 2008, p. 476)

A solution to this paradox was found in the increasing financialization of the highly industrialized countries' economies and the shift towards 'privatized Keynesianism' (Crouch 2009, p. 391). As others have pointed out, the problem of over-capacity in the highly industrialized countries not only resulted in the restructuring of economies and the emergence of global production chains. Their economies became ever more 'financialized', resulting in the 'growing weight of finance relative to production. Large corporations have come to rely less on banks, while becoming more engaged in financial markets. Households have become heavily involved in the financial system through assets (pension and insurance) and liabilities (mortgage and unsecured debt). Banks have been transformed, seeking profits through fees, commissions and trading, rebalancing their activities toward households rather than corporations. Financial profit has emerged as a large part of total profit' (Lapavitsas et al. 2012, pp. 1–2). Corporations became financiers in their own right, to a degree that some operated on a par with banks. For example, General

Electric's finance arm became 'one of America's largest financial entities, with assets of half a trillion dollars, about the same as Lehman Brothers had in the run-up to the financial crisis of 2008'. Dealing in 'everything from consumer loans to property', in 2001 it had 'a return on equity of 23% and contributed 41% of the company's profits' (The Economist 10 April 2015).

The spatio-temporal fix, therefore, not only involved a movement of capital to new sites with cheaper factors of production (the spatial dimension) often in the form of long-term investment (the temporal aspect), it also involved another temporal dimension. That is, the supply of immediate capital to consumers in the form of credit based on the promise of long-term repayment (as a substitute for substantial wage increases). On the one hand, industrialists invested across the world in the hope of improved rates of return on investment and, on the other hand, credit was extended to citizens within the highly industrialized countries to ensure that the demand for these products manufactured in these distant sites was maintained. In this way financialization became an essential element in maintaining the various circuits of capital.

Economies became ever more reliant on the expansion of credit that accompanied this financialization as a means to stimulate growth in an attempt to overcome the economic tensions that arose from the wage-cutting actions of firms. The shift towards financialization thus involved a form of 'privatized Keynesianism' which provided the engine for economic growth, but 'Instead of governments taking on debt to stimulate the economy, individuals did so' (Crouch 2009, p. 391). It is not being argued here that in tandem with this shift to privatized Keynesianism there was a concomitant reduction in state spending. However, given the already relatively high levels of debt and annual expenditure by the core industrialized countries, privatized Keynesianism, rather than Keynesian demand management by the state in the form of a fiscal stimulus, was politically far more preferable for those in government.

By relying upon the self-management of the financial markets, governments thought that they had come upon the holy grail of political economy. Not only did they benefit from abstaining from economic stimulation in downturns, they reaped a political dividend from segments of the population that had experienced a decline in their wages in relation to output, but that now had access to material goods that they could previously only dream of:

> An inability to share risks widely had been at the heart of the economic collapses of 1929 and the 1870s. In the 1940s it had seemed that only state action could solve this problem for the market. But now, absolutely in tune with neo-liberal ideology and expectations, there was a market solution. And, through the links of these new risk markets to ordinary consumers via extended mortgages and credit card debt, the dependence of the capitalist system on rising wages, a welfare state and government demand management that had seemed essential for mass consumer confidence, had been abolished. The bases of prosperity shifted from the social democratic formula of working classes supported by government intervention to the neo-liberal conservative one of banks, stock exchanges and financial markets. (Crouch 2009, p. 392)

By seeming to provide a means to escape the 'tyranny of earned income', mass consumption was once again married to the capitalist system, but this time without large-scale intervention of the state.[11] But, the increasing proportion of the population investing their wealth in the financial sector (either directly or indirectly—whether it be pensions or local government tax invested on a short-term basis) has meant that the spread of financial risk is now far more wide ranging.[12] As the potential impact of failure of these firms has grown, so too has the need for stronger regulation at the national, regional and international level.

Significantly, the tax revenue gathered from the financial sector was substantial and growing. For example, in the UK, 'financial services industry contributed only 15 per cent of corporation tax in the 1980s; by 2005 this had risen to over 30 per cent', and in the US, it rose from 10% to 40% by 2007 (Augur 2009, p. 33; *The Economist* 24–30 January 2009a, p. 20). The level of profits was disproportionate to its actual contribution to the overall economy. For example, in the US, the same financial services only accounted for 14% of US GDP and 5% of private sector jobs. It is easy to see why Western governments were reluctant to fetter such a prodigious cash cow. In a globalized world where tax extraction had become ever more difficult, any increase in revenue was welcomed.

The expansion of the securities market presented the opportunity of expanding credit provision, both in terms of value to those that already had access and in terms of breadth, thus extending it to those poorer income groups that previously had access denied. What were previously regarded as unacceptable levels of credit extension were now regarded as feasible through risk spreading. A win-win situation seemed to present itself with credit expanding to unprecedented levels, but at historically low interest rates. What had 'occurred initially by chance, a real case of market entrepreneurship…gradually became a matter for public policy so important as to threaten the entire neo-liberal project' (Crouch 2009, p. 391).

The problem was that a high degree of volatility attended this form of wealth generation. Looking back over the last few decades it can now be seen that a string of speculative bubbles arose eventually culminating in the great financial crisis. There was Mexico in 1994, then East Asia in 1997, Argentina in 2001, followed by the dotcom bubble of 2002—not to mention the individual corporate collapses of the Long Term Capital Management Company in 1998 and Enron in 2001 (Panitch et al. 2010). Ultimately the speculation in these economies fuelled classic asset bubbles with investment shifting from hedge, to speculative and finally to Ponzi financing (Minsky 1992). As Minsky pointed out, financial markets exhibit a repetitive cycle beginning with hedge or 'normal' financing in which the cash flow is 'more than sufficient to meet contractual payment commitments' (Minsky 2008, p. 230). However, the low profit yield associated with this type of lending leads to more speculative forms of financing in which income flows are enough to pay off the interest but not the principal leading to a 'rolling over of maturing debt' (Minsky 2008, p. 230). The assumption is that the financial asset will increase in value sufficiently to eventually cover the missed payments. The Ponzi form of finance is where the cash flow does not cover the interest or payment of principal due so that the actual 'face amount of outstanding debt increases' (Minsky 2008, pp. 230–31).

The housing market exhibited this exact tendency with constantly rising prices, ever more borrowers engaged in speculative financing by taking out interest only mortgages with the aim of paying the principal back once the loan matured (with the assumption that a profit could be made as a result of the house fetching a higher price than the original cost). The final part of the cycle before the bursting of the bubble (i.e. the 'Minsky Moment') was reached when lenders began to provide mortgages to borrowers who could not even pay the interest payments over time. Lenders provided mortgages on the basis of negative amortization, simply adding any unpaid interest payments onto the principal debt, involving the continual re-financing of the mortgage loan (McCulley 2009).

The Rise of the Neo-Liberal Subject

As several authors have previously pointed out, the restructuring of the production process, the retrenchment of the welfare state and the shift towards financialization 'entailed a range of attempts to shape and modulate the relations that individuals have with society's productive apparatus' (Miller and Rose 1990, p. 19). This is not to argue that there is an unmediated causal link between the restructuring of production and a shift towards financialization and the form that these regimes of governmentality took. The policies associated with these regimes 'do not happen automatically but have to be actively pursued in the policy realm' (Joseph 2012, p. 9). Moreover, these policies develop 'alongside these changes which contribute to the overall conditions of possibility' and are 'emergent aspects of a social whole' (Joseph 2012, p. 43).

What we can therefore say is that since the seventies we have witnessed the emergence of various regimes of neo-liberal governmentality in a multitude of countries. Each one may exhibit some unique characteristics but, at the same time, they exhibit a high enough degree of resemblance to be regarded as part of a neo-liberal family of regimes. Associated with these regimes are a particular set of norms aimed at promoting certain economic activities through the reconstitution of the subjectivities of the population (Rose 1993, p. 294; O'Malley 2004; Langley 2008).[13] The emergence of these subjectivities involved a complex process of norm and value formation that was influenced by the ongoing restructuring of the state and economy.

In relation to welfare retrenchment states sought to 'modify the relation of individuals to political power by seeking, in part, to get them to economize on their expectations of or demands on government' (Burchell 1991, pp. 145–6). More generally, this involved a move away from the notion of citizenship 'construed in terms of solidarity, contentment, welfare and a sense of security established through the bonds of organizational and social life' (Miller and Rose 1990, p. 24). Nowhere was this form of solidarity more apparent than in the socialization of risk in the form of social insurance as an 'inclusive technology of government' which involved 'collectivising the management of the individual and collective dangers posed by the economic riskiness of a capricious system of wage labour, and the corporeal riskiness of a body subject to sickness and injury' (Rose 1993, p. 294). Although welfare provision continued as an economic necessity, a new understanding of citizenship emerged, one 'manifested through the free exercise of personal choice amongst a variety of options' (Miller and Rose 1990, p. 24). Enterprise and entrepreneurship became the new watchwords with the worker 'no longer construed as a social creature seeking satisfaction of his or her need for security, solidarity and welfare, but as an individual actively seeking to shape and manage his or her own life in order to maximize its returns in terms of success and achievement' (Miller and Rose 1990, p. 9).

This new regime of governmentality no longer engaged in 'instructing individuals in all spheres of their existence, from the most intimate to the most public. Individuals themselves, as workers, managers and members of families can be mobilized in alliance with political objectives, in order to deliver economic growth, successful enterprise and optimum personal happiness' (Miller and Rose 1990, p. 28). The 'provider' state began to evolve into the 'enabler' state. The task of government began to be seen as providing a conducive environment in which individual capacities could flourish. Governments stressed the importance of investing in human capital: improving the education level of the population, providing them with the capability to adapt and learn new tasks; placing an emphasis on life-long learning; and providing the unemployed with the opportunity of re-training. As Cerny has pointed out, the objective of such state intervention is the 'insertion or reinsertion of such groups…into the market process through education, training etc.' (Cerny 2009, p. 378). The state has thus undertaken this restructuring in order to become pro-business in orientation, competing with other states for finance and investment from around the world.

At the same time, this new form of governmentality involved the constitution of neo-liberal financial subjects who were to be both entrepreneurial and responsible subjects rationally calculating the risks and benefits of the various financial positions they ventured into. The escape from the 'tyranny of earned income' was thus associated with the emergence of the entrepreneurial self and a shift in individual financial behaviour from thrift to investment so that the latter became seen as 'the socially desirable form of saving' (Froud et al. 2010; O'Malley 2004, p. 23). This form of saving is completely different to that of thrift which entails the setting aside of resources in relatively safe forms like bank deposits 'in order to provide for the effects of future harms' (O'Malley 2004, p. 23). Whereas thrift views risk negatively and, indeed, its emphasis on prudence derives from its concern to counter future uncertainties—investment treats risk and reward as inseparable (Langley 2008, p. 52). Associated with the shift away from socialized forms of risk towards self-management and the subject as entrepreneur was a positive re-evaluation of risk which was seen as a way to enhance an individual's security and freedom via 'calculative investments' (Langley 2008, p. 55).

The move from socialized risk to individual risk thus involved the taking on of various financial ventures by individuals to increase their wealth, but equally each individual was supposed to assume responsibility for their actions and to display self-discipline. As Paul Langley points out, this was not a shift from thrift to spendthrift, rather 'prudence and thrift are displaced by new moral and calculative self-disciplines of responsibly and entrepreneurially meeting, managing, and manipulating the outstanding obligations that arise from extended borrowing' (Langley 2008, p. 186).

Yet, this shift in governmentality towards inculcating populations with a spirit of entrepreneurialism was accompanied by a shift towards increasing individual debt to fuel both increased consumption and the acquisition of assets. Property was now viewed as an asset rather than a home and used either as a financial instrument to realize equity immediately as collateral on other financial ventures or as a speculative instrument in its own right. As Rob Aitken points out, such asset acquisition was a direct result of the rise of the investment economy and the shift in social security policies. Of course, previously, citizens had engaged in stock markets, houses and so on. But the fundamental difference was that asset accumulation was now seen as a form of social welfare policy. Asset accumulation was viewed as a policy of empowerment, one that would enable individuals through the ownership of various assets and 'introduce welfare recipients to the language of enterprise and to the concepts of choice and risk exposure' (Aitken 2007, p. 179). However, in so doing it produced an environment in which 'Risk exists as an inescapable and permanent condition' (Aitken 2007, p. 186).

It is also important to point out, in way of signposting to later chapters, that these endeavours to inculcate individuals with neo-liberal values did not go unchallenged and a variety of resistances have been apparent over the decades. Some were less successful than others, such as, the miners' strike in the UK and the US air traffic controllers strike during the Reagan/Thatcher periods. The anti-globalization protests at the WTO conference in Seattle helped place many developmental issues associated with WTO global trade agreements in the mainstream media. Others were even more successful, such as, the *cacerolazo* (pots and pans) protests against economic austerity in Argentina in 2001 which led to the resignation of President Fernando de la Rua and arguably laid the foundation for the decision to fully repay debts to the IMF at the beginning of 2006. The subjectification process associated with neo-liberalism is therefore often met with resistance and, as we will see in the following chapters, the neo-liberal austerity programmes rolled out after the financial crisis are no exception in this regard.

In the Aftermath of the Crisis: *Plus ça Change*?

This section argues that, after a brief period of Keynesian style government intervention in the highly industrialized economies, economic policy drifted back towards the neo-liberal rationalities after the financial crisis. Indeed, if anything, there was an intensification of state retrenchment and marketization of the social sphere—particularly in the sovereign periphery of Europe. In the case of finance, stricter regulations were put in place but these only differed in intensity with previous neo-liberal policies. There was an intensification in surveillance and pre-emptive policies in this sphere, alongside a greater emphasis on systemic resilience but these initiatives were enframed by the dominant neo-liberal discourse. This is equally true of the emergence of resilience thinking which more often than not resonated with the dominant discourse that views citizens as neo-liberal entrepreneurial subjects.

As mentioned in the Chapter Two, the continuance of neo-liberalism not only points to the abiding strength of the neo-liberal social imaginary but also points to the power and entrenched interests of political and economic elites. It also points to a high degree of ideational bankruptcy. Indeed, it is difficult to see how the economy can undergo a similar restructuring of production to that of the 1970s. The reconfiguration of industrial production from a national to a global scale involved major economic dislocation with swathes of the population in the highly industrialized countries either forced out of employment or re-skilled and re-employed outside the industrial sector. A historic shift towards employment in services therefore occurred, to the extent that over 75% of the population now works in services. The slower growth in wages associated with increased international competition and the shift to lower skilled jobs was partly compensated for by increased access to credit. Yet, if a similar transformation occurs in services through either shifting jobs to cheaper sites or the utilization of new technologies, it will simply increase unemployment and place further pressure on wages as well as increase our reliance on credit. We have yet to see whether companies will fully integrate new technologies into the service sector, but if they do, a crisis of even greater proportions is likely to happen.

In the aftermath of the 2008 financial crisis, two main views have emerged concerning its effects on economic policy. The first argues that the severity of the crisis has led to a fundamental rethink of neo-liberal practices because, 'Neo-liberalism has, quite simply, collapsed. It has shown itself not just to be unfair but also to be totally inadequate in doing what it claimed it could do — ensure prosperity for all' (Brown 2010, p. 12). At the other end of the spectrum, there are those that see the continuation of these economic policies and view the main task as explaining the 'strange non-death of neoliberalism' (Crouch 2011; Tomlinson 2011; Harvey 2009).

With the onset of the financial crisis, suddenly Keynes became flavour of the month once again. With \$3 trillion worth of write-downs in the financial sector and the possibility of meltdown staring them in the face, political leaders once again embraced Keynes (*The Economist* 16–22 May 2009b, p. 13). Nationalization/bail-outs of financial institutions on both sides of the Atlantic looks like a roll call of the great and the good: Freddie Mac and Fannie Mae, Citigroup, American International Group in the US; Northern Rock, Bradford and Bingley, Royal Bank of Scotland, Lloyds Banking Group in the UK; Hypo-Real Estate in Germany; Glitmir, Landsbanki, Kaupthing in Iceland; Dexia was rescued by Belgium, France and Luxembourg; and Ireland saved its banks by guaranteeing the payment of any of its banks' liabilities if need be. On 8 October 2008, three of the main central banks across the world (Federal Reserve, Bank of England, European Central Bank [ECB]) all cut their lending rates. Moreover, the ECB provided an unlimited credit line to banks and the Fed announced that it would provide unsecured loans to prop up the financial system (*The Economist* 11–17 October 2008a, p. 79). At the same time, in order to get financial institutions to lend not only to each other but to companies and individuals, the US absorbed over $700 billion of toxic assets (those loans that were most at risk of default). In the UK, banks were provided with 50 billion pounds in exchange for shares and 100 billion pounds worth of toxic assets were taken off their books by the Bank of England which also provided 250 billion pounds for new loans (*The Economist* 11–17 October 2008a, p. 79). Other countries followed suit with Germany setting up a 300 billion Euro fund, France 360 billion Euros and Holland 200 billion Euros (*The Economist* 19–24 October 2008b, p. 67). China responded to the crisis by opening up its coffers and setting aside $600 billion for what was hoped to be a one off spending spree to reverse its economic fortunes (*The Economist* 15–21 November 2008c, p. 30). The new Obama administration also passed a fiscal stimulus bill totalling $789 billion.

It may therefore seem like we have gone back to the future, but several points are worth noting. First, governments have made clear that their nationalization/part-nationalization of the banks is a temporary measure and will only last until calmer times return—not least because of the high level of government debt that such intervention generates. Second, financial markets accepted the fiscal stimulus that these states embarked upon because there was a clear imperative for radical action to save the system which was in everyone's interest. However, as the cases of the so-called PIIGS (Portugal, Italy, Ireland, Greece and Spain) demonstrate, normalcy has now returned and the usual limits upon government spending are currently being re-imposed by the financial markets. Third, a new round of privatization of state assets has now begun. Fourth, the highly industrialized states remain committed to an open world trade and investment order.

If this remains the case, it is highly likely that the neo-liberal form of governmentality will continue. In other words, these states will continue to promote the idea of a self-regulating market and entrepreneurship as the main driver of an open economy that is subject to international competition in an environment marked by over-capacity. A downward pressure on wages will continue to be exerted, but this time it will not only derive from international competition, but also from ever higher tax burdens aimed at reducing the long-term debts that have increased exponentially as a result of the crisis.

Colin Hay has remarked that the spending spree during the crisis represented 'foul-weather Keynesianism' rather than a return to Keynesian economic proper (Hay 2010, p. 23). This chimes with Crouch's observation that, 'The initial response of governments to the financial crisis has been a return to regulation and even temporary bank nationalization. However, this will not last…Governments will want to see a return to credit boom as the most effective way of restoring consumer confidence while they continue to pursue policies making labour markets more flexible' (2011 p. 120).

This would appear to be the case with large-scale cuts in public sector wages alongside a further shrinking of the state sector across Europe. Those states whose sovereign credit has been questioned because of their relatively high debt to GDP ratios have been the most severely affected, embarking upon another round of wholesale state privatization and further liberalization. As Chap. 6 argues, the post-financial crisis Eurozone is experiencing a transformation away from the more consensual and indirect methods of inculcating neo-liberal norms towards a regime based on surveillance, discipline and punishment. These structural adjustment programmes by the IMF and World Bank that were previously applied solely to industrially developing countries have now landed on the shores of the sovereign periphery of Europe (Merlingen 2003).

As we will see in Chap. 6, the 'solution' to the debt crisis in Europe has involved the usual push towards privatization and a raft of austerity measures, with the Greek Government agreeing to sell enough state assets to raise 50 billion Euros by 2015.[14] Such sell-offs provide huge economic opportunities for the struggling private sector. As the European Commission stated recently, 'The Greek government is one of the European sovereigns with the richest portfolio of assets. This portfolio includes listed and non-listed companies, concessions and commercially-viable real estate (buildings and land)' (European Commission 2011). The crisis and the concerns over the difficulties in securing credit has meant that the most vulnerable economies, Portugal, Italy, Ireland, Spain and Greece, have also embarked upon ambitious privatization and austerity programmes (Sakoui 22 September 2011). In tune with its neo-liberal leanings, this shift towards austerity includes the UK, even though its debt levels are not comparable to the Southern periphery (Watt 19 March 2012; *BBC News* 10 September 2010; Wintour 15 January 2012).

At the national level, the policy of privatized Keynesianism and neo-liberal governmentality with its emphasis on individuals as asset building entrepreneurial subjects remains relatively unchanged. The UK, for example, has recently endeavoured to promote further home ownership by offering from January 2014, 'five-year interest-free loans worth up to 20 per cent of the value of new-build homes costing less than £600,000' (Winnett March 2013). Similarly, at the same time as passing a new initiative to prevent further foreclosures, Obama announced a tax credit for any first-time homebuyer (Christie February 2009).

In the financial sphere, reform has been marked by both continuance and change. The rationalities of governance with regard to finance continue to enframe the financial system in a naturalistic manner. As such it is treated as if it is akin to naturally occurring homeostatic systems which should self-correct itself as long as appropriate limits to risk-laden behaviour are established and complied with. The assumption is that the 'wisdom of the market' will ensure that riskier financial operations will be correctly assessed as such by credit rating agencies and will therefore have greater costs (risk premiums) imposed upon them. In this regard, the post-financial crisis landscape is marked by one of degree rather than of kind. The emphasis has thus been less on establishing more restrictive risk parameters so that the outer limits of financial risk are narrowed and also that the markets will re-calibrate their spectrum of risk/cost calculations.

In addition, the perceived unpredictability of the financial system has led to a stronger emphasis on pre-emption, surveillance and resilience (O'Malley 2010, 2013). Of course, pre-emptive policies were present previously. Stress tests (preparedness/resilience) and early warning exercises had been used prior to the crisis (Berg et al. 2000, 2004). However, the intensity of such practices and degree of coordination between various supervisory bodies since the crisis are such that we can speak of the emergence of a pre-emptive regime of governance—one based on an extremely high degree of surveillance with the aim of identifying an emerging crisis and nipping it in the bud before it ramifies and threatens the global financial system. In the aftermath of the crisis, attention has also shifted towards resilience. This is not just focused at the level of individual subjectivities, but also on the way in which complex systems operate and the sources of instability within them. The focus has been on the 'performative adaptability' of the financial system to 'withstand, re-route and recombine in the wake of a potentially catastrophic event to maintain systemic operability' (Zebrowski 2009, p. 9) so that it can 'withstand, recover and bounce back from crisis' (Zebrowski 2016, p. 4). It is also hoped that stress testing and the introduction of living wills and so on will strengthen the resilience of the financial system and limit any damage if the aforementioned pre-emptive surveillance should fail in its objectives.

As mentioned previously in Chap. 2, governmentality refers not only to the rationalities of government, but also to the forms of subjectivity that issue from these rationalities of government and what forms of socialization are employed in attempts to regulate the conduct of the individual. Since the financial crises, neo-liberal subjectivities have continued alongside the re-assertion of neo-liberal rationalities with regard to economic and financial policies. However, alongside this continuation has emerged a new discourse centred on resilience thinking and the need to inculcate certain dispositions that enable the individual to adapt and survive when confronted by crises.

Although resilience discourses were very much apparent before the financial crisis, much of the emphasis was on large systems and ecology

(Hollings 1973; Gunderson and Pritchard 2002; Walker and Salt 2006). Whereas, since the financial crisis there has been much greater emphasis on citizens as resilient subjects and an emphasis on the inner qualities that will enable survival. Although resilience thinking is a relatively new discourse in economics, it is noteworthy that it coheres with the wider discourse of neo-liberalism and this is likely a key factor in its popularity. Indeed, compare the acceptance of this discourse in academic and policy circles compared to the subaltern discourse of resistance to welfare cuts, privatization and the lack of reform in the financial sector.

As O'Malley argues, since the 1970s, 'political and economic "security" had begun to diverge as exposure to uncertainty and insecurity in the economic domain were defined by neoliberals as beneficial and essential to freedom and security' (2013 pp. 191–2). For the entrepreneurial subject, the 'less the security, the greater the freedom' and uncertainty 'now came to mean increased opportunity for the enterprising' (2013 p. 192). Much of resilience thinking coheres with this interpretation, emphasizing the importance of embracing risk and adopting a '*risk-taking* attitude that regards uncertainty as opportunity' (O'Malley 2010, p. 499). The emphasis is on the constitution of subjects that '"thrive" on chaos and make every threat a challenge and opportunity' (O'Malley 2013, p. 192). As can be seen from earlier sections, this very much chimes with the constitution of citizens as entrepreneurial subjects. This coherence is covered in more detail in the next chapter, but it is worth noting here that, once again, these changes do not really challenge the wider precepts of neo-liberalism. So, unlike the 1970s which were marked by radical change, the crises since 2007/2008 have been tumultuous but they have not produced a watershed moment where governmentality has undergone radical change. The next chapter focuses on the rise of resilience, arguing that it chimes with, rather than, challenges the dominant neo-liberal discourse.

Conclusion

This chapter has argued that, contrary to expectations, there has been little change in the form of neo-liberal governmentality since the financial crisis. The chapter contends that the problem of productive over-capacity that arose in the late sixties and early seventies and the policies put into effect as a response continue to have deep ramifications for the economic system as a whole. In order to reverse the decline on the rate of return of investment, firms engaged in a three-pronged strategy: outsourcing/relocating labour-intensive parts of the production process, a greater reliance on financing and the renegotiation of labour relations—especially wages. The first two produced further pressure on the latter with a resulting decline, not only in terms of wage share of profits and in some countries real wages, but also in general employment conditions.

The slump in consumer demand which was no longer met through a Keynesian government-led demand stimulus was instead countered through privatized Keynesianism. This arose from a confluence of events: the emphasis by several states on promoting a form of citizenship that emphasized the subject as entrepreneur, financial deregulation, a recycling of Western currencies from the export-oriented economies of East Asia resulting in sources of cheap credit and the emergence of innovatory financial instruments that at the time were believed to ameliorate the risk of lending, even to the poorest deciles of the population. Ever greater amounts of money were invested in speculative activities across various financial sectors, producing ever-greater levels of wealth, but with attendant risks that were not fully appreciated at the time.

This book contends that there is little evidence that there is a wholesale shift away from this regime of neo-liberal governmentality. Institutions, individuals and governments have become highly dependent on the 'wealth effect' that cheap credit and asset accumulation created and it is difficult to see where an alternative form of stimulus will arise as long as states are unprepared to return to Keynesian style demand management alongside wholesale re-regulation and control of the financial world. Unless there is major civil disruption in the near future as the ramifications of the financial crisis continues to unfold, there seems to be no end in sight for the neo-liberal turn—at least for the foreseeable future.

Yet, some changes are apparent. The disciplinary mechanisms of neo-liberalism which were previously applied solely to industrially developing countries have landed on the shores of Europe and have been readily apparent in Portugal, Italy, Ireland, Greece and Spain. Moreover, although the financial system continues to be treated in a naturalistic manner, the possibility of an even more catastrophic financial crisis has prompted policy-makers to intensify surveillance of the financial sector whilst moving towards pre-emptive policies that seek to prevent crises before they ramify across the globe. At the same time, policy-makers have sought to shore up the resilience of the financial system through regular stress testing and the strengthening of the main nodal points (global significantly important financial institutions) in the financial system. Indeed, with regard to the economy, the emergence of the resilient subject is quite new—yet its immediate popularity is probably down to the fact that it coheres with, rather than challenges, neo-liberalism. These evolutions in neo-liberalism are further explored in the chapters that follow.

Notes

1. A broad definition of financialization would refer to the 'increasing role of financial motives, financial markets, financial actors and financial institutions in the operation of the domestic and international economies' (Epstein 2005b, p. 3).
2. Mark Watson quoted in Langley (2008, p. 9).
3. For example, just before the crisis, 40% of US corporate profits were derived from the financial sector.
4. Although since the financial crisis, this historical trend has reversed and in fact the majority of FDI inflows were to developing rather than developed countries, the historical trend has been around a 70/30 divide. Refer to World Investment Report (2011, p. 3).
5. Included within the processes of accumulation by dispossession are '(1) the commodification and privatization of land and the forceful expulsion of peasant populations; (2) conversion of various forms of property rights (common, collective, state, etc.) into exclusively private property rights; (3) suppression of rights to the commons; (4) commodification of labor power and the suppression of alternative (indigenous) forms of production and consumption; (5) colonial, neo-colonial, and imperial processes of appropriation of assets (including natural resources); (6) monetization of exchange and taxation, particularly of land; (7) the slave trade (which continues, particularly in the sex industry); and (8) usury, the national debt, and most devastating of all, the use of the credit system as radical means of primitive accumulation' (Dunn 2007, p. 5 and 9).

6. James Fallows, 'China Makes, the World Takes' quoted in Zakaria (2011).
7. Thus avoiding another cause of inflation. Devaluing a currency may lead to an increase in exports, but it also leads to domestic inflation as internal prices increase to reflect world prices (domestic prices × exchange rate = world prices).
8. UNCTAD lists Hong Kong as a separate entity and it is therefore difficult to ascertain how much of the inflow to China and Hong Kong is constituted from flows year on year and whether China really has overtaken the US as the primary recipient. However, it is estimated that in 2014, Hong Kong's contribution to inward FDI flows into China was around 17% and China's contribution to FDI inflows into Hong Kong was around 25% of total FDI inflows. Refer to *Global Trends on Inflows.* Online at http://chinaobs.eu/?tab=trendsin
9. The Johnston Administration had imposed controls on the outflow of capital in 1968. The first quote is from Lawrence Summers in 1998. Both quotes are in Panitch and Gindin (2012, p. 11).
10. Germany actually removed restrictions on capital outflows as early as 1958, but was reluctant to do so for capital inflows because of the potential appreciatory effect it would have on its currency. Refer to Quirk and Evans (1995, p. 11).
11. Although, of course, in reality it simply increased the levels of indebtedness in these countries (Froud et al. 2010; Montgomerie 2009, pp. 1–24).
12. As John Braithwaite has argued, 'The legal invention of the security in the seventeenth century was the most transformative moment in the history of corporations. It enabled the replacement of family firms with very large corporations based on pooled contributions of capital from thousands of shareholders and bondholders'. Braithwaite prefers the term regulatory capitalism because it emphasizes the fact that corporations also create regulatory capitalism. But here it is argued that it is useful to maintain a distinction between regulatory capitalism and regulation by states and other governance bodies (Braithwaite 2008, p. 21).
13. In terms of the economy, various authors have identified different regimes of governmentality associated with phases of capitalist transformation. The book uses the term regime because the argument is actually about a change in modality rather than change in the form of state or of capitalism. For the debate on state form versus governmental regime refer to du gay and Scott (2010), Jessop (2010) and Thompson (2010).

14. (Smith 2011). The second bailout in February 2012 not only led to fresh commitments to these privatizations, but also included agreements including 'sacking underperforming tax collectors to passing legislation to liberalise the country's closed professions'. (Chaffin and Hope 21 February 2012).

References

Aitken, R. 2007. *Performing Capital: Toward a Cultural Economy of Popular and Global Finance*. Basingstoke: Palgrave Macmillan.

Augur, P. 2009. *Chasing Alpha: How Reckless Growth and Unchecked Ambition Ruined the City's Golden Decade*. London: Bodley Head.

BBC News. 2010. Royal Mail Is to Be Privatised, Government Confirms, September 10. http://www.bbc.co.uk/news/business-11258649

Berg, A., E. Borensztein, G. Milesi-Ferretti, and C. Pattillo. 2000. Anticipating Balance of Payments Crises—The Role of Early Warning Systems, IMF Occasional Paper No. 186. https://www.imf.org/external/pubs/nft/op/186/index.htm

Berg, A., E. Borensztein, and C. Patillo. 2004. Assessing Early Warning Systems: How Have They Worked in Practice?. IMF Working Paper, WP/04/52.

Braithwaite, J. 2008. *Regulatory Capitalism: How It Works, Ideas for Making It Work Better*. Cheltenham: Edward Elgar.

Brenner, R. 2006. *The Economics of Global Turbulence: The Advanced Capitalist Economies from Long Boom to Long Downturn, 1945–2005*. London: Verso.

Brown, G. 2010. *Why the Right Is Wrong: Fabian Ideas 626*. London: Fabian Society.

Burchell, G. 1991. Peculiar Interests: Civil Society and Governing "The System of Natural Liberty". In *The Foucault Effect: Studies in governmentality*, ed. G. Burchell, C. Gordon, and P. Miller, 119–150. Chicago: Chicago University Press.

Burchell, G., C. Gordon, and P. Miller, eds. 1991. *The Foucault Effect: Studies in Governmentality*. Chicago: Chicago University Press.

Callinicos, A. 2003. *The New Mandarins of American Power*. Cambridge: Polity Press.

Cerny, P. 1990. *The Changing Architecture of Politics: Structure, Agency, and the Future of the State*. London: Age Publications.

———. 1995. Globalization and the Changing Logic of Collective Action. *International Organization* 49 (4): 595–625.

———. 1997. Paradoxes of the Competition State: The Dynamics of Political Globalization. *Government and Opposition* 32 (2): 251–274.

———. 2008. Embedding Neoliberalism: The Evolution of a Hegemonic Paradigm. *The Journal of International Trade and Diplomacy* 2 (1): 1–46.

———. 2009. Introduction: Financial Crisis and Renewal? Diversity and Convergence in Emerging Markets. *Review of International Political Economy* 16 (3): 371–381.

Chaffin, J., and K. Hope. 2012. Greece Races to Meet Bail-Out Demands. *Financial Times*, February 21. http://www.ft.com/cms/s/0/f7adc768-5cb8-11e1-8f1f-00144feabdc0.html#axzz1tTAsaNJ1

Christie, L. 2009. Final Score: $8,000 for Homebuyers First-Time Purchasers Get a Tax Credit Windfall if They Buy Before December. *CNN Money*, February 17. http://money.cnn.com/2009/02/13/real_estate/homebuyer_tax_credit_finalized

Christopher, M. 1992. *Logistics and Supply Chain Management: Strategies for Reducing Cost and Improving Service*. Harlow: Prentice Hall.

Crouch, C. 2008. What Will Follow the Demise of Privatised Keynesianism? *The Political Quarterly* 79 (4): 476–487.

———. 2009. Privatised Keynesianism: An Unacknowledged Policy Regime. *The British Journal of Politics and International Relations* 11 (3): 382–399.

———. 2011. *The Strange Non-Death of Neo-Liberalism*. Cambridge: Polity Press.

du gay, P., and P. Scott. 2010. State Transformation or Regime Shift?: Addressing Some Confusions in the Theory and Sociology of the State. *Sociologica* 2. http://www.sociologica.mulino.it/main/index

Dunn, B. 2007. Accumulation by Dispossession or Accumulation of Capital? The Case of China. *Journal of Australian Political Economy* 60: 5–27.

Epstein, G., ed. 2005b. Introduction: Financialization and the World Economy. In *Financialization and the World Economy*, ed. G. Epstein, 3–18. Cheltenham: Edward Elgar.

European Commission. 2011. *EU Economic Governance "Six-Pack" Enters into Force*. http://europa.eu/rapid/press-release_MEMO-11-898_en.htm

Froud, J., S. Johal, J. Montgomerie, and K. Williams. 2010. Escaping the Tyranny of Earned Income? The Failure of Finance as Social Innovation. *New Political Economy*. 15 (1): 147–164.

Glenn, J. 2016. *China's Challenge to US Supremacy: Economic Superpower Versus Rising Star*. London: Palgrave Macmillan.

Gowan, P. 1999. *The Global Gamble: Washington's Faustian Bid for World Dominance*. London: Verso.

Gunderson, L., and L. Pritchard Jr., eds. 2002. *Resilience and the Behavior of Large-Scale Systems (Scientific Committee on Problems of the Environment)*. London: Island Press.

Harvey, D. 2003. *The New Imperialism*. Oxford: Oxford University Press.

———. 2006. *Spaces of Global Capitalism: Towards a Theory of Uneven Geographical Development*. London: Verso.

———. 2009. Is This Really the End of Neoliberalism? *Counterpunch*. http://www.counterpunch.org/harvey03132009.html

———. 2010. Pathology Without Crisis? The Strange Demise of the Anglo-Liberal Growth Model. *Government and Opposition* 46 (1): 1–31.

Helleiner, E. 1996. *States and the Reemergence of Global Finance: From Bretton Woods to the 1990s*. Ithaca/New York: Cornell University Press.

Holling, C.S. 1973. Resilience and Stability of Ecological Systems. *Annual Review of Ecology and Systematics* 4 (1): 1–23.

Hoogvelt, A. 2001. *Globalization and the Postcolonial World*. 2nd ed. Basingstoke: Palgrave.

Jessop, B. 1990. *State Theory: Putting Capitalist States in Their Place*. Cambridge: Polity.

———. 1999. The Strategic Selectivity of the State: Reflections on a Theme of Poulantzas. *Journal of the Hellenic Diaspora* 25 (1–2): 41–77.

———. 2010. Comment on Paul du Gay and Alan Scott/2: On Historical Semantics, State Forms, and Political Regimes. *Sociologica* 2. http://www.sociologicamulino.it/main/index

Joseph, J. 2012. *The Social in the Global: Social Theory, Governmentality and Global Politics*. Cambridge: Cambridge University Press.

———. 2013. Resilience as Embedded Neoliberalism: A Governmentality Approach. *Resilience: International Policies, Practices and Discourses* 1 (1): 38–52.

Kiely, R. 2007. *The New Political Economy of Development: Globalization, Imperialism, Hegemony*. London: Palgrave Macmillan.

———. 2010. *Rethinking Imperialism*. London: Palgrave.

Langley, P. 2008. *The Everyday Life of Global Finance: Saving and Borrowing in Anglo-America*. Oxford: Oxford University Press.

Lapavitsas, C., A. Kaltenbrunner, G. Labrinidis, D. Lindo, J. Meadway, J. Michell, J. Paincera, E. Pires, J. Powell, A. Stenfors, N. Teles, and L. Vatikiotis. 2012. *Crisis in the Eurozone*. London: Verso Books.

Lardy, N. 2002. *Integrating China into the Global Economy*. Washington, DC: Brookings Institution Press.

McCulley, P. 2009. The Shadow Banking System and Hyman Minsky's Economic Journey. http://www.pimco.com/LeftNav/Featured+Market+Commentary/FF/2009/Global+Central+Bank+Focus+April+2009+Money+Marketeers+Solitaire+McCulley.htm

McNally, D. 2011. *Global Slump: The Economics and Politics of Crisis and Resistance*. Oakland: PM Press.

Merlingen, M. 2003. Governmentality Towards a Foucauldian Framework for the Study of IGOs. *Cooperation and Conflict* 38 (4): 361–384.

Miller, P., and N. Rose. 1990. Governing Economic Life. *Economy and Society* 19 (1): 1–31.

Minsky, H. 1992. The Financial Instability Hypothesis. *Levy Economics Institute*, Working Paper 74: 1–10.

———. 2008. *Stabilizing An Unstable Economy*. New York: McGraw and Hill.

Mohun, S. 2006. Distributive Shares in the US Economy: 1964–2001. *Cambridge Journal of Economics* 30 (3): 347–370.

Montgomerie, J. 2009. The Pursuit of (Past) Happiness? Middle-Class Indebtedness and American Financialisation. *New Political Economy* 14 (1): 1–24.

Morrison, W. 2013. *China's Economic Rise: History, Trends, Challenges, and Implications for the United States*, 1–38. Washington, DC: Congressional Research Service.

O'Malley, P. 1996. Risk and Responsibility. In *Foucault and Political Reason*, ed. Andrew Barry, Thomas Osborne, and Nikolas Rose, 189–208. London: UCL Press.

———. 2004. *Risk, Uncertainty and Government*. London: Glass House Press.

———., ed. 2005. *Governing Risks*. Aldershot: Ashgate.

———. 2010. Resilient Subjects: Uncertainty, Warfare and Liberalism. *Economy and Society* 39 (4): 488–509.

———. 2013. Uncertain Governance and Resilient Subjects in the Risk Society. *Oñati Socio-Legal Series* 3 (2): 180–195.

OECD. 2004. *Employment Outlook*. Paris: OECD.

Panitch, L., and S. Gindin. 2012. *The Making of Global Capitalism: The Political Economy of American Empire*. London: Verso.

Panitch, L., G. Albo, and V. Chibber. 2010. *The Crisis This Time*. Ponty Pool: Merlin Press.

Peters, J. 2010. The Rise of Finance and the Decline of Organised Labour in the Advanced Capitalist Countries. *New Political Economy* 16 (1): 73–99.

Quirk, P., and O. Evans. 1995. *Capital Account Convertibility: Review of Experience and Implications for IMF Policies*. Washington, DC: IMF.

Rose, N. 1993. Government, Authority and Expertise in Advanced Liberalism. *Economy and Society* 22 (3): 283–299.

The Economist. 2008a. Global Finance: Lifelines, October 11–17, p. 74.

———. 2008b. Rescuing the Banks: But Will It Work?, October 19–24, p. 68.

———. 2008c. The Global Economic Summit: After the Fall, November 15–21, p. 61.

———. 2009a. The Uneven Contest: Financial Regulation Is Essential. That Does not Make It Easy, January 24–30, p. 78.

———. 2009b. Three Trillion Dollars Later, May 16–22, p. 73.

———. 2015. Electric Shock: An Iconic Firm Abandons Its Finance Business, April 10. http://www.economist.com/news/business-and-finance/21642356-iconic-firm-abandons-its-finance-business-electric-shock

Thomas, C. 2000. *Global Governance, Development and Human Security*. London: Pluto Press.

Thompson, G. 2010. Comment on Paul du Gay and Alan Scott/3. *Sociologica* 2. http://www.sociologicamulino.it/main/index

Tomlinson, J. 2011. Out of Recession? *New Political Economy* 16 (5): 655–665.

Walker, B., and D. Salt. 2006. *Resilience Thinking: Sustaining Ecosystems and People in a Changing World*. Washington, DC: Island Press. http://www.guardian.co.uk/world/2011/aug/01/greece-50bn-privatisation-drive

Watt, N. 2012. David Cameron Unveils Plan to Sell Off the Roads. *The Guardian*, March 19. http://www.guardian.co.uk/politics/2012/mar/19/david-cameron-sell-off-roads

Western, B., and K. Mealy. 1999. Explaining the OECD Wage Slowdown Recession or Labour Decline? *European Sociological Review* 15 (3): 233–249.

Winnett, R. 2013. Budget 2013: George Osborne Pins Hopes on Housing Boom, *The Telegraph*, March 20. www.telegraph.co.uk/finance/budget/9944688/Budget-2013-George-Osborne-pins-hopes-on-housing-boom.html

Wintour, P. 2012. Labour Steps Up Opposition to NHS Privatisation Plans. *The Guardian*, January 15. http://www.guardian.co.uk/politics/2012/jan/15/labour-opposition-nhs-privatisation-plans

World Investment Report. 2011. *Non-Equity Modes of International Production and Development*. New York: UNCTAD.

Zakaria, F. 2011. *The Post American World*. London: Penguin Books.

Zebrowski, C. 2009. Governing the Network Society: A Bio-political Critique of Resilience. *Political Perspectives* 3 (1): 1–36.

———. 2016. *The Value of Resilience: Securing Life in the Twenty-First Century*. London: Routledge.

Zhang, K.H. 2002. Why Does China Receive So Much Foreign Direct Investment. *China: An Economics Research Study Series* 2: 39–57.

4

Neo-Liberalism Rebooted: Resilience Versus Resistance

Introduction

The previous chapter identified two historic economic moments in the last half century, where it was argued that historic moments should be understood as 'spaces of time within which a particular combination (or conjunction) of causes exercises a predominant (causal and imaginative) influence over the course of events and the production of ideas' (Rosenberg 2005, p. 29).[1] The crisis of the 1970s was resolved by the rise of neo-liberalism involving the scaling back of the welfare state, the ever-increasing encroachment of economic rationality into the management of society and the emphasis on laissez-faire economics on a world scale with the aim of producing new production and speculative opportunities for global capital.

Although the 2007/2008 financial crisis had altogether different causes, it gave rise to the popularity of resilience thinking. Resilience discourse was very much apparent before the financial crisis, but much of the emphasis was on large systems and ecology (Holling 1973; Gunderson et al. 2002). However, since the crisis it has gained traction

J. G. Glenn, *Foucault and Post-Financial Crises*, International Political Economy Series, https://doi.org/10.1007/978-3-319-77188-5_4

in the political/economic field. Emblematic of this trend is the launch of several new journals in the last few years including *Resilience: A Journal of the Environmental Humanities, Resilience: Interdisciplinary Perspectives on Science and Humanitarianism* and the launch in 2013 by David Chandler of *Resilience: International Policies, Practices and Discourses.* This trend has not been limited to academic circles with the likes of Jean-Claude Juncker telling Greece that, 'Throughout all these years I have been feeling your pain. I know well how much many Greeks have been suffering. But I also know well the resilience of the Greek people in the face of adversity' (Juncker 2014). Around the same time, George Osborne, the UK Chancellor of the Exchequer, announced a 'Budget for building a resilient economy' (UK Government 19 March 2014).

Several of these writings have highlighted the importance of the individual as resilient subject, strengthening the individual characteristics that will enable 'each and all to live freely and with confidence in a world of potential risks' (Lenztos and Rose 2009, p. 243). For some, this entails nothing less than the 'constitution of new subjectivities' inculcating individuals with 'the positive attitude that regards high uncertainty as opportunity and challenge' (O'Malley 2013, p. 190). For others, it is more of a question of tapping into the 'existing embedded and relational capacities of ordinary people', using 'our natural abilities to cooperate with each other, to innovate and to construct communities of shared interest' (Chandler 2014b, p. 60 and 61).

This chapter identifies two strands of thought that are apparent in these recent writings on resilience: the first views resilience as an extension of neo-liberal *governmentality*; the second approach associates resilience with the emergence of a post-modern episteme.[2] The chapter goes on to argue that resilience thinking is best understood as a sub-discourse whose popularity can be explained by its fit with neo-liberalism. As Jonathan Joseph points out, 'resilience is best understood in the context of rolling-out neoliberal governmentality. Its meaning varies depending on the place and the level where this occurs and the aims and objects of governance' (Joseph 2013, pp. 51–2). In other words, the exact form of resilience thinking will be context and time dependent—yet, it has come to the fore because it chimes with rather than challenges neo-liberalism. Although the post-modern variant of resilience thinking may be logically coherent (if one accepts its initial premises), as will become apparent, its conclusions are at odds with ensuring that the various circuits of capital continue to function. What is also striking is that the most recent crisis has not spawned a 'meta-evaluation' replacing neo-liberalism, thus helping 'to resolve doubt and restore certainty' (Davies 2014, p. 154). Instead neo-liberalism is increasingly defended 'purely via contingent acts of preservation of the status quo', and resilience serves to assimilate opposition to this state of affairs (Ibid. p. 155).

This chapter is divided into four parts. The first section takes issue with the post-modernist version of resilience thinking which is elaborated (although not necessarily endorsed) by Chandler.[3] According to Chandler, resilience thinking 'can be understood as the first post-liberal or post-modern episteme' (Chandler 2014a, p. 47). Moreover, resilience discourse is said to provide a solution to the radical uncertainty and unknowability of our social and natural worlds—one that relies on local communities and local knowledges. Indeed, it asserts that 'all knowledge can only be local, contextual and time and place specific' (Chandler 2014a, p. 42). Chandler argues that current resilience thinking interprets the contemporary period as marking a shift towards a post risk society where we fully acknowledge our own self-entanglement within the world and government is through society rather than over society. However, two major issues arise concerning resilience thinking. First, there is no in-depth analysis of power arising from the stratification of society. Indeed, and as Chandler points out, post-modern resilience discourse argues that rather than 'understanding capitalism as a social system that can be opposed or struggled against, resilience ethics suggest that we see ourselves as in part responsible for the market and its outcomes' (Chandler 2014a, pp. 139–40). This levelling of responsibility paradoxically supports the neo-liberal project of responsibilization rather than challenges it, since it systematically fails to accord blame for capitalism's negative consequences to those most responsible and instead emphasizes the responsibility of all individuals. Second, post-modern resilience discourse provides no method by which to differentiate between local knowledges (is all local knowledge to be supported regardless of its political content simply because it is local?) nor how to identify whether such knowledge is really local or influenced by/constituted within a wider dominant discourse.

The second section of the chapter argues that rather than representing some radical rupture with current practices heralding the dawn of a new era, the manner in which resilience has been practically interpreted has effectively led to its incorporation into a larger neo-liberal framework. Following Joseph, the chapter argues that the 'recent enthusiasm for the concept of resilience across a range of policy literature is the consequence of its fit with neoliberal discourse', rather than signalling a radical divergence from it.[4] By emphasizing our supposed inability to intervene effectively in a complex, economic system, resilience thinking represents an ideological behavioural prescription promoting political passivity. As such, it helps mask the failure of political elites to put forward radical policy prescriptions in the face of neo-liberal crises.

The chapter then follows Chandler in developing a Foucauldian analysis of resilience thinking, but one that goes beyond a description of resilience thinking as a 'regime of truth' and one that views it as supplementing rather than supplanting neo-liberal governmentalities (Chandler 2014a, p. 48). One that emphasizes the importance of comparing knowledges through the archaeological and genealogical methods enabling us to go beyond the 'theoretical and political singularity' of post-modernism (Hay 2002, p. 250). We can do so, Foucault avers, because critical investigation exhibits a certain structure via its homogeneity, generality and systematicity, arising from the questions motivating such critical investigations (Foucault 1984a, p. 47). Using such methods, it is argued that resilience thinking represents an expansion of neo-liberal governmentality, rather than the emergence of a new episteme. In addition, although often overlooked in the literature, Foucault recognized the importance of understanding social structures, but, clearly, he did not view these in a deterministic manner.[5] By understanding the power relations associated with these social differentiations, we can better grasp how some discourses become dominant whilst others are subjugated.

The final section of this chapter situates the emergence of resilience discourse in the context of neo-liberalism-in-crisis. This crisis has multiple dimensions,[6] but since 2007/2008 two are key: first, there is, for capital, a 'realisation problem', that is, a problem of generating profitable investment opportunities; and, second, a governance crisis over the legitimacy of neo-liberalism per se. As a result, and as William Davies argues, neo-liberal political-economic arrangements are increasingly defended 'with no appeal to common humanity, but purely via contingent acts of preservation of the status quo' (Davies 2014, p. 154). The chapter argues that resilience, from a Foucauldian perspective, serves to assimilate opposition to this state of affairs. Indeed, the emphasis on individuals as resilient subjects represents a new phase in the neo-liberal shift from the state as provider to state as enabler and promoter of self-reliance. Resilience has emerged in tandem with a further reduction in state welfare commitments, a further rolling back of employment rights and an intensification of the privatization of national assets.

Resilience: A New Mantle for Neo-Liberalism

Several authors writing on risk have distinguished between policies centred around precaution, pre-emption and resilience (O'Malley 2010, 2013; Lenztos and Rose 2009). These policies, it is argued, have emerged as a result of the sheer enormity of catastrophic events associated with late modernity combined with a heightened sense of uncertainty in which direct causal relationships are harder to identify and may only become apparent after the event leading to a situation where we postulate relationships of 'possibility, eventuality, plausibility or probability without being able to provide the proof of its validity' (Ewald 2005, p. 61).

Such writings bring to our attention the greater emphasis on precaution and the need to 'intervene in emergence precisely because of uncertainty linked to massive consequences' (O'Malley 2013, p. 188). As Lentzos and Rose point out, whereas pre-emption operates in a highly uncertain environment in which emergent threats are identified and counteracted before they have become actual and realizable, resilience, in contradistinction to these policies, emphasizes the quality of adaptability that enables rapid recovery after catastrophes. They identify two aspects that have been historically associated with the term: 'the mental state of being able to withstand stress or adverse circumstances or to recover quickly from their effects'; and, 'the capacity of systems, structures or organizations to resist being affected by shock or disaster, and to recover quickly from such events' (Lenztos and Rose 2009, p. 242). Resilience is thus said to involve

> a systematic, widespread, organizational, structural and personal strengthening of subjective and material arrangements so as to be better able to anticipate and tolerate disturbances in complex worlds without collapse, to withstand shocks, and to rebuild as necessary…a logic of resiliency would aspire to create a subjective and systematic state to enable each and all to live freely and with confidence in a world of potential risks. (Lenztos and Rose 2009, p. 243)

According to Joseph, its recent popularity has arisen from 'literature on the adaptability of ecological systems… These ideas come from applied mathematics and resource ecology and are used to examine the interaction of ecological resilience and human adaptability in complex large systems. This approach emphasizes such things as complexity, self organisation, functional diversity and nonlinear ways of behaving… Resilience provides these complex systems with the ability to withstand and survive shocks and disturbances. It also emphasizes the capacity for renewal' (Joseph 2013, p. 39).

Two strands of thought are apparent in recent writings on resilience: the first views resilience as an extension of the neo-liberal governmentality outlined at the beginning of the book; the second approach associates resilience with the emergence of a post-liberal world. With regard to the first approach, Pat O'Malley sees the roots of resilience discourse in the 'entrepreneurial, neo-liberal business models such as were developed in the 1970s' (O'Malley 2013, p. 189). Such models viewed uncertainty and insecurity as 'beneficial and essential to freedom and security. The less the security, the greater the freedom. Increased uncertainty now came to mean increased opportunity for the enterprising' (O'Malley 2013, p. 191). O'Malley argues that resilience emphasizes the importance of embracing risk and adopting a '*risk-taking* attitude that regards uncertainty as opportunity' (O'Malley 2010, p. 499). This interpretation of resilience accepts that this is part of a larger neo-liberal mentality that 'valorizes self-reliance and responsibility in an uncertain world' (O'Malley 2010, p. 505). One that creates subjects that '"thrive" on chaos and make every threat a challenge and opportunity' (O'Malley 2013, p. 192).

Others agree that the sedimentation of resilience thinking as a dominant discourse should be understood as an extension of neo-liberalism, arguing that 'the success of this ecological concept in colonizing multiple arenas of governance is due to its intuitive ideological fit with a neoliberal philosophy of complex adaptive systems' (Walker and Cooper 2011, p. 144). The latter is traced back to Friedrich Hayek's view of society (and markets) as 'complex, adaptive and non-linear' and the limitation of our understanding of such systems. His anti-interventionist position with regard to the economy derives from this appreciation of our limited knowledge alongside an ontological stance that views the market as endowed with 'immanent law-making powers' (Walker and Cooper 2011, p. 150). These laws of the market only reveal themselves after the event, their very survival serves 'as proof of concept, in much the same way as the law of natural selection constantly proves or disproves the viability of chance mutations in nature' (Walker and Cooper 2011, p. 150).

Risk analysis is premised on the calculability of events in probabilistic terms. Such calculations enable us to respond to the vicissitudes of life either through insurance—recompensing those affected through collective compensation schemes—or altering our behaviour to decrease the likelihood of such events. The promotion of resilience, on the other hand, has arisen in reaction to our uncertainty with regard to unexpected often one-off catastrophic events that do not necessarily exhibit probabilistic patterns. Given this uncertainty, the emphasis shifts to how well systems/communities/individuals respond to crises and the *post-facto* environments that emerge. In an age of complexity and uncertainty, the ability to adapt and rebound to unexpected events is said to be of paramount importance—because 'we can survive better through knowing how to adapt' (Joseph 2013, p. 43).

Chandler, on the other hand, has provided one of the best accounts to date of those that view resilience as representing the emergence of a post-liberal world, arguing that our growing appreciation of complexity is also leading to a post-modern framework of governance:-

> *emergent complexity—or life as the object of governance conceived as complex*—necessarily calls forth a new 'resilience' agenda of governance. It seeks to unpack the nature of that 'life' which is seen to evade liberal forms

> of representation and of government and to dictate new forms of governing…while it is understood in precisely the relational terminology immune to liberal reductionist and linear understandings, complex life is also understood to demand governance through other—nonlinear and non-reductionist—approaches. Complex emergent life is governable but on a very different basis to liberal and neoliberal 'life'. (Chandler 2014b, pp. 47–8)

In making the claim that resilience thinking is post-modern, Chandler makes a sharp distinction between resilience thinking and previous modes of thought that, whilst viewing the world as complex, still assume that 'it is possible to intervene instrumentally to shape the outcome of these processes and to realign them to liberal rationalist understandings of progress and development' (Chandler 2014a, p. 37). For Chandler, resilience thinking accepts that, 'Calculation or control and direction become impossible in general complexity theory…The problematic of a complex emergent order is not that of knowing more, "filling in the gaps" of knowledge, but an ontological problem, i.e. the problem exists at the level of what is to be known (it is not linear and law-bound) rather than at the level of how we might know the underlying reality' (Chandler 2014b, p. 50).

As a result, it is argued that, the 'world is not amenable to appropriation within liberal frameworks of representation with their…universal understandings of causal connections, structures and rationalities' (Chandler 2014b, p. 50). For post-modern resilience thinking, 'State-based reasoning works on crude linear cause-and-effect understandings which cannot account for unintended consequences and side-effects, while market reasoning is just as reductionist, excluding all the relational "externalities" outside the concerns of the contracting parties' (2014a, p. 204). With regard to policy-making, the key aspects that differentiate post-modern resilience from modernist forms of governance are its 'post-modern ontological assumptions about the nature of the world as complex and the consequences for governance as a process of self-reflexive policy responses' (Ibid.)

Chandler's view is that this post-modern version of resilience thinking is emphatically rooted in ontological complexity, arguing that resilience thinking arises from the very complexity of life itself—'Without complexity there would be no demand for resilience' (2014a, p. 19). This post-modern version of resilience thinking represents 'a radically distinctive approach to governing complexity (bringing complexity into governmental reason) through reposing complexity as an ontological rather than an epistemological problem' (Chandler 2014b, p. 56). Complexity renders the world unknowable in terms of discernible patterns and predictability, it is the '"unknown unknowns" that have the central role in emergent causation meaning that contingent outcomes only reveal concrete causality after the event and are impossible to know beforehand' (Chandler 2014b, p. 50).

As a result, post-modern resilience thinking asserts that we must radically rethink present forms of governance, to 'humble ourselves before the altar of life as complexity' and take the 'unknown unknowns' as the basis of governmental reason itself (Chandler 2014b, pp. 51–2; 2014a, p. 184). Governance based on resilience thinking must reject the subject/object divide of liberal thinking and take full account of our 'being in the world'—that we are inseparably entangled in the complex world that we have previously treated as the object of our analysis. Instead, post-modern resilience thinking posits an external world that 'is not passive or objective and lacking in creative agency. Ergo, humans are not the only agents or subjects in the world and—in a world where agency is spread more widely or thinly—humans now have the possibility of recognising, rejoining and re-embedding themselves in the world. The historic struggle for human mastery of necessity in the name of collective human freedom (as a 'war' against nature) is thereby declared over. There is no longer an 'outside' to be conquered; there is 'no more environment', 'no more nature': Political philosophy abruptly finds itself confronted with the obligation to internalize the environment that it had viewed up to now as another' (Chandler 2014a, p. 183).

With the emergence of resilience thinking, we are told that the 'divide between subject and object is elided through understanding that the governing/knowing subject is not external to the problematic but always and already "entangled" or embedded in this relationship' (Chandler 2014a, p. 27). Post-modern resilience thinking believes the traditional subject/object divide will be replaced by radical critique which will be 'framed by the ontology of resilience-thinking, [which] thus becomes the dominant discourse of power, legitimising and reproducing governing authority on the basis of the unknowability of the world' (Chandler 2014a, p. 226).[7] Such critique is said to 'no longer operate on the basis of revealing "unifying principles" such as the inner-workings of power or the supposed structures of domination' (Ibid., p. 221). Instead, this radical critique based on resilience thinking is 'critical of states (all forms of state power are seen to be a barrier to accessing the reality of complex life), it is critical of the market (its reductionist focus on profit and exclusion of 'externalities'—the relational consequences of putting profits before life itself); it is critical of universal, fixed and reductionist forms of thought (real complex life is fluid and ever changing)' (Ibid., p. 226).

We are told that the implication of complexity is that 'governments cannot be expected to know what policies do or do not work and certainly cannot impose these policies on the world' (Chandler 2014b, p. 62). How then to govern in a post-modern world? The key, according to Chandler, is self-reflexivity and an appreciation of our entanglement in the world around us (Chandler 2014a, p. 27). When engaged in policy-making we must always be cognisant of 'the nature of the world as complex and the consequences for governance as a process of self-reflexive policy responses' (Chandler 2014a, p. 204). The latter involves 'the consideration of the multiple consequences of our actions which guide and enable the process of revising our judgements in line with our self-reflection' (Chandler 2014a, p. 202). Thus, resilience thinking ensures that, 'the "real" processes of complex life, as the object of rule, can be enabled through the indirect process of governance, understood as a process of reflexive self-knowledge of the complex embedded nature of power....the ethical injunction of resilience is externally orientated towards others and the consideration of the multiple consequences of our actions which guide and enable the process of revising our judgements in line with our self-reflection on these outcomes which can never be known fully in advance' (Chandler 2014a, p. 202).

Such governance should be based on 'everyday democracy', which 'is not about governing from the top-down or the bottom-up but about social resilience, understood as the existing embedded and relational capacities of ordinary people. It is these capacities that are perceived to be bypassed or muted by instrumentalized neoliberal interventions in the social sphere' (Chandler 2014b, p. 61) This 'everyday democracy' by 'focusing on recognising the role of the existing practices and understandings of the public themselves, can constitute a productive way forward' beyond modernist/liberal forms of governance (Chandler 2014b, p. 60).

This form of resilience thinking chimes, to some degree, with Ulrich Beck's work on the emergence of a risk society in which the unintended consequences of our actions and the risks that attend these consequences predominate. As a result, we are beginning to appreciate our inability to truly know the world we live in and the attendant uncertainty of the consequences of our actions (Chandler 2014a, p. 121). Indeed, Chandler himself positions his interpretation in this way, acknowledging that it 'is here that the "life politics" of Giddens and Beck or the actor-network theorising of Latour can be seen to provide models for resilience as a framework for governing in a non-linear world' (Chandler 2014a, p. 176).

The world risk society approach introduces a dichotomy between reflective and reflexive modernization that is very similar to Chandler's liberal-modernist/resilience-post-modernist dichotomy (Rasmussen 2004, p. 101; Beck 1994, pp. 5–8). Reflective modernization is associated with the first phase of modernity where 'calculating risks is part of the master narrative' (Beck 2002, p. 39) and involves 'improving our knowledge of cause-effect relations and control of the world' (Griner 2002, p. 149), whereas the latter is associated with self-confrontation and an acceptance of 'our own *inability* to know' (Beck 1999, p. 131). The former attempts to reduce potential vulnerabilities through improved scientific technical knowledge, while the latter involves an appreciation of the uncontrollable risks that lead to catastrophic events, prompting full recognition of the unknowability of the future effects of our current activities. Risks become 'de-bounded', 'not limited by political borders or calculable time frames' and are said to be of 'low probability but potentially cataclysmic' (Hameiri 2011, p. 382).

As with post-modern resilience thinking, Beck argues that the 'assignment of causes and consequences is no longer possible with any degree of reliability' (Beck 2007, p. 52). Beck suggests that the enormity of these risks will inevitably generate sufficient awareness within global society to prompt such critical self-reflection on our existing practices (Beck 1999,

p. 81). This critical reflection—or reflexivity—is said to involve self-confrontation 'with the effects of risk society that cannot be dealt with and assimilated in the system of industrial society' and an acceptance of 'our own *inability* to know' the unintended consequences of our own actions (Beck 1994, p. 6; 1999, p. 131). Reflexive modernization thus goes beyond simply 'improving our knowledge of cause-effect relations and control of the world' and actually involves 'a process of reflection by which the foundations of modernity are questioned and revised' (Griner 2002, p. 149).

This shift, it is argued, prompts a major political movement towards what Beck calls a '*Cosmopolitan form of statehood*' in which an alliance of the state and civic movements is forged to confront the issues that arise from such risks (Beck 2007, p. 66). This is because in a world risk society, the traditional nationally based solutions are no longer feasible because, 'instead of solving problems, it contributes to producing and exacerbating them' (Beck and Grande 2007, p. 254). It is argued by Beck that the cosmopolitan solution is likely to succeed precisely because it proposes a realistic solution to today's problems (Beck and Grande 2007, p. 21). Most recently, Beck has argued that we are already witnessing the emergence of 'cosmopolitanized risk collectivities' that 'are engendered through the anticipation of endangered futures' that may act as a stepping stone towards cosmopolitan statehood (Beck and Levy 2012, p. 6 and Abstract).

Although Chandler does not speak of cosmopolitan forms of statehood, both writers see the loss of faith in scientific methods as having deep social implications because, 'The individual must cope with the uncertainty of the global world by him- or herself. Here individualization is a default outcome of a failure of expert systems to manage risks. Neither science, nor the politics in power, nor the mass media, nor business, nor the law or even the military are in a position to define or control risks rationally. The individual is forced to mistrust the promises of rationality of these key institutions. As a consequence, people are thrown back onto themselves, they are alienated from expert systems' (Beck 2006, p. 336).

They both also see the solution in terms of communities rather than expert knowledge. For Beck, the distant other is 'becoming the inclusive other not through mobility but through risk. Everyday life is becoming cosmopolitan: human beings must find the meaning of life in the exchange with others' (Beck 2006, p. 331). Similarly, for post-modern resilience thinking, in 'resilience-framings, parochial or local knowledges are not a limit but a policy goal, once it is understood that all knowledge can only be local, contextual and time and place specific' (Chandler 2014a, p. 42). In many ways, then, we can understand Chandler's version of resilience as a shift towards a post risk society where we fully acknowledge our own self-entanglement within the world and government is through society rather than over society, by 'recognising the capacities and capabilities that already exist' (Chandler 2014b, p. 61). We therefore need To draw upon the resilient characteristics of communities, our 'natural abilities to cooperate with each other, to innovate and to construct communities of interest' (Chandler 2014a, p. 217).

Governmentality and the Rise of the Resilient Subject

Foucauldian analysis, like Chandler's post-modern understanding of resilience, also emphasizes the importance of local knowledges, by focusing on the way in which such knowledges are subjugated by dominant discourses and, specifically for this paper, governmental enframings. In contrast to post-modern resilience thinking, however, Foucault established a method to uncover such dominance. Through the archaeological method and genealogical design, he sought to uncover the various power mechanisms that worked to support the emergence of dominant discourses. The archaeological method seeks to discover the rules governing the enframement of knowledge in different periods. As such, it examines those governing statements 'that concern the definition of observable structures and the field of possible objects, those that prescribe the forms of description and the perceptual codes that it can use, those that reveal the most general possibilities of characterization, and thus open up a whole domain of concepts to be constructed' (Foucault 2002, p. 113). Genealogy complements this by tracing 'the struggles, displacements and processes of repurposing out of which contemporary practices emerged, and to show the historical conditions of existence upon which present-day practices depend' (Garland 2014, p. 373). By letting 'knowledge of the past work on the experience of the present', we can then establish 'a historical knowledge of struggles and…make use of this knowledge tactically today'.[8] By tracing the subjugation of alternative knowledges, genealogical analysis thus provides us with a 'history of the present' because 'its intent is to problematize the present by revealing the power relations upon which it depends and the contingent processes that have brought it into being' (Garland 2014, p. 372).

The combination of the two methods not only reveals the subjugation of other knowledges, but also exposes our conditioning and limitations as a result of past and present systems of knowledge and alerts us to the potential power relations associated with these knowledges. This critical attitude applies to both dominant and local knowledges and entails a historical investigation into 'the events that have led us to constitute ourselves and to recognize ourselves as subjects of what we are doing, thinking, saying' (Foucault 1984a, p. 46). In order to transgress the limits of the current and past epistemes, we need to interrogate 'what is given to us as universal, necessary, obligatory' to understand what in fact is 'singular, contingent, and the product of arbitrary constraints'.[9] This will enable us to determine what is 'no longer indispensable for the constitution of ourselves as autonomous subjects' (Foucault 1984a, p. 43).

In addition, Foucault warns against concluding that the impossibility of attaining complete and definitive knowledge means 'that no work can be done except in disorder and contingency' (Foucault 1984a, p. 47). Rather, critical investigation exhibits a certain structure via its homogeneity, generality and systematicity, arising from the questions motivating such critical investigations (Ibid.). The latter emerges along the three axes of power, knowledge and ethics–'How are we constituted as subjects of our own knowledge? How are we constituted as subjects who exercise or submit to power relations? How are we constituted as moral subjects of our own actions?' (Foucault 1984a, p. 49). Homogeneity refers to the way in which the discursive and non-discursive elements of practices are 'articulated by forms of rationality … that cohere in particular social orders and historical epochs' (Sugarman 2015, p. 168). Generality, in this context, does not refer to some 'metahistorical continuity', but to the fact that the 'problematics of these practices continue to recur in our own time' (e.g. 'the problem of the relationship between sanity and insanity, or sickness and health, or crime and the law').[10]

Using a Foucauldian perspective, the chapter questions the argument that the uncertainty surrounding cataclysmic events leads to a process of self-confrontation through which the foundations of modernity are questioned and a post-modern episteme emerges. When confronted by cataclysmic events, this chapter argues that policy has followed a far more pragmatic path such that reflexivity takes the form of 'governmentalization of government' or 'reflexive government' whereby 'the mechanisms of government themselves are subject to problematization, scrutiny and reformation' (Dean 1999, p. 193). As Foucault's earlier work suggests, epistemic ruptures do occur and new systems of knowledge may emerge, but the evidence thus far suggests that resilience thinking does not represent the emergence of such a new (post-modern) episteme (Foucault 1984b).

Instead, resilience thinking exhibits a certain homogeneity with neo-liberalism in that it is constituted from the familiar forms of rationality that articulate the discursive and non-discursive practices of neo-liberalism. Moreover, it is clear that the crisis did not unsettle pre-crisis social differentiations, rather the lack of serious reform points towards the sedimentation of these differentiations in institutional forms and that the enframing of resilience thinking did not emerge in a power vacuum. In terms of systematicity, resilience subjectivities represent both a continuation and extension to those of neo-liberalism—the subject *qua* responsible self and a corresponding silence surrounding those who have the greatest influence on society and how they benefit most from the social differentiations that are maintained within it. In terms of generality, we can see that there is a continuation of focus on familiar binary tropes: strivers versus skivers, profligacy versus thrift, responsibility versus irresponsibility. Resilience thinking is thus 'an interpretation of social behaviour determined by, and supportive of, neoliberalism' (Zebrowski 2016, p. 88).

Uncertainty has as its referent object infrequently occurring and often unique events that can 'only be "likened" to other cases' (O'Malley 2013, p. 13). As such, one can only 'formulate, between a cause and its effect, a relationship of possibility, eventuality, plausibility or probability without being able to provide the proof of its validity' (Ewald 2005, p. 561). There is thus an 'absence of certainties, having taken into account the scientific and technical knowledge of the time' (Ibid.). However, this does not mean that uncertainty should be elided with incalculability (Jarvis 2011, p. 308). Rather, new forms of governmentality emerge using new technologies of control, 'taming the infinities of risk and integrating it within a *dispositif* of governance' (Aradau and Van Munster 2007, p. 100). Enframing new challenges within a given form of governmentality using our new or existing knowledges and technologies of control inevitably involves impacting upon our physical and social worlds so that the subject can never be treated as separated from its object. Of course, this knowledge is limited and fallible, but its effects are reflexively monitored and changed prompting new frameworks of knowledge and new governmental rationalities.

Such resilience thinking seeks 'to invest life with the capacity to quickly and efficiently adapt, regenerate and transform in the presence of an emergency event' (Zebrowski 2016, p. 13). Hence, the emphasis on individual/community/system capacities that encourage 'malleability, adaptability, flexibility and regeneration' in order to enable society to bounce back, from unexpected set-backs' (Zebrowski 2016, p. 7). With resilience thinking, order is 'understood to be "complex", mutable and dynamic rather than merely complicated' (Dillon and Reid 2001, p. 41). As a result, resilience thinking promotes individual and system's capacities to overcome shocks (Zebrowski 2009, p. 8). At the individual level, becoming resilient subjects involves an interpellative process whereby individuals rely on their existing capacities to bounce back from unexpected events and are encouraged to learn and adapt to new environments (Joseph 2013, p. 29). Indeed, resilience thinking 'is not simply a call to ignite some base-level human instinct for survival. It is an ideological project that is informed by political and economic rationalities which offer very particular accounts of life as an ontological problem, that is, a problem which emanates from the potentiality of life as ontologically conceived, along with the types of epistemic communities which now scientifically verify the need to become resilient as a fait *accompli*. Resilience, in other words, is a key strategy in the creation of contemporary regimes of power which hallmark vast inequalities in all human classifications' (Evans and Reid 2013, p. 92). For the subject to increase its resilience, argue Brad Evans and Julian Reid, it

> must disavow any belief in the possibility to secure itself and accept, instead, an understanding of life as a permanent process of continual adaptation to threats and dangers which are said to be outside its control. As such, the resilient subject is a subject which must permanently struggle to accommodate itself to the world, and not a subject, which can conceive of changing the world, its structure and conditions of possibility. However, it is a subject which accepts the dangerousness of the world it lives in as a condition for partaking of that world and which accepts the necessity of the injunction to change itself in correspondence with threats now presupposed as endemic. (Evans and Reid 2013, p. 85)

As Joseph points out, neo-liberal governmentality 'works by telling us to be enterprising, active and responsible citizens…Resilience contributes to this through its stress on heightened self-awareness, reflexivity and responsibility'(Joseph 2013, p. 42). However, this emphasis on self-organization and responsibilization also usually promotes non-intervention by the state (Joseph 2013, p. 43). With resilience thinking, responsibilization still operates by shifting the onus away from the state providing a social safety net and intervening in the economy towards individual and community self-help, but the emphasis is on *post-facto* adaptation—there is therefore a shift towards promoting adaptive capacities in order that subjects can meet their responsibilities after crises. Whether individuals/communities simply survive or thrive will depend upon their degree of self-reliance, flexibility and adaptability.

Instead of witnessing a shift towards a post-modern resilient society or a cosmopolitan risk society, crises and catastrophes are said to produce reflexive moments through which the governance of our natural and social environments is modified to meet the challenges that confront us. Crises and catastrophes are said to produce reflexive moments through which the existing security *dispositif*—the 'discourses, institutions, architectural forms, regulatory decisions, laws, administrative measures, scientific statements, philosophical, moral and philanthropic propositions'—adopted by state and non-state actors to govern and manage our natural and social environments are modified to meet the challenges that confront us, thereby sustaining the 'authority of their authority' (Aradau and Van Munster 2007, p. 97).

Resilience thinking fits with neo-liberalism, because it also 'encourages the idea of active citizenship, whereby people, rather than relying on the state, take responsibility for their own social and economic well-being' (Joseph 2013, p. 42). But this emphasis on self-organization and responsibilization also usually promotes non-intervention by the state (Joseph 2013, p. 43). With resilience thinking, responsibilization still operates by shifting the onus away from the state providing a social safety net and intervening in the economy towards individual and community self-help, but the emphasis is on *post-hoc* adaptation—there is therefore a shift towards promoting adaptive capacities in order that subjects can meet their responsibilities after crises. Whether individuals/communities simply survive or thrive will depend upon their degree of self-reliance, flexibility and adaptability.

This can be seen clearly in the post-crisis reforms of the financial system, which have been orientated towards ensuring that in the event of another financial collapse, states will not be forced to step in and bail-out bankrupt entities. Instead, such financial entities will be allowed to fail in the belief that the post-reform financial system is resilient enough to withstand such closures. Equally, individual/community resilience has been orientated to survival in an era of austerity. Rather than stepping in and providing a welfare safety net for the population, states have tended to act in the opposite direction, reducing their welfare support at the time of greatest need. The result, it is argued, is a more productive and efficient economy enabling growth to return. Thus, Jean-Claude Juncker, during the elections for the President of the European Commission, could tell Greece that, 'Throughout all these years I have been feeling your pain. I know well how much many Greeks have been suffering. But I also know well the resilience of the Greek people in the face of adversity. The result is that efforts are paying off. The signs of recovery are getting stronger' (Juncker 2014). Resilience thinking, then, is not only indicative of just how deeply embedded neo-liberal thinking has become, but also the inability of mainstream politicians to embrace other political alternatives. The final next section argues, therefore, that far greater emphasis should be placed on resistance—particularly with regard to austerity, but also to the lack of radical reform of the financial system and the economy in general that all too often acts as an iron cage preventing alternative policies from emerging.

Explaining the Emergence of Resilience Thinking

The previous section argued that resilience thinking should be viewed as part of a wider practice of neo-liberal enframing, one which typically involves a process of responsibilization. In the particular case of catastrophes, the emphasis is on the post-hoc adaptability of individuals/communities and the various capacities they possess to enable them to bounce back from such shocks. With regard to finance, such enframing has centred around a 'naturalistic fallacy' whereby these systems have been treated as analogous to systems we find in nature. The emphasis has thus been on establishing more restrictive risk parameters and strengthening the nodal points of the system in order that they can withstand economic shocks and the homeostatic 'norm' can be reinstated.

Several issues arise with regard to the economy from such enframing. First, there is an implicit levelling of responsibility, where individuals and communities are expected to mine their own resources and capacities in order to survive such shocks. But it also transforms our understandings of resistance, promoting a high degree of political passivity by emphasizing adaptability over opposition and transformation—'Resistance here is transformed from being a political capacity aimed at the achievement of freedom from that which threatens and endangers to a purely reactionary impulse aimed at increasing the capacities of the subject to adapt to its dangers and simply reduce the degree to which it suffers. This conflation of resistance with resilience is not incidental but indicative of the nihilism of the underlying ontology of vulnerability at work in contemporary policies concerned with climate change and other supposedly catastrophic processes' (Evans and Reid 2013, p. 85).

In addition, resilience thinking has little to say with regard to social structures/agency concerning positions of power and the benefits that accrue from such positions as well as responsibility for the policies that greatly exacerbate the contradictions inherent within the capitalist system. In practice, this is clearly seen in the current austerity policies implemented across Europe. Those least responsible for the crisis have felt the greatest economic deprivation. The aforementioned 'naturalistic fallacy' with regard to the economic order also promotes such a perspective. By viewing finance as something akin to an organic homeostatic system, a social construction permeated by power relations and agents who have an interest in maintaining the economic order is rendered agentless and self-perpetuating.

Indeed, post-modern resilience thinking's understanding of resilience thinking is a prime example of such an approach. Although people are viewed as 'always and already … relationally entangled' with one another, this entanglement is purely on a contingent basis (Chandler 2014a, p. 14). The assemblage approach adopted by post-modern resilience thinkers emphasizes the emergent nature of the social world but in so doing it presents society as pluralist in nature where, with regard to actors/agents, 'there are no internal relations, only relations of exteriority' (Sayer 2013, p. 22). It is argued that it is 'relations, associations and assemblages of the unknown and the unseen that are held to have real agency, rather than knowledgeable human subjects' (Chandler 2014a, p. 198). Post-modern resilience thinking's ontology means that actors are placed in a position of exteriority to one another, they are contingently rather than internally and necessarily interconnected (Chandler 2014a, p. 39). Such an approach has far reaching implications, for example, capitalism becomes a 'complex system of associative relations which we are all to different extents responsible for because we are all unequally embedded in the global market system which forms a network of interconnectivity stretching from our smallest private choices to the largest global political problems. Rather than understanding capitalism as a social system that can be opposed or struggled against, resilience ethics suggest that we see ourselves as in part responsible for the market and its outcomes' (Chandler 2014a, pp. 139–40).

Instead of viewing the social world as both infused with different actors/agents that are internally related (and, as a result, embedded in a network of power relations) as well as actors that are in a position of exteriority to one another, post-modern resilience thinking argues that the world of becoming 'is an ontologically flat world without the traditional hierarchies of existence and a more shared conception of agency' (Chandler 2014a, p. 196). In such an approach, we are told that 'While there may not be agential hierarchies, there is no assumption of equality either, merely interactions and associations of humans and non-humans within the complex assemblages of the world of becoming' (Chandler 2014a, p. 191). As a result, we can 'no longer operate on the basis of revealing "unifying principles" such as the inner-workings of power or the supposed structures of domination' (Chandler 2014a, p. 221). Analysis should no longer concern itself with 'unearthing "essences" or structures but about tracing surface connections…Empiricism is the new method of critique because the reality of the world is seen to have been obscured by social science' (Chandler 2014a, p. 56). Moreover, it is argued that the 'world which cannot be comprehended meaningfully by us; the world of complex life and emergent causality, which offers the promise of post-human "freedom", constitutes the end of our world, precisely because it is not amenable to our appropriation as a meaningful structure within which we can consciously engage' (Chandler 2014a, p. 198).

By failing to examine the internal relations of social structures, post-modern resilience thinking occludes any analysis that provides insights into the way in which power operates—through forms of domination, exploitation and subjection (Foucault 1982, p. 781). For example, by treating social relations as external and contingent it forgoes an analysis of capitalist relations of production and the complex networks of production, consumption and exploitation associated with them. Moreover, such an approach occludes our understanding of neo-liberalism's rise as a result of the contradictions and crises associated with such relations, nor does it explain our present preoccupation with uncertainty and resilience. Yet, uncertainty in the present epoch can only be understood in the general context of a 'neoliberal insurgency' that has successfully 'critiqued and dismantled earlier modernist technologies of protection and social insurance' (Duffield 2015, p. 31). As a result, resilience thinking fails to see 'in vulnerability a critique of capitalist exploitation and dispossession', instead it is 'parasitic upon their existence' (Duffield 2015, p. 31).

Despite post-modern resilience thinking's criticism of approaches that investigate the structural relations within society and the power that attends such relations, post-modern resilience thinking's exposition is infused with such assumptions. In a rather contradictory move, according to Chandler's interpretation of post-modern resilience thinking, the roots of social problems 'lie deep within the social texture of society. Social problems are thereby re-presented as problems which are deeply social, rather than as problems of social policy-making at the level of state regulation or intervention' (Chandler 2014a, p. 4). According to Chandler, resilience thinking 'sees the most marginal or oppressed as the agents of policy solutions through the understanding and channelling of their differentiated rationalities and local knowledges and understandings' (Chandler 2014a, p. 51). Yet, at the same time, we are told that, 'Concepts which previously had meaning for us—space, time, value, capital, states, democracy, rights, oppression, and so on' become 'unfit for purpose: understood as fetishised (fixed) forms of representation and as barriers to the technical and pragmatic (already existing) solutions to problems' (Chandler 2014a, p. 225).

Second, with regard to the wider literature, resilience thinking tends to be reactive in nature. Rather than reform orientated, the emphasis is upon survival and the capacities required to do so. Equally, treating finance as analogous to natural systems and attempting to re-instate a homeostatic system is an inherently conservative endeavour—one which restores the previous order, albeit with stricter risk parameters and pre-emptive policies that attempt to shore up such homeostasis. Finally, as the analysis below argues, the continuation of neo-liberal policies, such as austerity and increased competition, will greatly exacerbate the contradictions of capitalism (greater reliance on credit and personal debt increasing the risk of a crash, further declines in the rate of profit, unemployment/low wages) and it is therefore likely that another crisis will emerge within the near future.

This section therefore argues that a more fruitful avenue is to examine the emergence of resilience thinking through a Foucauldian lens that emphasizes the exclusionary procedures of discourses and the strategic selectivity of institutions. Although Foucault did acknowledge the structural biases and stratifications within institutions and society in general, a greater emphasis on what Bob Jessop refers to as strategic selectivity provides us with a better understanding as to why certain discourses are given precedence over others.

Yet, Foucault also has a contribution to make with regard to how particular dominant discourses hold sway over societies. Foucault's 1970 inaugural lecture at the *College de France* where he lectured until his death is a typical example of this. In *L'Ordre du Discours*, Foucault sets out various procedures of exclusion that help maintain established discourses. Such discourses exhibit a high degree of stability through prohibition—'the taboo on the object of speech…the ritual of the circumstances of speech, and the privileged or exclusive right of the speaking subject' (Foucault 1981, p. 52). They are also maintained through divisive practices, establishing exclusion through discourses founded on binary opposites, such as, true and false or reason and madness (Foucault 1981, p. 55). But exclusion is also associated with the internal procedures of discourses themselves. The hierarchical division between 'sacred' texts and those texts that are relegated to the status of mere commentary—this hierarchy is supported by identifying such texts with a particular author and their revered system of thought (Foucault 1981, p. 58). In addition, the establishment of specific disciplines with their particular internal rules for establishing what is to be regarded as true or false act as 'a principle of control over the production of discourse' (Foucault 1981, p. 61). Again, such exclusion is supported through the appropriation of subjects through 'societies of discourse' establishing 'the expert'—who is qualified to speak on a subject and who is not (Foucault 1981, p. 62).

These procedures of exclusion cannot be treated in isolation—societies are saturated by relations of power and such procedures of exclusion will be predominantly exercised by those in dominant positions of power. Foucault thus provides a useful counter to post-modern resilience thinking because of his emphasis on the relationality of power, on the 'manifold relationships of force that take shape and come into play' between the multitude of actors within society (Foucault 1978, p. 94). Thus, when he speaks of the 'structures or the mechanisms of power, it is only insofar as we suppose that certain persons exercise power over others. The term "power" designates relationships between partners' (Foucault 1982, p. 786). In contradistinction to a post-modern resilience approach that places actors in a position of exteriority to one another, Foucault explicitly states that, 'relations of power are not in a position of exteriority with respect to other types of relationships (economic processes, knowledge relationships, sexual relations), but are immanent in the latter; they are the immediate effects of the divisions, inequalities, and disequilibriums which occur in the latter, and conversely they are the internal conditions of these differentiations' (Foucault 1978, p. 94).

For Foucault, although there is a multitude of multifaceted relations of power, he argues that we can identity three main types of struggles—'either against forms of domination (ethnic, social, and religious); against forms of exploitation which separate individuals from what they produce; or against that which ties the individual to himself and submits him to others in this way (struggles against subjection, against forms of subjectivity and submission)' (Foucault 1982, p. 781).

In a move that echoes the later works of Jessop on strategic selectivity and the structurally inscribed biases of institutions, Foucault argues that

> In most societies, organizations are created to freeze the relations of power, hold those relations in a state of asymmetry, so that a certain number of persons get an advantage, socially, economically, politically, institutionally, etc. And this totally freezes the situation. That's what one calls power in the strict sense of the term: it's a specific type of power relation that has been institutionalized, frozen, immobilized, to the profit of some and to the detriment of others. (Foucault 3 November 1980, p. 11)

Foucault's view of society is thus one in which a network of power issues forth from this multitude of social structures or 'mechanisms of power'—but equally so does resistance (Heller 1996, p. 85). As Kevin Heller points out, it is through this image of a complex stratified society that we can understand Foucault's assertion that 'power relations are both intentional and non-subjective' (Foucault 1978, p. 94). This Janus-faced nature arises from the fact that 'while the decision to exercise power is always intentional, *the mechanisms of power that individuals use to exercise power are inherently non-subjective, because they do not depend on the existence of those individuals for their own existence.* Power-mechanisms, because they are structured and reproduced by a multiplicity of power-relations that are not reducible to the individuals who exercise them, are necessarily incapable of being controlled by any particular individual' (Heller 1996, p. 85).[11]

As a result, Foucault makes a clear distinction between tactics and strategies. Tactics are said to be the '*intentional* actions carried out in determinate political contexts by individuals and groups' (Heller 1996, p. 87). Whereas strategies are the '*unintentional*—but institutionally and socially regularized—effects produced by the non-subjective articulation of different individual and group tactics' (Heller 1996, pp. 87–88). Both tactics and strategies are said to 'involve power, because both create social change; only strategies, however, involve non-subjective power' (Heller 1996, p. 88).

If Heller is correct when he argues that Foucault does not mean to say that the structural position of certain individuals or groups does not enable them to control certain mechanisms of power, but it does imply that no particular individual/group can control the whole social formation, then we need to investigate this subjective and non-subjective aspect a little further (Heller 1996, p. 86). We need to explain the non-randomness of strategies and their associated discourses. What is proposed here is a more 'structural' understanding of policy formation using Jessop's work on strategic selectivity. This approach has the merit of capturing both the discursive and extra-discursive elements that influence the sedimentation of certain discourses over others—the way in which we frame our understandings of issues and the policy solutions that subsequently arise and the social configurations with their attendant biases that will favour some of these framings over others.

Jessop's work highlights the way in which certain strategies (in Foucault's terminology tactics) are selected over others because institutions exhibit a certain social bias, positioning 'agents in certain ways, allowing them to exercise power, but also exercising bias in favour of some projects and against others' (Joseph 2012, p. 36). They thus exhibit certain strategic selectivities that 'privilege the access of some forces over others, some strategies over others, some interests over others, some spatial and temporal horizons of action over others, and some coalition possibilities over others' (Jessop 1990, p. 54). But this is not to say that even when such strategies are successfully pursued that unforeseen consequences do not arise as a result of actions associated with these strategies (as Foucault points out).

The emphasis is therefore on both the selectivity of our social environment and agents as strategic actors. Differential influence over proceedings by certain social/class forces will issue from institutional biases that favour 'some actors, some discourses, some identities, and some strategies over others' (Jessop and Ngai-Ling 2006, p. 166). Yet, at the same time, actors are 'conceptualised as conscious, reflexive and strategic' (Hay 2002, p. 131). The approach emphasizes that actors act strategically towards the context in which they find themselves, agents are said to 'take account of this differential privileging through "strategic-context" analysis when choosing a course of action' (Jessop and Sum 2006, p. 325). The result is a duality involving 'recursive interaction of structurally inscribed strategic selectivity and strategically calculated, structurally oriented action'. The recursive nature of this interaction produces a reflexive reorganization of structural configurations and recursively selected strategies that 'co-evolve over time' (Sum and Jessop 2012, p. 114; Jessop 1999, p. 54).

As actors recursively interact with each other in a given social configuration, they learn about the context in which they are operating and the intended/unintended consequences of their actions. It is assumed that 'agents are reflexive, capable of reformulating within limits their own identities and interests, and able to engage in strategic calculation about their current situation' (Jessop 1996, p. 124). If their initial understanding of either the issue or the strategic context does not align with their actual experience, then it is likely that their ideas, concepts and discourses will be modified so that they accord with their experiences. But these modifications may also be more strategic in orientation, altering their discursive framings in order that they dovetail with the discourses of other coalitions in order to achieve specific ends.

In such a way, Foucault's insights on intentional and unintentional actions and subjective/non-subjective power can be taken into account, but Jessop's work helps us to better understand why some discourses are favoured over others. So Jessop's work emphasizes the point made by Heller that successful strategies qua articulation of various tactics do not become successful completely randomly. Rather, the success of particular strategies and their associated discourses will depend both on structurally inscribed biases and how well agents re-orient their strategies to this strategic context. Given the domination of capitalist classes within society in general, the form of state will be capitalist in nature and biased towards strategies pursued by them. The tendency will be for their strategies and discourses to be favoured over others. Other groups may adapt to this selective environment and it is possible that under certain conditions their strategies are successful in a particular issue area. However, the overall tendency is that institutions operate in such a way as to favour the dominant class or fractions within it. Moreover, in the absence of some epochal transforming event, strategies and associated discourses that challenge or obstruct the various circuits of capital will not rise to the fore.

For the post-financial crisis period, we can see that the regulatory capture associated with the reforms of the financial system provides a good example of institutional bias and strategic selectivity that has resulted in a general strategy of limiting reforms. Although each individual/firm's tactic exhibits a degree of variance, the overall strategy that emerged was one of fairly limited reforms. Even though this strategy will likely result in another financial crisis in the near future, the individual tactics of financiers pursuing their own self-interest by minimizing the reforms appears perfectly rational within their habitus. It is also important to note that the condensation of class forces within the highly industrialized countries is such that the financial class fraction continues to have greater influence than the industrial class fraction, thus ensuring the success of a limited reform strategy. For sure, a degree of path dependency also influenced this state of affairs with state mandarins and politicians favouring incremental solutions that did not challenge the overall framework that they were familiar with. But the policy outcomes were clearly influenced by the fact that most highly industrialized states had become reliant upon revenue generated by the financial sector. Moreover, the use of so-called privatized Keynesianism has clearly become a key economic instrument of the state, boosting the economy in downturns through the provision of cheap credit.

Inextricably intertwined with this strategy has been the emergence of resilience thinking, because it chimes with rather than challenges neo-liberalism. Rather than examine radical solutions that would prevent another financial crisis, resilience thinking promotes an acceptance that uncertainty and crises are part of the social fabric. Yet, the more radical post-modern version of resilience has not taken hold in policy circles. From a Jessopian perspective, this is relatively easy to explain. Governing on the basis of the unknowability of the world and its emphasis on non-intervention palpably fails to ensure the smooth running of the circuits of capital and protection against instability. Whereas neo-liberal resilience thinking has gone hand in hand with limited (interventionist) reforms that are believed to shore up the stability of capitalist society. Yet, it has also helped shift the onus away from those responsible for the crisis towards each individual by emphasizing the need for *post-facto* adaptability.

Beyond Neo-Liberal Resilience

As Foucault stressed, those who 'resist or rebel against a form of power cannot merely be content to denounce violence or criticise an institution. Nor is it enough to cast the blame on reason in general. What has to be questioned is the form of rationality at stake'.[12] The concluding part of this chapter uses a Foucauldian framework to demonstrate how understandings of, and solutions to, the financial crises have been enframed in such a manner that they fit within a wider neo-liberal discourse. In addition, Foucault's acknowledgement of social differentiations and the way in which these are often sedimented in institutional forms serve to remind us that the discourses associated with these enframings do not emerge in a power vacuum. We can therefore understand the emergence of resilience, in part, as a result of the conditioning effect of an abiding neo-liberal imaginary and as a result of the entrenched interests of political and economic elites. The outcome has been that, far from representing a radical departure, resilience serves to support the continuation of a highly volatile financial system, the further reduction of welfare commitments and employment rights and further privatization of national assets.

At first glance, the financial reforms, promulgated by institutions such as the Basel Committee on Banking Supervision (BCBS) and the Financial Stability Board (FSB) appear to resonate with post-modern resilience thinking's argument that ontological complexity is leading to new forms of resilience governance. Following the financial crisis, attention did shift towards complex systems analysis, the sources of instability within them and how to make them more resilient. Indeed, as Melinda Cooper highlights, such work tentatively began in 2006 but came to the fore after the crisis with several papers analysing the banking system as analogous to natural ecosystems (Cooper 2011, pp. 371–2). Although this work fully recognizes the Knightian uncertainty and unpredictability of complex financial systems, rather than abandon modernist notions of intervention, such reforms have focussed on instilling 'order in far from equilibrium conditions' (Cooper 2011, p. 381; Jarvis 2011, p. 308).

Accordingly, the focus of post-financial crisis reforms has been on resilience and the 'performative adaptability' of the financial system to 'withstand, re-route and recombine in the wake of a potentially catastrophic event to maintain systemic operability' so that it can 'withstand, recover and bounce back from crisis'.[13] Systems with high degrees of connectivity are said to be highly vulnerable to network spill over effects and therefore less systemically resilient, that is, where the failure of one financial institution or nodal point has negative knock-on effects throughout the system. In order to increase the resilience of the financial system overall, those financial institutions that have the potential for being 'superspreaders' (Global Systemically Important Banks) of instability in times of stress have been identified (Haldane and May 2011, p. 354).[14] The emphasis is on increasing the 'absorptive capacity of each of the nodes in the financial network in response to external shocks' in order to reduce systemic risk (Ibid.). One consequence of this systemic concern is that the capital adequacy requirements for banks have been significantly increased. The GSIBs as critical nodes within a complex banking system also have far more stringent requirements, with the FSB requesting a total loss absorbing capacity of 16–20% of risk-weighted assets for the 30 banks so identified.

The state continues to take a back seat role; it conducts the conduct of financial institutions through the setting of acceptable risk levels (e.g. through adherence to the Basle Accords), the monitoring of risk exposure by auditors and the rating of their activities by the credit rating agencies. Key to maintaining the free circulation of capital is the way in which the market ensures that financial activity is delimited—financial institutions must limit their risk exposure to within what are deemed acceptable levels lest they be punished by capital flight in reaction to credit rating downgrades. States establish maximum risk levels through the setting of capital adequacy ratios (increasingly through international agreements such as the Basle Accords). But the actual judgement of the day-to-day health of a financial institution is conducted through the process of auditing, risk assessments and credit ratings (Vestergaard 2009).

In part, as a result of regulatory capture by those with most to lose from more radical reforms but also, in part, as a result of the conditioning effect of an abiding neo-liberal imaginary, the enframing of finance is still conditioned by the modernist episteme, with its emphasis on organic structures that develop in 'accordance with autochthonous laws' (Foucault 2007, p. 245).[15] Rather than the introduction of radical reform, we have witnessed the re-balancing of what is regarded as a homeostatic system that establishes 'an average considered as optimal on the one hand, and, on the other, a bandwidth of the acceptable that must not be exceeded' (Foucault 2007, p. 21). Such enframing involves the implementation of a biopolitical strategy establishing new parameters of risk that are thought to be 'within socially and economically acceptable limits and around an average that will be considered as optimal for a given social functioning' (Foucault 1989, p. 20). So-called Minsky moments are to be prevented by reducing risk through increasing banks' capital buffers during economic booms thus pre-empting heightened speculation in various asset classes.[16] Finance is still presented as analogous to an organic homeostatic system, rather than a system permeated by power relations with agents who have an interest in maintaining the extant economic order. In this way, the economy continues to be framed as self-regulating and self-perpetuating. The reforms thus continue to embrace risk taking as a foundation stone of economic behaviour that O'Malley refers to below, while at the same time trying to delimit the extent of risk associated with such activities. In the felicitous phrase of Martijn Konings, the reforms should thus be understood 'not as involving a transcendence of risk, but precisely in terms of the principles endogenous to it' (Konings 2016, p. 273).

Equally, the emphasis on resilient subjects is best understood as the expansion and reconfiguration of extant neo-liberal subjectivities. The various neo-liberal regimes that emerged in the aftermath of the seventies crisis promoted a particular set of economic norms with the purpose of reconstituting the subjectivities of the population (Rose 1993, p. 294; O'Malley 2004). In relation to welfare retrenchment, states sought to 'modify the relation of individuals to political power by seeking, in part, to get them to economize on their expectations of or demands on government' (Burchell 1991, pp. 145–6). More generally, this involved a move away from the notion of citizenship 'construed in terms of solidarity, contentment, welfare and a sense of security established through the bonds of organizational and social life' (Miller and Rose 1990, p. 24). Enterprise and entrepreneurship became the new watchwords with the worker 'no longer construed as a social creature seeking satisfaction of his or her need for security, solidarity and welfare, but as an individual actively seeking to shape and manage his or her own life in order to maximize its returns in terms of success and achievement' (Miller and Rose 1990, p. 9).

At the same time, neo-liberal governmentalities involved the constitution of neo-liberal financial subjects who were to be both entrepreneurial and responsible subjects rationally calculating the risks and benefits of the various financial positions they ventured into. The escape from the 'tyranny of earned income' was thus associated with the emergence of the entrepreneurial self and a shift in individual financial behaviour from thrift to investment so that the latter became seen as 'the socially desirable form of saving' (O'Malley 2004, p. 23; Froud et al. 2010). As O'Malley argues, resilience resonates with these earlier neo-liberal discourses because it continues to emphasize the importance of embracing risk and adopting a '*risk-taking* attitude that regards uncertainty as opportunity' (O'Malley 2010, p. 499). Hence, resilience creates subjects that '"thrive" on chaos and make every threat a challenge and opportunity' (O'Malley 2013, p. 192). Yet, just like previous neo-liberal discourses, resilience emphasizes the importance of the responsibilization of the self. This is most clearly seen in the European Union's increasing emphasis on 'bail-ins' (in contrast to bail-outs) ensuring that shareholders and creditors of the failing institution suffer appropriate losses and bear an appropriate part of the costs capsulated in its Bank Recovery and Resolution Directive (BRRD) which ensures 'that shareholders and creditors of the failing institution suffer appropriate losses and bear an appropriate part of the costs' of a failed bank—this will include citizens with deposits of €100,000 or over.[17]

Resilience is therefore best understood as part of a larger neo-liberal mentality that 'valorizes self-reliance and responsibility in an uncertain world' (O'Malley 2010, p. 505). As Ronen Shamir points out, for instance, the neo-liberal project

> operates at the level of individual actors, reconfiguring roles and identities (employees, welfare recipients, managers, civil servants, citizens, consumers and so on) so as to mobilize designated actors actively to undertake and perform self-governing tasks. Accordingly, multiple sources of authority, including governmental units, non-governmental organizations and commercial enterprises are responsibilizing their relevant clients to adjust to the harsh realities of the free market by adopting 'a certain entrepreneurial form of practical relationship to themselves as a condition of their effectiveness'. (Shamir 2008, p. 8)

The Organisation for Economic Cooperation and Development (OECD), for example, encourages firms to adopt an entrepreneurial form which enables them to enhance 'productive efficiency' in an unpropitious global environment, whereas resilience for workers is understood to be about weathering 'economic downturns with limited social costs' (OECD 2012, p. 57). The partisan character of these reforms, however, is demonstrated by the creation of new opportunities for investment capital, provided through the further commodification of the social sphere in the form of privatization of utility and other nationalized companies. Such privatizations may promote the further valorization of capital, but this deepening of marketization and the emphasis on profit making, more often than not, leads to the eradication of subsidies for necessities such as warmth and water. Resilience thinking, then, is indicative not only of just how deeply embedded neo-liberal thinking has become, but also of the inability of mainstream politicians to embrace other political alternatives.

As Davies suggests, the global financial crisis of 2007/2008 is best understood as a 'historical punctuation of normality'—a period in which the tried-and-tested tools of neo-liberal governance and 'principles of judgement' were thrown into doubt (Davies 2014, p. 154). However, this period of 'meta-evaluation' has not, unlike the crisis of Fordism in the

1970s given rise to a political-economic programme able 'to resolve doubt and restore certainty' (Davies 2014, p. 154). Unable to restore profitability through the expanded reproduction of capital, mechanisms of exploitation and domination have been intensified at every level of society. Under these conditions, as Maurizio Lazzarato argues, there is no distinction between working people and the unemployed, between consumers and producers, between working and non-working populations, between retirees and welfare recipients. All are cast as 'debtors', 'accountable to and guilty before capital' (Lazzarato 2011, p. 7). This, the book submits, is a key driving force of austerity and its conjunctural discursive counterpart, resilience.

Under such austerity, we have seen the usual pattern of policy proposals surrounding fiscal balance, financial stability and structural reforms to restore competitiveness. However, loan conditionality now goes much further in terms of broadening and deepening market relations within a state. The policies foisted upon loan recipients through economic adjustment programmes by the Troika, for example, are part of a wider supranational disciplinary mechanism that seeks to instil neo-liberal patterns of behaviour at the state level, entailing a 'policy of coercions that act upon' the state that enters a 'machinery of power that explores it, breaks it down and rearranges it' (Foucault 2007, p. 138). Fiscal balances are produced through the shrinking of state commitments, leading to reductions in pensions, social welfare provision, public sector employment, public sector wages, education and health and so on. As part of this process, worker protections are understood by the OECD to be 'particularly damaging' to firms' profitability because they 'undermine long-run labour supply, leading to lower potential growth' (Sánchez et al. 2015).

More generally, macroeconomic reforms have as their objective the broadening and deepening of market relations with the privatization of state enterprises, attacks on collective bargaining rights and the opening up of hitherto closed professions and protected industries to market forces. Loan recipients must discipline themselves and adhere to these severe structural adjustments and fiscal targets if they are to continue to receive loan disbursements. Indeed, in the Greek case, the potential for almost immediate punishment is inscribed in the loan conditionalities in the form of *ex-ante* prior actions that the state must enact. In its most recent Third Economic Adjustment Programme, the Memoranda of Understanding stipulates 35 prior actions for the Greek state to take before loans are disbursed.[18]

Yet, we can see that resistance to both the activities of financiers by the occupy movement and the resistance to various austerity policies resemble the articulation of a plethora of tactics from which a complex of strategies emerge that Foucault points to.[19] Although there is evidence, therefore, of an emergent counter-hegemonic movement, we are as yet unable to divine the overall strategy that will emerge because this will depend on how such struggles become articulated with other resistances. But the use of archaeological and genealogical techniques will at least help us in our 'investigation into the events that have led us to constitute ourselves' and will help us understand that radical economic alternatives may also be conditioned by previous epistemes (Foucault 1984a, p. 46). For example, worker self-management and local trade exchanges are to be lauded as alternatives, yet still often have at their heart labour theories of value (equality based on wages or exchange tokens solely with regard to hours worked) that hark as far back as the Physiocrats (and such a perspective may well remain until artificial intelligence and automation become the predominant mode of production). Neither do these approaches overcome the problem of non-equivalence between utility value, exchange value nor labour value that has occupied economists for centuries (Foucault 1984b, Chapters 6 and 7).

Conclusion

This chapter has examined two main strands of resilience thinking in the literature. The first strand argues that, we are now confronted with such a degree of radical uncertainty that it is prompting a philosophical re-orientation that eschews the subject/object of liberal thinking in favour of viewing the human species as inextricably entangled in a web of complexity. Moreover, because complexity gives rise to a multitude of 'unknown unknowns' we must accept the highly contingent nature of final outcomes and can therefore never know the causalities of events before they occur. This is said to lead to a truly post-modern form of politics where we are self-reflexive of being part of a complex world, governing through society rather than over society.

The second strand argues that, although the emergence of resilience thinking has relatively independent origins it quickly gained traction in the political and economic realms. Moreover, the reason that it became sedimented into the wider neo-liberal economic discourse is because many of its assumptions and arguments cohered rather than challenged the tenets of neo-liberalism. This is not to say that there is nothing new about resilience thinking. The emphasis on building human capacities that promote the ability to withstand shocks through *post-hoc* adaptability and the even greater emphasis on self-reliance even in times of crisis are of interest precisely because they are new.

But one has to ask why resilience thinking has become so popular in academic and policy circles rather than, say, resistance thinking. Resilience thinking fails to challenge neo-liberalism on any front and, indeed, has been absorbed into this dominant discourse in such a manner that it reinforces neo-liberal policies, such as, further flexibilization of the work force. The responsibility for overcoming crises of capitalism is placed firmly at the individual/community level—often directed towards those that are least able to cope with crises and least responsible for causing such crises. Moreover, resilience thinking tends to promote a high degree of political passivity through its emphasis on uncertainty, rather than viewing capitalism and its inherent tendencies that lead to such crises as socially constructed and therefore transformable. Its emphasis on *post-facto* adaption, rather than proactive change, fits with the general lack of radical reform since the crises began in 2008. Its popularity and incorporation into the wider neo-liberal discourse can therefore be partly understood as resulting from the structural biases within society itself—the dominant social forces favouring resilience thinking because it does not entail radical reform and chimes with their wider interests.

The chapter concludes by examining how resilience thinking has in practice not challenged but supported neo-liberalism. Clearly, although the crises since 2008 have had devastating economic consequences throughout the world, this has not translated into the degree of political upheaval required to break the grip that the dominant social forces have over the stewardship of the economy and society itself. At the same time, neo-liberal discourse still maintains a dominant influence in policy-making and political thought in general. The next two chapters provide a more detailed exposition of the issues covered in the latter section of this chapter. Chapter 5 examines the financial reforms after the crises arguing that neo-liberal rationalities continue to hold sway, particularly the enframing of the financial system as analogous to a natural homeostatic system. Chapter 6 demonstrates not only the continuance but the expansion of neo-liberal disciplines both in their scale and geographical reach since the crises, to the extent that structural adjustment policies have become a feature of the political/economic landscape in the sovereign periphery of Europe.

Notes

1. This work has heavily drawn upon material from within: A. Mckeown and J. Glenn. 'The rise of resilience after the financial crises: A case of neoliberalism rebooted?', *Review of International Studies,* pp. 1–22, 2017 © British International Studies Association, published by Cambridge University Press. Reprinted with permission.
2. Post-modernism is most often associated with deconstructivism, intertextuality and ontological complexity and the challenges to knowledge of the world that these present. Chandler essentially argues that a post-modernist episteme is emerging as a result of our evolving recognition that the world is so complex that it renders it impossible to predict and control. As a result, top-down 'modernist' conceptions of social dynamics no longer work and that governance should shift to the grassroots level relying on situated 'local' knowledge.
3. It should be noted that Chandler may not necessarily be advocating resilience thinking himself. See for example, Chandler and Reid (2016).
4. As Joseph contends, 'resilience is best understood in the context of rolling-out neoliberal governmentality. Its meaning varies depending on the place and the level where this occurs and the aims and objects of governance'. In other words, the exact form neoliberalism takes will be

context and time dependent—yet there are certain commonalities (2013, pp. 38 and 51–2). See also, Macartney (2010), Peck and Theodore (2007), Brenner, Peck and Theodore (2010, pp. 182–222) and Jessop (2012, pp. 91–111).

5. Hence his comment that 'certain half witted "commentators" persist in labelling me a "structuralist"' (Foucault 1984b, p. xiii).
6. For an overview, see Gill (2012).
7. Word in parenthesis added.
8. First quote is from Foucault (2008, p. 130), quoted in Garland (2014, p. 373). Second quote is from Gordon (1980, p. 83).
9. Kristina Zolatova, 'Part II: Fanon and Foucault on Humanism and Rejecting the "Blackmail" of the Enlightenment'. http://percaritatem.com/2011/02/23/part-ii-fanon-and-foucault-on-humanism-and-rejecting-the-%e2%80%9cblackmail%e2%80%9d-of-the-enlightenment/
10. Birmingham (1989, p. 211). Second quote from Foucault (1984a, p. 49).
11. Italics in original.
12. M. Foucault, 'Omnes et Singulatim: Towards a Criticism of 'Political Reason", *Tanner Lectures on Human Values*, (1979), available at http://tannerlectures.utah.edu/_documents/a-to-z/f/foucault81.pdf, p. 254.
13. First quote is from Zebrowski (2009, p. 9) and second is from Zebrowski (2013, p. 4).
14. See also Haldane (2009) and Gai, Haldane and Kapadia (2011, pp. 415–536).
15. On regulatory capture, refer to Underhill, Blom and Mügge (2010), Porter (2005), Porter and Ronit (2006, pp. 41–72). With regard to possible policies to address these issues, refer to Pagliari (June 2012).
16. As Minsky pointed out, financial markets exhibit a repetitive cycle beginning with hedge or 'normal' financing in which the cash flow is 'more than sufficient to meet contractual payment commitments'. However, the low profit yield associated with this type of lending leads to more speculative forms of financing in which income flows are enough to pay off the interest but not the principal leading to a 'rolling over of maturing debt'. The assumption is that the financial asset will increase in value sufficiently to eventually cover the missed payments. The Ponzi form of finance is where the cash flow covers neither the interest nor payment of principal due so that the actual 'face amount of outstanding debt increases' (Minsky 2008, pp. 230-31; Minsky May 1992, pp. 1–10).

17. Directive 2014/59/Eu Of The European Parliament And Of The Council, 15 May 2014, Point 67 of the Preamble.
18. This is very clear from the various memoranda of understanding that the Troika have signed with various national governments setting out bail-out conditions. For example refer, to Greek MOU (August 11, 2015) and Portuguese MOU (17 May, 2011). For an overview of the various policies, refer to Pisani-Ferry, Sapir and Wolff (2013).
19. Foucault in Gordon (1980, p. 77).

References

Amoore, L., and M. De Goede. 2008. *Risk and the War on Terror*. London: Routledge.

Aradau, C., and R. Van Munster. 2007. Governing Terrorism Through Risk: Taking Precautions, (un)knowing the Future. *European Journal of International Relations* 13 (9): 89–115.

Beck, U. 1994. The Reinvention of Politics. In *Reflexive Modernization: Politics, Tradition and Aesthetics in the Modern Social Order*, ed. U. Beck, A. Giddens, and S. Lash, 1–55. Cambridge: Polity Press.

———. 1999. *World Risk Society*. Cambridge: Polity.

———. 2002. The Terrorist Threat: World Risk Society Revisited. *Theory, Culture and Society* 19 (4): 39–55.

———. 2006. Living in the World Risk Society. *Economy and Society* 35 (3): 329 345.

———. 2007. *World at Risk*. Cambridge: Polity Press.

Beck, U., and E. Grande. 2007. *Cosmopolitan Europe*. Cambridge: Polity Press.

Beck, U., and D. Levy. 2012. Cosmopolitanized Nations: Re-imagining Collectivity in World Risk Society. *Theory, Culture and Society* 30 (2): 3–31.

Birmingham, P. 1989. Local Theory. In *The Question of the Other: Essays in Contemporary Continental Philosophy*, ed. A. Dallery and C. Scott, 203–230. Albany: State University of New York Press.

Brenner, N., J. Peck, and N. Theodore. 2010. Variegated Neo-Liberalization: Geographies, Modalities, Pathways. *Global Networks* 10 (2): 182–222.

Burchell, G. 1991. Peculiar Interests: Civil Society and Governing "The System of Natural Liberty". In *The Foucault Effect: Studies in Governmentality*, ed. G. Burchell, C. Gordon and P. Miller, 119–150. Chicago: Chicago University Press.

Burchell, G., C. Gordon, and P. Miller, eds. 1991. *The Foucault Effect: Studies in Governmentality*. Chicago: Chicago University Press.

Chandler, D. 2014a. *Resilience: The Governance of Complexity*. London: Routledge.

———. 2014b. Beyond Neoliberalism: Resilience, the New Art of Governing Complexity. *Resilience: International Policies, Practices and Discourses* 2 (1): 47–63.

Chandler, D., and J. Reid. 2016. *The Neoliberal Subject: Resilience, Adaptation and Vulnerability*. London: Rowman & Littlefield International.

Cooper, M. 2011. Complexity Theory After the Financial Crisis: The Death of Neoliberalism or the Triumph of Hayek? *Journal of Cultural Economy* 4 (4): 371–385.

Davies, W. 2014. *The Limits of Neoliberalism: Authority, Sovereignty and the Logic of Competition*. London: Sage.

Dean, M. 1999. Risk, Calculable and Incalculable. In *Risk and Sociocultural Theory: New Directions and Perspectives,* ed. D. Lupton. Cambridge: Cambridge University Press.

de Goede, M., ed. 2006. *International Political Economy and Poststructural Politics*. Basingstoke: Palgrave Macmillan.

Dillon, M., and J. Reid. 2001. Global Liberal Governance: Biopolitics, Security and War. *Millennium* 30 (1): 41–66.

Duffield, M. 2015. From Protection to Disaster Resilience. In ed. Ginty and Peterson, 26–37.

Evans, B., and J. Reid. 2013. Dangerously Exposed: The Life and Death of the Resilient Subject. *Resilience* 1 (2): 83–98.

Ewald, F. 2005. The Return of the Crafty Genius: An Outline of a Philosophy of Precaution. In ed. O'Malley, 535–567.

Foucault, M. 1978. *History of Sexuality Vol. 1: Translated by Robert Hurley*. New York: Pantheon Books.

———. 1980. The Confession of the Flesh. In *Power/Knowledge: Selected Interviews and Other Writings 1972–1977,* ed. C. Gordon, 194–228. New York: Pantheon Books.

———. 1981. The Order of Discourse. In *Untying The Text: A Post-Structuralist Reader*, ed. R. Young. London: Routledge, Kegan Paul.

———. 1982. The Subject and Power. *Critical Inquiry* 8 (4): 777–795.

———. 1984a. What Is Enlightenment. In *The Foucault Reader*, ed. P. Rabinow, 32–50. New York: Pantheon Books.

———. 1984b. *The Order of Things: An Archaeology of the Human Sciences*. New York: Vintage Books.

———. 2002. *The Archaeology of Knowledge*. London: Routledge.
———. 2007. *Security, Territory, Population: Lectures at the College de France 1977–78*. Basingstoke: Palgrave Macmillan.
———. 2008. *The Birth of Biopolitics: Lectures at the College de France, 1978–79*. Basingstoke: Palgrave Macmillan.
Froud, J., S. Johal, J. Montgomerie, and K. Williams. 2010. Escaping the Tyranny of Earned Income? The Failure of Finance as Social Innovation. *New Political Economy* 15 (1): 147–164.
Gai, P., A. Haldane, and S. Kapadia. 2011. Complexity, Concentration and Contagion. *Journal of Monetary Economics* 58 (5): 415–536.
Garland, D. 2014. What Is a "History of the Present"? On Foucault's Genealogies and Their Critical Preconditions. *Punishment & Society* 16 (4): 365–384.
Gill, S., ed. 2012. *Global Crises and the Crisis of Global Leadership*. Cambridge: Cambridge University Press.
Ginty, R., and J. Peterson, eds. 2015. *The Routledge Companion to Humanitarian Action*. London: Routledge.
Gordon, C. 1980. *Power/Knowledge: Selected Interviews and Other Writings 1972–1977*. New York: Pantheon Books.
Greek MOU. 2015. Greece: Memorandum of Understanding for a Three-Year ESM Programme, August 11. http://online.wsj.com/public/resources/documents/greecedoc.pdf
Griner, S. 2002. Living in a World Risk Society: A Reply to Mikkel V. Rasmussen. *Millennium: Journal of International Studies* 31 (1): 149–160.
Gunderson, L., and L. Pritchard Jr., eds. 2002. *Resilience and the Behavior of Large-Scale Systems (Scientific Committee on Problems of the Environment)*. London: Island Press.
Haldane, A. 2009. Why Banks Failed the Stress Test. Marcus-Evans Conference on Stress-Testing, February 13, pp. 1–23.
Haldane, A., and T. May. 2011. Systemic Risk in Banking Ecosystems. *Nature* 469: 371–355.
Hameiri, S. 2011. State Transformation, Territorial Politics and the Management of Transnational Risk. *International Relations* 25 (3): 381–397.
Hay, C. 2002. *Political Analysis: A Critical Introduction*. London: Palgrave Macmillan.
Heller, K. 1996. Power, Subjectification and Resistance in Foucault. *Substance* 25 (1): 78–110.
Holling, C.S. 1973. Resilience and Stability of Ecological Systems. *Annual Review of Ecology and Systematics* 4 (1): 1–23.

Jarvis, D. 2011. Theorising Risk and Uncertainty in International Relations: The Contributions of Frank Knight. *International Relations* 25 (3): 296–312.
Jessop, B. 1990. *State Theory: Putting Capitalist States in Their Place*. Cambridge: Polity.
———. 1996. Interpretive Sociology and the Dialectic of Structure and Agency. *Theory, Culture, & Society* 13 (1): 119–128.
———. 1999. The Strategic Selectivity of the State: Reflections on a Theme of Poulantzas. *Journal of the Hellenic Diaspora* 25 (1–2): 41–77.
———. 2012. The World Market, Variegated Capitalism, and the Crisis of European Integration. In *Globalisation and European Integration: Critical Approaches to Regional Order and International Relations*, ed. P. Nousios, H. Overbeek, and A. Tsolakis. London: Routledge.
Jessop, B., and N. Sum. 2006. Towards a Cultural International Political Economy: Poststructuralism and the Italian School. In ed. de Goede, 157–176.
Joseph, J. 2012. *The Social in the Global: Social Theory, Governmentality and Global Politics*. Cambridge: Cambridge University Press.
———. 2013. Resilience as Embedded Neoliberalism: A Governmentality Approach. *Resilience: International Policies, Practices and Discourses* 1 (1): 38–52.
Juncker, J. 2014. Main Messages of Jean-Claude Juncker During His Campaign Visit to Athens, Greece. http://juncker.epp.eu/press-releases/main-messages-jean-claude-juncker-during-his-campaign-visit-athens-greece
Konings, M. 2016. Governing the System: Risk, Finance and Neoliberal Reason. *European Journal of International Relations* 22 (2): 268–288.
Lazzarato, M. 2011. *The Making of the Indebted Man: An Essay on the Neoliberal Condition*. Los Angeles: Semiotext(e).
Lenztos, F., and N. Rose. 2009. Governing Insecurity: Contingency Planning, Protection, Resistance. *Economy and Society* 38 (2): 230–254.
Macartney, H. 2010. *Variegated Neoliberalism: EU Varieties of Capitalism and International Political Economy*. London: Routledge.
Miller, P., and N. Rose. 1990. Governing Economic Life. *Economy and Society* 19 (1): 1–31.
Minsky, H. 1992. The Financial Instability Hypothesis. *Levy Economics Institute*. Working Paper 74, pp. 1–10.
———. 2008. *Stabilizing An Unstable Economy*. New York: McGraw and Hill.
O'Malley, P. 2004. *Risk, Uncertainty and Government*. London: Glass House Press.

———., ed. 2005. *Governing Risks*. Aldershot: Ashgate.

———. 2010. Resilient Subjects: Uncertainty, Warfare and Liberalism. *Economy and Society* 39 (4): 488–509.

———. 2013. Uncertain Governance and Resilient Subjects in the Risk Society. *Oñati Socio-Legal Series* 3 (2): 180–195.

OECD. 2012. What Makes Labour Markets Resilient During Recessions. http://www.oecd-ilibrary.org/employment/oecd-employment-outlook-2012/what-makes-labour-markets-resilient-during-recessions_empl_outlook-2012-3-en

Pagliari, S., ed. 2012. The Making of Good Financial Regulation Towards a Policy Response to Regulatory Capture, June. http://www.icffr.org/assets/pdfs/June-2012/ICFR-Regulatory-Capture-Book-25-June---The-Making-.aspx

Peck, J., and N. Theodore. 2007. Variegated Capitalism. *Progress in Human Geography* 31 (6): 731–772.

Pisani-Ferry, J., A. Sapir, and G. Wolff. 2013. *EU-IMF Assistance to Euro-Area Countries: An Early Assessment*. Belgium: Bruegel Blueprint Series.

Porter, T. 2005. *Globalization and Finance*. Cambridge: Polity Press.

Porter, T., and K. Ronit. 2006. Self-Regulation as Policy Process: The Multiple and Criss-Crossing Stages of Private Rule-Making. *Policy Sciences* 39: 41–72.

Portugal. 2011. Memorandum of Understanding on Specific Economic Policy Conditionality, May 17. http://ec.europa.eu/economy_finance/eu_borrower/mou/2011-05-18-mou-portugal_en.pdf

Rasmussen, M.V. 2004. It Sounds Like a Riddle: Security Studies, the War on Terror and Risk. *Millennium* 33 (2): 381–395.

Rose, N. 1993. Government, Authority and Expertise in Advanced Liberalism. *Economy and Society* 22 (3): 283–299.

Rosenberg, J. 2005. Globalization Theory: A Post Mortem. *International Politics* 42 (1): 2–74.

Sánchez, A., M. Rasmussen, and O. Röhn. 2015. Economic Resilience: What Role for Policies? *OECD Economics Department Working Papers, No. 1251*. Paris: OECD Publishing.

Sayer, D. 2013. Looking Forward to New Realist Debates. *Dialogues in Human Geography* 3 (1): 22–25.

Shamir, R. 2008. The Age of Responsibilisation: On Market Embedded Morality. *Economy and Society* 37 (1): 1–19.

Sugarman, J. 2015. Historical Ontology. In *The Wiley Handbook of Theoretical and Philosophical Psychology: Methods, Approaches and New Directions for Social Sciences*, ed. J. Martin, J. Sugarman, and K. Slaney, 166–182. West Sussex: Wiley.

Sum, N., and B. Jessop. 2012. *Towards a Cultural Political Economy*. London: Edward Elgar Publishing Ltd.

UK Government. 2014. Chancellor George Osborne's Budget 2014 Speech, March 19. https://www.gov.uk/government/speeches/chancellor-george-osbornes-budget-2014-speech

Underhill, G., J. Blom, and D. Mügge. 2010. *Global Financial Integration Thirty Years On: From Reform to Crisis*. New York: Cambridge University Press.

Vestergaard, J. 2009. *Discipline in the Global Economy?: International Finance and the End of Liberalism New Political Economy*. New York: Routledge.

Walker, J., and M. Cooper. 2011. Genealogies of Resilience: From Systems Ecology to the Political Economy of Crisis Adaptation. *Security Dialogue* 42 (2): 143–160.

Zebrowski, C. 2009. Governing the Network Society: A Bio-political Critique of Resilience. *Political Perspectives* 3 (1): 1–36.

———. 2013. The Nature of Resilience. *Resilience International Policies, Practices and Discourses* 1 (3): 159–173.

———. 2016. *The Value of Resilience: Securing Life in the Twenty-First Century*. London: Routledge.

5

Securing Finance: Risk, Pre-emption and Resilience

Introduction

This chapter examines the changes that were made to the new financial architecture in the aftermath of the financial crisis.[1] In so doing, the chapter argues that, although there is much discussion concerning resilience with regard to the financial system, the reforms were actually marked more by continuation than change. Rather than challenging the management of finance, the reforms have relied mainly upon previous methods albeit in more intensive form. Resilience thinking is apparent, but not the radical post-modern version discussed in Chap. 4. Rather, resilience thinking in policy-making tends to dovetail with other neo-liberal policy reforms and is quite interventionist in its approach in contrast to that predicted by the post-modernist variant of resilience thinking.

Indeed, this chapter argues that, with regard to the financial system, neo-liberal governmentality continues to adopt policies that are analogous to biopolitical strategies. The enframing of the financial system has centred around a 'naturalistic fallacy'. Neo-liberal rationalities of

J. G. Glenn, *Foucault and Post-Financial Crises*, International Political Economy Series, https://doi.org/10.1007/978-3-319-77188-5_5

governing, that is, 'styles of thinking, ways of rendering reality thinkable in such a way that it [is] amenable to calculation and programming', have thus treated finance as analogous to homeostatic systems that we find in nature (Rose and Miller 2008, p. 16).[2] This mode of thinking has clearly continued after the crisis, so that the emphasis has been less on radical reform and more on establishing more restrictive risk parameters and strengthening the nodal points of the system in order that it can withstand economic shocks and the homeostatic 'norm' can be reinstated.

In addition, the perceived unpredictability of the financial system has led to a stronger emphasis on pre-emption and surveillance (O'Malley 2010, 2013). Pre-emptive policies were present previously. For example, in the mid-nineties the Federal Reserve attempted to pre-empt negative market reactions by announcing possible shifts in policy in advance (Krippner 2011, p. 127). Similarly, stress tests and early warning exercises (EWEs) had been used prior to the crisis (Berg et al. 2000, 2004). However, the intensity of such practices and degree of coordination between various supervisory bodies since the crisis are such that we can speak of the emergence of a new pre-emptive regime. Moreover, the emphasis on pre-emption and surveillance may partly compensate for the lack of fundamental reforms that one would have expected given the profound ramifications of the financial crisis. The chapter therefore argues that despite much debate on the emergence of resilience thinking, in the financial sphere at least, there has been little in the way of radical new policy changes of the post-modernist variant discussed in Chap. 4. Rather, resilience thinking in practice actually works symbiotically with and relies upon an array of neo-liberal policies. The chapter also concludes that, although the policy of pre-emption has the potential to reinforce the regulatory mechanism, it fails to overcome the paradoxes associated with intervention in a highly complex system.

Securing Finance

This chapter uses the insights from Foucault's work on regulatory power to map out the changes in financial governance that have arisen since the crisis. As mentioned in Chap. 2, Foucault added to his earlier work with his analysis of biopolitics, security and regulatory power in his later 1975–1979 lectures at the *Collège de France* which focused on the evolution of governing populations. In so doing, he argued that a general recognition emerged of the limits of state knowledge and control (Gordon 1991, p. 16). The population was viewed as placing 'constraints upon political governance by means of an arena of naturalistically conceived laws, including those of capital, population and subsistence, that it would be foolish for the state to ignore' (Dean 1994, p. 190).

As a result of these constraints, a mode of government developed that provided a high degree of individual freedom whilst maintaining a certain level of security, so that 'Liberalism turns into a mechanism continually having to arbitrate between the freedom and security of individuals by reference to' the notion of danger (Foucault 2008, p. 66).[3] Liberal forms of government thus promote individual freedom whilst at the same time ensuring a level of protection for the population. In practice, liberalism actually involves 'an entire series of interventions and regulatory controls: a biopolitics of the population', 'a power whose task is to take charge of life needs continuous regulatory and corrective mechanisms' (Foucault 1978, p. 139 and 144).

Liberal security governance is thus said to work through the 'delimitation of phenomena within acceptable limits' (Foucault 2007, p. 93). In any given area of activity, a spectrum of behaviours are possible, but some constitute a greater danger to the population than others—'There are therefore differential risks that reveal, as it were, zones of higher risk and, on the other hand, zones of less or lower risk. This means that one can thus identify what is dangerous' (Foucault 2007, p. 89). Security is not viewed as a binary division of the permitted and prohibited, but 'an average considered as optimal on the one hand, and, on the other, a bandwidth of the acceptable that must not be exceeded. In this way a completely different distribution of things and mechanisms takes shape' (Foucault 2007, p. 20). Liberal governance therefore works through regulatory mechanisms to 'establish an equilibrium, maintain an average, establish a sort of homeostasis, and compensate for variations within this general population and its aleatory field' (Foucault 2003, p. 246).

This regulatory technique, it is argued, is readily apparent in attempts to ensure stability within the financial system. Indeed, it can be argued that the financial governance regimes represent particular security apparatuses of a much larger security *dispositif* which attempts to balance the need for complex financial transactions and calculations that facilitate the circulation of capital with the dangers that crises clearly present (Langley 2013, p. 60).[4] What has emerged over decades is a regulatory form of regulation (rules that delimit modulation) which seeks to modulate financial behaviour within certain given risk parameters that are supposed to prevent financial meltdowns while allowing the freest possible movement for finance itself. Moreover, this regulatory mechanism relies on the supposed self-correcting mechanism of the market. Risk parameters are set, but how well states and financial institutions comply to these codes is assessed by credit rating agencies (CRAs). Risk premia increase as ratings fall below the best (AAA) thus increasing the costs of their financial operations (Vestergaard 2009).

Given that this form of mechanism constitutes the basis for many of the reforms that we have recently witnessed, the chapter takes this as part of its object of focus. But, furthermore, it argues that the unpredictability of the financial system has led to an emphasis on pre-emption and an associated set of intensive surveillance techniques which have as their object the curtailment of embryonic crises alongside an emphasis on the survival of the financial system through improved preparedness should such policies fail.

Several authors writing on risk have distinguished between policies centred around precaution, pre-emption and resilience (O'Malley 2010, 2013; Lenztos and Rose 2009). Such writings bring to our attention the greater emphasis on precaution and the need to 'intervene in emergence precisely because of uncertainty linked to massive consequences' (O'Malley 2013, p. 188). Complexity often produces radical uncertainty, which goes beyond the realms of risk calculations and recognizes the possibility of 'unknowable contingencies—events for which it is impossible to assign a probability distribution on the basis of past frequencies' (Cooper 2010, p. 173). As a result, the precautionary principle often requires pre-emptive or 'weatherman' (sic) policies identifying potential dangers and attempting to reduce the probability of them turning into actual threats by acting in advance of the event (Rasmussen 2006, p. 101). As Melinda Cooper points out, such pre-emption 'exhorts us to respond to what we suspect without being able to discern; to prepare for the emergent, long before we can predict how and when it will be actualized; to counter the unknowable, before it is even realized' (2006, p. 120).

The precautionary principle is associated with our lack of knowledge concerning certain activities. Under conditions of radical uncertainty, the precautionary principle thus invokes action 'even before a causal link has been established by absolutely clear scientific evidence' (O'Malley 2013, p. 186). Pre-emptive policies associated with such precaution, it is argued, have emerged as a result of the sheer enormity of catastrophic events associated with late modernity combined with a heightened sense of uncertainty in which direct causal relationships are harder to identify and may only become apparent after the event leading to a situation where we postulate relationships of 'possibility, eventuality, plausibility or probability without being able to provide the proof of its validity' (Ewald 2005, p. 61). Pre-emption differs from prevention as it involves 'pre-emptive judgement' and engagement in speculative activities, acting without knowing if the conditions identified will actually develop into a full-blown crisis (Andenas and Chiu 2014, pp. 456–8). Temporally, pre-emption focuses on imminent crises, attempting to identify the emergence of an event and nipping things in the bud so that potential issues are identified and dealt with before they have an impact. As is demonstrated below, this therefore requires a highly intensive form of surveillance for two reasons: in an environment of uncertainty, as much information as possible needs to be acquired; and the imminent nature of threats means that such information needs to be gathered in as rapid a fashion as possible.

As Lentzos and Rose point out, resilience, in contradistinction to these policies, emphasizes the quality of adaptability that enables rapid recovery after catastrophes. They identify two aspects that have been historically associated with the term: 'the mental state of being able to withstand stress or adverse circumstances or to recover quickly from their effects'; and, 'the capacity of systems, structures or organizations to resist being affected by shock or disaster, and to recover quickly from such events' (Lenztos and Rose 2009, p. 242).

Since the crisis, we have witnessed a much greater emphasis on the above preemptive policies. In addition to strengthening the regulatory mechanisms, we have witnessed the broadening and deepening of the financial surveillance regime, combined with frequent and extensive stress testing of banks to ensure their resilience during a sudden crisis. The chapter thus begins with the efforts to strengthen the financial system through regulatory mechanisms and then moves on to examine reforms that have sought to increase the level of pre-emptive surveillance, preparedness and resilience of the financial system.

Reinforcing the Global Regulatory Regime

Financial risk analysis is essentially concerned with calculating the 'mathematical commodification of contingency' (Dillon 2008, p. 282). However, the recent financial crisis highlighted one of the ways in which such calculations are error prone. Essentially, a multitude of micro-calculations of risk covering the vast array of financial activities occurring in the contemporary world produced a macro-risk at the level of the system itself. As the IMF points out, 'today macrofinancial feedback effects have reached a level of complexity that has become difficult to capture in such models, requiring new analytical frameworks to be developed that explore the interdependencies of real-financial sectors within and across countries' (IMF August 2012c, p. 9). As a result, the financial reforms have introduced a more intensive form of economic surveillance alongside stricter risk parameters and attempts to improve the performance of credit rating and auditing bodies.

Mirroring Foucault's work on security and regulatory power, changes to the financial system have tended to concentrate on the resetting of what is considered to be a homeostatic system that establishes 'an average considered as optimal on the one hand, and, on the other, a bandwidth of the acceptable that must not be exceeded' (Foucault 2007, p. 21). The focus has thus been on the recalibration of financial risk parameters that are thought to be 'within socially and economically acceptable limits and around an average that will be considered as optimal for a given social functioning' (Foucault 2007, p. 20).

The reforms continue to employ modulatory techniques that establish 'acceptable' risk parameters with regard to capital adequacy ratios, leverage ratios and levels of proprietary trading. In addition, the reforms have focused on the removal of conflicts of interest for CRAs and auditing companies in order to ensure that these risk parameters are adhered to. This form of economic governance can, therefore, be understood through Foucault's explanation of regulatory (modulatory) mechanisms that, in the case of finance, have been implemented at the international, national and regional levels. Operating within these risk parameters is ensured primarily through surveillance by the other two legs of a triadic relationship—auditors and CRAs (Vestergaard 2009).

Governing bodies continue to take a back seat role; they conduct the conduct of financial entities through the setting of acceptable risk levels (e.g. through adherence to the Basle Accords), the monitoring of risk exposure by auditors and the rating of their activities by the CRAs. Key to maintaining the free circulation of capital is the way in which the market ensures that financial activity is delimited—financial institutions must limit their risk exposure to within what are deemed acceptable levels lest they be punished by capital flight in reaction to credit rating downgrades. States establish maximum risk levels through the setting of capital adequacy ratios (increasingly through international agreements such as the Basle Accords). But the actual judgement of the day-to-day financial health of a financial institution is conducted through the process of auditing, risk assessments and credit ratings.

Across the industrialized world, states have enacted legislation that raises liquidity requirements for financial institutions (*The Economist* 2009e, p. 67). Basel III builds upon the first two accords (Basel I and II) by increasing the levels of capital adequacy so that they continue to hold a minimum capital equivalent to 8% of risk-weighted assets (RWA), 6.0% must be Tier 1 and 4.5% of this must be Common Equity Tier 1. There is also a conservation buffer of Tier 1 common equity equivalent to 2.5% of RWA. These requirements have been 'extended to off-balance sheet vehicles, reducing the incentive for banks to avoid existing charges by moving assets off their balance sheet' (Helleiner and Pagliari 2009, p. 277). With regard to Global Systemically Important Banks (GSIBs), the Financial Stability Board (FSB) has established a standard of total loss absorption capacity (which includes instruments other than Tier 1 capital) equivalent to 16% of RWA which will come in to force in 2019 (FSB 2014b).

The soon-to-arrive Basle IV attempts to standardize the capital adequacy levels by reducing the reliance on internal ratings. It looks like there is now agreement that those banks using an internal ratings based approach can continue to do so as long as they don't go below an established floor based on a standardized method of calculation. As this book went to print, the agreed floor looked like it would be set around 72.5–75% of capital levels established by using the standardized approach (McKinsey and Company, April 2017). Furthermore, all banks, when calculating their operational risk, must now use a standardized model (the Standardised Model Approach). Both of these initiatives will make the degree of risk exposure clearer whilst also helping to produce a more level playing field.

A second aim of Basle III is to attenuate the negative effects economic cycles can have on economies—producing an oversupply of credit in boom times and a credit squeeze in downturns. As the deputy governor of the Bank of England, Paul Tucker, put it, governments are currently attempting to 'make a regime of taking away the punch bowl [as the party gets going]' (Giles and Pimlott 2009) The idea is 'to build larger capital buffers in good times and allow them to be drawn down—but not below prudent levels—during more-stressed periods' (*The Financial Times* 2009). By curtailing highly speculative activity through the reduction of credit supply, it is hoped that any emergent Minsky moment is nipped in the bud. In order to do this, capital adequacy ratios will have an in-built flexibility in the form of a discretionary counter-cyclical buffer made up from common equity ranging from 0 to 2.5% of RWA depending upon economic conditions (*Bank of International Settlements* 2010). Basle III thus aptly illustrates the continuing reliance on risk calculus as the lynch pin in the arms-length control of financial activity.

Given the centrality of risk analysis to the current financial system, the reforms have also sought to ensure that risk assessment is accurate and reliable. With regard to homeostasis, it is essential that the risk assessment by CRAs—as key nodal points in the financial system—performs correctly. Previously, there were three problems associated with the ratings process:

> First, the agencies are paid by the issuers of the securities they rate rather than by the investors who use the ratings. Second, CRAs largely base their ratings on information provided by issuers of the securities they are rating. Third, CRAs act as advisers to issuers on how to structure their offering to achieve the best ratings and then rate the same securities. (Helleiner and Pagliari 2009, p. 280)

The G20 called for CRAs that provide public ratings to be registered and that they avoid conflicts of interests (e.g. providing advice to issuers concerning the structure of their offerings) while at the same time encouraging greater transparency and reducing reliance on these entities. (G20 2012). Attempts have been made to make the rating agencies themselves subject to the self-correcting power of the market with the Dodd-Frank Act attempting to make them 'subject to so-called expert liability' (Acharya et al. 2010, p. 456). The act sought to ensure that investors could 'bring a suit against rating agencies for a knowing or reckless failure to conduct a reasonable investigation of the rated security' (Ibid.). CRAs were supposed to, therefore, be kept in check via the market through individual economic actors having recourse to liability proceedings. Previously under the 1933 Securities Act, credit ratings were not part of the required registration statement given to the Securities and Exchange Commission (SEC) with regard to the issuance of securities, but the new requirement that they be registered meant this was no longer the case thus making them liable (Lehmann 2014, p. 15). However, regulatory capture has once again re-emerged—these CRAs threatened to withhold their rating opinions which would have led to a complete seizure of the securities market. As a result, the SEC withdrew the obligation that such ratings had to be a constituent element of the registration process, essentially letting the American CRAs off the hook (Brummer and Loko 2014, p. 167).

In January 2011, the European Union (EU) created the European Markets and Securities Authority tasked with supervising the registration and oversight of CRAs in Europe. To begin with, Germany and Italy proposed having an EU-run CRA, but it soon became apparent that this would probably produce an equally problematic conflict of interest as the funding for the proposed CRA would be reliant upon EU financing, yet the CRA's rating of European sovereign bonds could negatively affect European states and the EU itself, that is, forcing it to step in and bail-out distressed members (Brummer and Loko 2014, p. 170). Instead, the EU focused on reducing reliance on CRAs, increasing visibility of their activities (particularly with regard to methodologies) and competition. It also sought to increase accountability by exposing these bodies to liability—it proposes to make such agencies liable for damage to an investor if it infringes 'intentionally or with gross negligence' the new EU regulations (EC 18 June 2013). In order to reduce conflicts of interest, the new regulation requires 'at least two different CRAs for the rating of structured finance instruments' (EC 18 June 2013). At the same time, it insisted upon the rotation of CRAs every four years where they were involved in rating structured finance products which include underlying re-securitized assets (Singapore Risk Management Institute 2013, p. 27).

In the US, the Office of Credit Ratings has been created within the SEC. The rating systems of the CRAs are now subject to review, with the SEC empowered to 'temporarily suspend or permanently revoke the registration' of a CRA (Dodd-Frank Act 2010, p. 499). Moreover, CRAs must disclose whether they 'provided services other than determining credit ratings to the person that paid for the rating' if the credit rating was solicited (SEC 2013, p. 14).

One of the other central elements underpinning the regulatory and corrective mechanism of the financial system that regulators have sought to rectify is the auditing process. In fact, less than a decade before the financial crisis, major reforms had already been introduced in the US and other countries (in the US in the form of the Sarbanes-Oxley Act—SOX) following the collapse of Enron, WorldCom and so on.[5] SOX established the Public Company Accounting Oversight Board (PCAOB) to inspect accounting firms on a regular basis (annually for large companies and triennially for smaller ones). There were also efforts to reduce conflicts of interest by prohibiting auditors from offering additional services such as bookkeeping, designing financial information systems, act as an investment banker or legal expert (Bainbridge 2012, p. 186).[6] Moreover, SOX sought to protect whistle-blowers and ensure the creation of internal procedures within auditing firms to ensure 'the confidential, anonymous submission by employees … of concerns regarding questionable accounting or auditing matters' (Bainbridge 2008, p. 185). It also aimed to make the rotation of audit partners every five years mandatory.[7] However, it has been argued that due to a lack of rigorous statistical analyses, the PCAOB has 'failed in making audit firm quality more transparent' and one study has indicated that 'less is now known about audit firm quality than was the case under the pre-SOX regime' (Bainbridge 2012, p. 186).

In the aftermath of the financial crisis of 2007/2008, the issue of conflicts of interest with regard to accounting firms and their relations with clients gained salience. In 2011, the PCAOB attempted to broaden its scope through the introduction of not only mandatory audit partner rotation, but full audit firm rotation (Campbell-Verduyn 2014, p. 192). This attempt failed, however, as private interests and the issue of regulatory capture came to the fore once again when the House of Representatives passed, by an overwhelming majority, a bi-partisan bill that killed off these reforms in their infancy. The bill prevented the PCAOB from making the rotation of auditing firms mandatory, thus completely undermining its attempts to break long-term accounting firm-client relations (Tysiac 2013).

In reaction to the Eurozone crisis, the European Commission also floated the idea of regular rotation of auditors, joint audits combining smaller accounting firms with the Big Four and introducing greater transparency. Yet, its 2014 directive simply proscribed some non-auditing activities that had previously been carried out by accountancy firms for clients, 'including tax advice and services linked to the financial and investment strategy of the audit client' (European Commission 3 April 2014). However, it did set up the Committee of European Auditing Oversight Bodies tasked with ensuring that auditors conduct themselves ethically and that their internal quality controls meet certain standards. But, regulatory capture, yet again, prevailed during the policy-making process with large amounts of funds spent by the 'Big Four' campaigning against much of the proposed legislation (Campbell-Verduyn 2014, p. 191).[8] It is difficult, of course, to measure the degree of influence that this activity had on the final outcome, but in the agreed directive the initiative for joint audits was notable by its absence. A limit on the client-audit company relationship limit was set at ten years in the first instance, but European Member States are allowed to 'choose to extend the 10-year period up to 10 additional years if tenders are carried out' (European Commission 3 April 2014).

In the post-crisis environment, there was also much discussion and divergence of opinion concerning actual accounting principles. Both the validity of using mark-to-market fair value accounting and its inherent procyclicality were questioned. At the international level, these differences continue with regard to the mark-to-market accounting approach. Although the International Accounting Standards Board accepted a modified form of this approach for certain assets in June 2009, the reforms have been fiercely opposed by America and the UK (Campbell-Verduyn 2014, p. 191).

The Emergence of a Pre-emptive Regime

As was pointed out at the beginning of the chapter, current literature on crises (whether financial or otherwise) brings to our attention the greater emphasis on precaution and pre-emption and the need to 'intervene in emergence precisely because of uncertainty linked to massive consequences' (O'Malley 2013, p. 188). This differs to prevention as it involves 'pre-emptive judgement' and engagement in speculative activities, acting without knowing if the conditions identified will actually develop into a full-blown crisis (Andenas and Chiu 2014, pp. 456–8). Temporally, pre-emption focuses on imminent crises, attempting to identify the emergence of an event and nipping things in the bud so that potential issues are identified and dealt with before they have an impact. As is demonstrated below, this therefore requires a highly intensive form of surveillance for two reasons: in an environment of uncertainty as much information as possible needs to be acquired; and the imminent nature of threats means that such information needs to be gathered in as rapid a fashion as possible.

This chapter argues that a form of financial governance at the global, regional and national levels is emerging that focuses on surveillance, pre-emption and resilience. As is outlined below, this has involved a mixture of early warning exercises (EWEs), stress tests and an emphasis on GSIBs nodal points. These policies are inextricably intertwined, so that stress tests not only provide pre-emptive indicators of systemic vulnerability but also indicate the degree of resilience of each bank. Similarly, an emphasis on the GSIBs ensures that their resilience is higher than other financial institutions, but the emphasis is also on ensuring that the financial system as a whole is resilient to crises thus ensuring its continuance even in the event that some GSIBs go bankrupt.

Some of the elements of surveillance can be found in earlier reforms in the aftermath of the Asian crisis, with the IMF implementing early warning models since 1999 for emerging economies in an attempt to predict currency and balance of payments crises (Berg et al. 2004, p. 4). At the same time, the period after the Asian crisis also witnessed a widening of IMF surveillance from a 'relatively narrow focus on fiscal, monetary, and exchange rate policies to a broader purview encompassing external vulnerability assessments, external debt sustainability analyses, financial sector vulnerabilities, and structural and institutional policies that have an impact on macroeconomic conditions' (IMF August 2004, p. 5). Similarly, stress testing by the IMF under its Financial Sector Assessment Programme (FSAP) was under way by 2001 (Haldane 13 February 2009, p. 4).

The revision of the IMF's Article IV in 1977 focused on both multilateral surveillance so that the IMF oversees the 'international monetary system to ensure its effective operation' and bilateral surveillance that oversees 'the compliance of each member with its obligations under Article IV, Section I' (Foot and Walter 2011, p. 79).[9] However, since the crisis of 2007/2008, the intensity, breadth and coordination of these practices have grown substantially. Key amongst such reforms is a new emphasis on multilateral surveillance and the Integrated Surveillance Decision to implement this that took effect in January 2013. This reform includes a new emphasis on 'global economic and financial stability' at the global and individual level, but also focuses on 'spillovers arising from policies of individual members' that may affect global stability (such as exchange rate, monetary, fiscal and financial sector policies) (IMF June 2012b, p. 12). In 2009, the vulnerability exercises which were previously limited to emerging markets were expanded to include advanced economies (the new Vulnerability Exercises for Advanced and Emerging Economies—VEAEE) and the IMF has further introduced a Low-Income Country Vulnerability Exercise to assess the impact of external shocks (IMF 2009, p. 39; IMF March 2011a). In addition, these vulnerability exercises have been incorporated into the EWEs which will be conducted on a semi-annual basis (Independent Evaluation Office 2011, p. 18).

The IMF and FSB are now cooperating on conducting EWEs with the FSB taking the lead in analysing vulnerabilities in the financial sector and the IMF concentrating on macro-economic analysis (Lombardi 2011, p. 7). The FSB is charged with attempting to identify issues before they become too much of a threat, pre-empting possible problems by engaging in remedial action through either recommending adjustments to risk exposure or warning entities that they have failed to comply with international standards. Such surveillance now involves the detection of 'problems proactively and intervene early to reduce the impact of potential stresses on individual firms and therefore on the financial system as a whole' (*Financial Stability Board* November 2010b). In so doing, it not only relies on the FSAPs and RAMs) but also, echoing Foucault's supervision of supervisors, conducts peer reviews regarding the implementation of reforms by states thus providing 'an opportunity for FSB members to engage in dialogue with their peers and to share lessons and experiences' (Vestergaard 2009, p. 110; Financial Stability Board 7 February 2011a, p. 2). The FSB thus plays a key role in the surveillance of the global economy as it is tasked with identifying and monitoring potential risks, plus conducting 'early warning' stress tests to spot any potential problems.

In terms of fiscal risks, the EWEs concentrate on public debt, persistent fiscal imbalances, sovereign default risk and the probability of fiscal crises. The EWEs also examine the balance sheets of the corporate sector in order to gauge the leverage, liquidity and profitability as a whole. Moreover, they now closely monitor real estate and stock prices for the possible emergence of asset bubbles. In determining financial market risk attitudes, the risk assessment matrices (EWEs assess both the prices of assets but also takes on board the judgement of its staff regarding general market sentiment (IMF September 2010, pp. 20–7).

The EWEs also now incorporate spillover and contagion analysis, systemically important financial institutions and macro-economic scenario mapping of potential shocks to the economic system. With regard to contagion, the EWEs cover three areas. In the first of these areas, the

EWEs examine the dependence 'among major financial institutions, corporations or sovereigns' with regard to various financial instruments (credit, equity, exchange rates and interest rates) by estimating the possible effects of distress of one entity on the others (IMF 2010, p. 34). In addition, it examines cross-border lending and the systemic effects arising from the effects of financial problems in debtor countries, the resulting losses and deleveraging by international banks and the ramifications for inter-bank lending, that is, amplification of deleveraging (IMF 2010, pp. 35–6).

The problems of dealing with uncertainty through such intense surveillance and pre-emption are not lost on these institutions. Indeed, the report on EWEs' methodologies points out that 'in a complex global economy, there is almost no limit to the range of conceivable risks, and IMF staff are under no illusions that the EWEs could capture all those to which policy-makers should remain alert. There is clearly a possibility that global developments could yet again take an unexpected turn, despite best intentions and efforts behind the exercise' (IMF 2010, p. 41). Yet, despite this uncertainty and the possibility of generating 'misses' as well as 'hits', the report stresses that 'it is better to be prepared for risks that do not materialize than to count on luck to see one through' (Ibid.).

Similar moves are afoot at the European level. The President of the European Commission announced the creation of a European Systemic Risk Board (ESRB) and the European Supervisory Authorities (ESAs) as part of the new European System of Financial Supervision. The former includes the head of each national central bank and will oversee macro-prudential policy providing both early warning with regard to systemic threats at the national and regional level and recommendations to counter such trends.[10] To this end, it receives regular analysis from the European Central Bank identifying systemic risks and 'possible "triggers" that could lead to the crystallization of those risks' and benefits from the European Commission's notes on macro-economic surveillance and systemic risk (McPhilemy and Roche 2013, p. 33). Just as important is the reliance on the aforementioned ESAs conducting system-wide stress tests and providing bi-annual reports on identifiable risks in each of the sectors and producing risk dashboards in their area of competence.[11] Although the ESRB cannot issue binding instructions to European national authorities, it can make its warnings and recommendations public to increase its 'compliance pull' (McPhilemy and Roche 2013, p. 20). In addition, its surveillance powers are relatively strong given that it is within its mandate to make requests for data from individual financial institutions, which they must reveal (McPhilemy and Roche 2013, p. 21).

From these various inputs, alongside work by their Advisory Technical Committee, the ESRB analyses overall macro-risk arising from GDP growth, public finances, current account balances, levels of debt, unemployment rates, commodity prices and so on (McPhilemy and Roche 2013, p. 35). It also assesses credit risk—not only arising from the creditworthiness of industry and households, but also residential property prices, yields on corporate bonds and lending in foreign currencies (McPhilemy and Roche 2013, p. 35). At the same time, it is tasked with identifying market risks, such as, equity price volatility, short- and long-term interest rates and price to earnings ratios (McPhilemy and Roche 2013, p. 33). As the Chair of the ESRB has made clear on several occasions, it is essential for the organization to have 'the scope to act early and effectively before the build-up of significant imbalances or unstable interconnections, having regard for unintended consequences. This requires a framework that supports the use of the most effective policy tools, for a given risk, in a pre-emptive, timely and efficient manner' (Draghi 29 March 2012).

During the Euro crisis it became ever more apparent how vulnerable some banks in the Eurozone actually were. This combined with the issue of sovereign debt which had led to ever higher yields being offered on government bonds eventually resulted in the recognition that the mutualization of debt and therefore a banking union for the Eurozone was inevitable if the Union was to survive (Djankov 2014, p. 148). In 2012, this resulted in the European Stability Mechanism (ESM), which relies on contributions from Eurozone members and seeks to address the instability the Eurozone has confronted by providing not only loans in support of macro-economic adjustment programmes, but also precautionary loans, bank refinancing (through loans to governments who then pass the funds on) and intervention in primary and secondary bond markets.

As part of the shift towards an EU Banking Union, a single supervisory mechanism through which the ECB will monitor the largest banks was also established, alongside the single resolution mechanism set up in order to ensure the orderly resolution of failing banks and a common rulebook establishing a legal framework that all Eurozone banks should abide by (Pisani-Ferry 2014, pp. 16–20). Much of the surveillance of the single supervisory mechanism will involve cooperation with the member states of the Eurozone and it will also involve its own on-site inspections of banks (EU 15 October 2013, Art 12(1)). It will also bring greater consistency across the Eurozone by developing standard frameworks of analysis, particularly a common risk assessment analysis. Such harmonization is required if this new body is to fulfil one of the key responsibilities it is tasked with—the establishment of an early warning mechanism—to ensure 'early intervention where a credit institution or group in relation to which the ECB is the consolidating supervisor, does not meet or is likely to breach the applicable prudential requirements' (EU 15 October 2013: Art 4(1)i). Alongside its interventionary powers and the single resolution mechanism, it is hoped that the new body will help pre-empt any emerging crisis (Ravoet March 2014, p. 13).

Such pre-emptive surveillance is also apparent at the national level and indeed much of the surveillance at the higher tiers of governance depend upon so-called National Competent Authorities in the financial sphere. In the UK, new regulation will herald the creation of both a macro-prudential Financial Policy Committee and a micro-prudential Prudential Regulatory Authority. The former will be tasked with attempting to identify systemic risks and cyclical imbalances while the latter's main objective will be to 'promote the stable and prudent operation of the financial system through the effective regulation of financial firms' (Freshfields, Bruckhaus & Deringer 2010, p. 2). Although such authorities play an instrumental role in providing information and conducting stress tests that feed into these higher tiers of governance, they may, of course, carry out such exercises separately. For example, the UK carries out a more severe stress test on its banking sector which will overlap with the one that has to be carried out for the ESRB. In so doing, its last stress test presented a scenario of residential property prices falling by 35% and commercial property falling by 30%, interest rates rising from 0.5% to 4%, a fall in sterling of 30% and almost a doubling in the unemployment rate (Fleming 29 April 2014).

In the aftermath of the crisis, attention has shifted towards the way in which complex systems operate in nature, the sources of instability within them and how to improve the resilience of the system itself. Such analysis has tended to treat the financial system as analogous to these natural complex systems (Haldane and May 2011). The focus has thus been on the 'performative adaptability' of the financial system to 'withstand, re-route and recombine in the wake of a potentially catastrophic event to maintain systemic operability' (Zebrowski 2009, p. 9) so that it can 'withstand, recover and bounce back from crisis' (Zebrowski 2016, p. 4). Complex systems in nature with high degrees of connectivity tend to be highly vulnerable to network spillover effects and are therefore less systemically resilient. Using this analogy, policy-makers have focused on the way financial institutions or nodal points have negative knock-on effects throughout the system. In order to increase the resilience of the financial system overall, those financial institutions that have the potential for being 'superspreaders' (GSIBs) of instability in times of stress have been identified (Haldane and May 2011, p. 354). The emphasis is on increasing the 'absorptive capacity of each of the nodes in the financial network in response to external shocks' in order to reduce systemic risk (ibid.). But, in practical terms, the implementation of this has relied on classic neo-liberal strategies of risk delimitation. In order to increase the resilience of each 'nodal point', the capital adequacy requirement for globally systemically important banks has been significantly increased. At the same time, each of these GSIBs will have to introduce plans for an orderly wind-down of their operations should they fail.

As explained at the start of this section, stress testing has the dual utility of providing a picture of the risk levels at the systemic level and gauging the degree of resilience of each bank (and thus providing an opportunity to improve the degree of preparedness). Although, the ESRB was not so active in the first round of European stress tests in 2011, it is now playing a stronger role (as was actually originally intended) alongside the European Banking Authority in setting up the adverse scenarios in order to test the banking sectors resilience to financial shocks (McPhilemy and Roche 2013, p. 47). These stress tests involve 124 banks across all 28 member states (European Banking Authority 2014). The most recent scenario which was developed for the 2014 stress test, established a hypothetical case where GDP dropped by 7% by 2016 in the core EU countries, unemployment rose to 13%, banks were confronted with a jump in bond yields ranging from 137 to 380 basis points and house prices fell by 20% (European Banking Authority 2014). Any banks failing these tests are required to increase their capital adequacy levels within nine months of the results (European Banking Authority 2014).

At the same time, in the US, the Federal Reserve has led the way in conducting adverse scenario stress tests under the Supervisory Capital Assessment Program (SCAP). In fact, the first test after the crisis in 2009 had a major stabilizing effect throughout the financial system, despite the severity of the more adverse scenario (Langley 2013). This was not an unintended outcome and was largely due to the transparent nature of the process and 'making capital available to banks that were unable to raise from private sources the amounts necessary for them to continue to function as effective financial intermediaries' (Tarullo 2008, p. 2).

In the US, banks regarded to be too big to fail will be limited in size through the Dodd-Frank restriction on mergers which states that, for any merger, total liabilities must not 'exceed 10 per cent of aggregate consolidated liabilities of all financial companies in the United States' (Acharya et al. 2010, p. 186). Moreover, the Act places significant restrictions on emergency bail-outs, with lending prohibited for any 'individual, partnership, or corporation', and limited to 'participant(s) in any program or facility with broad-based eligibility' (Acharya et al. 2010, p. 186). The objective is thus to take away the safety net of individual bail-outs in the hope that this ensures financial rectitude and a high degree of preparedness for financial shocks.

In the US, systemically important financial institutions will now be monitored by the Financial Stability Oversight Council (FSOC) which is tasked with 'supervision of all firms big enough to threaten overall stability' (*The Economist* 20–26 June 2009d). The powers invested in the FSOC will be substantial, capable of significantly lowering the leverage levels at any company deemed to pose a significant threat to the system as a whole and, in general, can make recommendations to the Federal Reserve concerning capital, leverage, liquidity and risk management if it identifies unacceptable risks within the system (Brief Summary of The Dodd-Frank 2010).

The FSB is also playing a central role in addressing the 'too big to fail' question of GSIBs (Helleiner 2010). Its central tasks are to identify those financial institutions said to be systemically important (30 have been identified), to ensure they are prepared for worst case scenarios and that effective resolution regimes have been put in place in the case of bankruptcy ('living wills'). To this end, the FSB is introducing higher capital adequacy ratios for these institutions to ensure that during difficult times they have a greater loss absorption capacity (16–20% of RWA). It has also established an international standard for resolution in the case of a critical failure of any one of these financial institutions. This essentially entails making sure all national resolution arrangements are such as 'to enable authorities to resolve failing financial firms in an orderly manner and without exposing the taxpayer to the risk of loss' (FSB 2011b, p. 2). These increases in loss absorption capacity and effective winding down arrangements are essentially aimed at lowering the overall vulnerability of the international system (FSB October 2010a; European Commission 2010). Financial collapse is made less likely, but should it happen it is hoped that the orderly resolution of financial affairs will limit the possibility of contagion from these so-called superspreaders.

Not only have the nodal points been strengthened through increasing their absorptive capacity, but also functional differentiation has been re-introduced. There is now a greater appreciation that homogeneity with regard to financial strategy may 'minimize risk for each individual bank, but maximize the probability of the entire system collapsing' (Haldane and May 2011, p. 353). As a result, there have been some attempts to increase modular differentiation within the system by both the US and Europe reinstating the distinction between commercial (UK retail) and investment banking thus creating an essential firewall between the two sectors reducing the possibility of contagion (although, of course, Goldman Sachs and Morgan Stanley became bank holding companies anyway in order to apply for government assistance). As part of the Dodd-Frank Act, the Volcker Rule was originally supposed to prohibit commercial banks from proprietary trading altogether, thus producing a firebreak between themselves and the vagaries of the financial markets. However, it will now limit investment in hedge and private-equity funds to 3% of their Tier 1 capital.

Conclusion

This chapter has sought to demonstrate how resilience thinking and its understandings of/solutions to the financial crises have been enframed in such a manner that they fit within a wider neo-liberal discourse. In practice, resilience building has relied on many of the same techniques that were in use prior to the crisis. The financial system is still treated as a homeostatic system, the main difference being that such activities are further constricted by narrower risk parameters. The emphasis has thus been on establishing new parameters of risk that are thought to be 'within socially and economically acceptable limits and around an average that will be considered as optimal for a given social functioning' (Foucault 2007, p. 20). Indeed, rather than transcending risk calculus the reforms have consolidated our reliance on it (Konings 2016, p. 273).

Similarly, surveillance and pre-emptive policies were apparent before the crisis. There is greater acknowledgement that financial complexity brings with it high levels of uncertainty. The aim of pre-emption is to search 'over the horizon' for activities that may potentially produce systemic risk and to take remedial action, such as recalibrating risk parameters, increasing capital adequacy or monitoring innovatory financial instruments. One could see the positive effects of such monitoring and coordinated action with regard to Central Bank intervention to ensure dollar liquidity in September 2011 to counter the negative impact of the Euro crisis (Atkins 15 September 2011). Regular stress tests have the objective of providing a map of systemic risk while at the same time providing timely feedback to financial institutions in order that they be better prepared if confronted by a new crisis.

Pre-emption does resonate to a certain degree with resilience thinking's emphasis on the unpredictability of complex systems, but policies have been directed towards *ex-ante* pre-emption—the very antithesis of the post-modernist version of resilience thinking's emphasis on non-intervention. This emphasis on pre-emption may also be a reflection of the relative weakness of the other reforms. One of the areas where there has been a clearer focus on resilience is the identification of key nodal points within the financial system, the GSIBs, and their loss absorption capabilities whilst ensuring an orderly wind-down if they should fail thus reducing the possibility of spillover effects. But this not only dovetails into neo-liberalism's emphasis on moral hazard and the unforeseen negative consequences that intervention may produce, the solutions put forward continue to rely on the pre-crisis interventionist biopolitical strategies, albeit in a more stringent manner.

By establishing a set of bodies that constantly look out for activities that may potentially produce systemic risk, the reforms provide an opportunity for introducing remedial action before they induce a crisis, such as recalibrating risk parameters, increasing capital adequacy or monitoring innovatory financial instruments. However, although this surveillance combined with pre-emptive policies is designed to complement the regulatory mechanism, it also introduces certain contradictory tendencies into this form of financial governance, the full consequences of which are yet to be seen.

There are several paradoxes associated with the reforms as they stand now. The plethora of governing bodies and the detailed surveillance that is carried out may themselves be focusing too much on the complexity of the financial system, rather than identifying the most important sources of instability. Their analysis may end up being precisely wrong rather than roughly right (Haldane 13 February 2009, p. 2). Worse still, their actual activities may induce instability rather than the converse. As Cooper points out, the paradox of pre-emptive policies is that 'catastrophe risk places us in the uncomfortable position of having to take drastic and immediate action in the face of an inescapably elusive, uncertain threat, decisions which may in turn generate their own incalculable dangers' (2006, p. 119). One only needs to examine market reactions to the Federal Reserve's stress tests in 2009 and 2014 to see this paradox at work. In a highly volatile environment in the aftermath of the financial crisis, the highly transparent stress test had the effect of calming the financial market. Yet, in March 2014, it had precisely the opposite effect. With a greater emphasis on qualitative factors with regard to banks' ability to evaluate their own risks and with Citigroup and the American operations of HSBC, RBS Citizens and Santander having their plans rejected, shares plunged and volatility ensued (*The Economist* 29 March 2014, p. 75). It may be for this reason that in an emergency, the recently created ESRB 'will issue a confidential warning to the European Council', rather than make its analysis public (CMS March 2012). Additionally, the reliance on tighter risk parameters may increase the levels of correlation risk throughout the system because it still relies on assessing RWA to capital ratios. The herd-like behaviour that occurs during crises may be amplified as each individual institution reassesses its risk exposure upwards with an ensuing credit freeze similar to that experienced in 2007/2008.

Rather than triggering a radical reconstitution of the economic realm, the reforms do not represent a radical rupture with the past. The one area that is markedly different is the increased emphasis on surveillance and pre-emption. But once again, the difference is in degree rather than kind. In part, the lack of radical reforms may be a result of the conditioning effect of an abiding neo-liberal imaginary, but it is also clearly a result of the entrenched interests of political and economic elites. Since the crisis, there have been clear examples of private actors using their financial clout to lobby governments and/or using their functional power (i.e. the power that derives from them providing a critical function for the smooth operation of the financial system) to influence various financial reforms. Such influence was clearly seen in attempts at credit rating and auditing reforms and the watering down of the Volcker Rule alongside the dilution of the Lincoln Amendment in extremis in 2013 (banks would have become ineligible for Federal Deposit Insurance and the deposit window if they continued to engage in riskier swap activities) (Schultz 2014, p. 228). As a result, the reforms have struggled to ensure that the self-corrective mechanisms that are so essential for the smooth running of the financial system are fit for purpose.

The influence of these financial elites has become even more evident since the inauguration of President Trump. Shortly thereafter, the Financial Choice Bill was introduced to the House of Representatives. The bill represents a rolling back of many of the reforms mentioned in this chapter. The proposals are sweeping and include the repeal of the Volcker Rule; removing the FSOC's authority to 'designate non-bank financial institutions and financial market utilities as "systemically important"' (thus eliminating the stricter operating practices for these entities; and allowing banks to exempt themselves from 'specified regulatory standards if they maintain a certain ratio of capital to total assets' (Congress.

Gov 2017). Although the bill has passed the lower house, it is unlikely that it will pass the Senate unaltered. However, it does indicate the direction of things to come and it is highly likely that even the moderate reforms that we have witnessed in the last decade will either be further diluted or rolled back altogether.

Notes

1. This work has heavily drawn upon material from within: J. Glenn. 'In the aftermath of the financial crisis: Risk governance and the emergence of pre-emptive surveillance', *Review of International Studies, 40*(2), pp. 227–246, 2014 © British International Studies Association, published by Cambridge University Press. Reprinted with permission.
2. The verb has been changed from the past as it appeared in the original to the present.
3. Foucault further adds, there is 'the appearance in this new art of government of mechanisms with the function of producing, breathing life into, and increasing freedom, of introducing additional freedom through additional control and intervention' (Foucault 2008, p. 67).
4. 'The field of interventions for security *dispositifs* is organized around the following question: "How should things circulate or not circulate?"'. Foucault defines a security dispositif as a 'heterogeneous ensemble consisting of discourses, institutions, architectural forms, regulatory decisions, laws, administrative measures, scientific statements, philosophical, moral and philanthropic propositions' (Foucault 1980, p. 194).
5. For example, the German Corporate Governance Code of 2002, the French Financial Security Law of 2003 and the Japanese Financial Instruments and Exchange Act of 2006.
6. Although they could still prepare a client's tax returns.
7. Although it should be pointed out that a seven-year rotation was supposed to be a commonly adopted standard in the industry anyway.
8. It is estimated that the Big Four spent approximately $9.4 million in campaigning in order to dilute the European Commission's initiative (Campbell-Verduyn 2014, p. 191).
9. That is, that states will (i) endeavour to direct its economic and financial policies towards the objective of fostering orderly economic growth with reasonable price stability, with due regard to its circumstances; (ii) seek

to promote stability by fostering orderly underlying economic and financial conditions and a monetary system that does not tend to produce erratic disruptions; (iii) avoid manipulating exchange rates or the international monetary system in order to prevent effective balance of payments adjustment or to gain an unfair competitive advantage over other members; and (iv) follow exchange policies compatible with the undertakings under this section.

10. 'Whilst ESRB recommendations are not legally binding they cannot simply be ignored. Addressees of recommendations must state whether they agree with the recommendation or not. If they agree, the addressees are expected to communicate what action they are taking whilst if they disagree and choose not to act, the reasons for inaction must be properly explained'. Refer to Section 3, point 49 in House of Commons Treasury Committee (November 2011).
11. The ESA is made up of three constitutive elements arising from the transformation of previous committees: the European Banking Authority (EBA), the European Insurance and Occupational Pensions Authority (EIOPA) and the European Securities and Markets Authority (ESMA).

References

Acharya, V., T. Cooley, M. Richardson, and I. Walter, eds. 2010. *Regulating Wall Street: the Dodd-Frank Act and the New Architecture of Global Finance.* Hoboken: Wiley.

Amoore, L., and M. De Goede. 2008. *Risk and the War on Terror.* London: Routledge.

Andenas, M., and H.-Y.I. Chiu. 2014. *The Foundations and Future of Financial Regulation.* London: Routledge.

Atkins, R. 2011. Central Banks Act to Help Europe Lenders. *Financial Times,* September 15. Online at http://www.ft.com/cms/s/0/11039e2c-dfa0-11e0-845a-00144feabdc0. html

Bainbridge, S. 2008. *The New Corporate Governance in Theory and Practice.* Oxford: Oxford University Press.

———. 2012. *Corporate Governance After the Financial Crisis.* Oxford: Oxford University Press.

Bank of International Settlements. 2010. *Group of Governors and Heads of Supervision Announces Higher Global Minimum Capital Standards,* September 12. http://www.bis.org/press/p100912.htm

Berg, A., E. Borensztein, G. Milesi-Ferretti, and C. Pattillo. 2000. Anticipating Balance of Payments Crises—The Role of Early Warning Systems. IMF Occasional Paper No. 186. https://www.imf.org/external/pubs/nft/op/186/index.htm

Berg, A., E. Borensztein, and C. Patillo. 2004. Assessing Early Warning Systems: How Have They Worked in Practice? IMF Working Paper, WP/04/52.

Brief Summary of The Dodd-Frank Wall Street Reform And Consumer Protection Act 2010. Online at http://banking.senate.gov/public/_files/070110_Dodd_Frank_Wall_Street_Reform_comprehensive_summary_Final.pdf

Brummer, C., and R. Loko. 2014. The New Politics of Credit Rating Agency Regulation. In Porter, ed. 2014, 154–176.

Burchell, G., C. Gordon, and P. Miller, eds. 1991. *The Foucault Effect: Studies in Governmentality*. Chicago: Chicago University Press.

Campbell-Verduyn, M. 2014. Conflicting Trends and Tensions in Post-Crisis Reforms of Transnational Accounting Standards. In Porter, ed. 2014, 177–199.

CMS. 2012. *The New European System of Financial Supervision – Institutional Reform Within the EU*, March. http://www.law-now.com/cmck/pdfs/nonsecured/ neweuropean reform.pdf

Congress.Gov. 2017. *H.R.10 – Financial CHOICE Act of 2017115th Congress (2017–2018)*. https://www.congress.gov/bill/115th-congress/house-bill/10

Cooper, M. 2006. Pre-empting Emergence: The Biological Turn in the War on Terror. *Theory, Culture & Society* 23 (4): 113–135.

———. 2010. Turbulent Worlds: Financial Markets and Environmental Crisis. *Theory, Culture & Society* 27 (2–3): 167–190.

Dean, M. 1994. *Critical and Effective Histories: Foucault's Methods and Historical Sociology*. London: Routledge.

Dillon, M. 2008. Biopolitics of Security in the 21rst Century: An Introduction. *Review of International Studies* 34 (2): 265–292.

Djankov, S. 2014. *Inside the Euro Crisis: An Eyewitness Account.* Washington, DC: Institute for International Economics.

Dodd-Frank Act - Dodd-Frank Wall Street Reform And Consumer Protection Act 2010, http://www.sec.gov/about/laws/wallstreetreform-cpa.pdf. Accessed 14 Jan 2014.

Draghi, M. 2012. *Principles for the Development of a Macro-Prudential Framework in the EU in the Context of the Capital Requirements Legislation*, March 29. https://www.esrb.europa.eu/pub/pdf/2012-03-29_CRR-CRD_letter.pdf?bde429ab505746d6cac9325fca3fca58

European Banking Authority. 2014. *EBA Publishes Common Methodology and Scenario for 2014 EU-Banks Stress Test.* https://www.eba.europa.eu/-/eba-publishes-common-methodology-and-scenario-for-2014-eu-banks-stress-test

European Commission. 2010. *Communication from the Commission to the European Parliament, the Council, the European Economic and Social Committee and the European Central Bank – Bank Resolution Funds*, May. http://ec.europa.eu/internal_market/bank/docs/crisismanagement/funds/com2010_254_ en.pdf

———. 2013. *New Rules on Credit Rating Agencies (CRAs) Enter into Force*, June 18. http://europa.eu/rapid/press-release_MEMO-13-571_en.htm

———. 2014. *European Parliament Backs Commission Proposals on New Rules to Improve the Quality of Statutory Audit*, April 3. http://europa.eu/rapid/press-release_STATEMENT-14-104_en.htm

European Union. 2013. *Council Regulation (EU) No 1024/2013 – Conferring Specific Tasks on the European Central Bank Concerning Policies Relating to the Prudential Supervision of Credit Institutions*, October 15. http://eur-lex.europa.eu/legal-content/EN/TXT/;ELXSESSIONID=8D94JLLNvydKyyQZPGGFPCJQfkVNGjs7QGQQ6TvQ7Q1wzrTpGLc5!-197644489?uri=CELEX:32013 R1024

Ewald, F. 2005. The Return of the Crafty Genius: An Outline of a Philosophy of Precaution. In O'Malley, ed. 2005, 535–567.

Financial Stability Board. 2010a. *Reducing the Moral Hazard Posed by Systemically Important Financial Institutions: FSB Recommendations and Time Lines*, October. http://www.financialstabilityboard.org/publications/r_101111a.pdf?frames=0

———. 2010b. *FSB Letter to G20 Leaders on Progress of Financial Regulatory Reforms*, November. http://www.financialstabilityboard.org/publications/r101109.pdf

———. 2011a. *FSB Completes Peer Review of Italy*, February. http://www.financialstabilityboard.org/press/pr_110207b.pdf

———. 2011b. *Policy Measures to Address Systemically Important Financial Institutions*, November. http://www.financialstabilityboard.org/publications/r_111104bb.pdf

———. 2014a. *Thematic Review of the FSB Principles for Reducing Reliance on CRA Ratings (Final Report)*, May. http://www.financialstabilityboard.org/publications/r_140512.htm

———. 2014b. *Adequacy of Loss-Absorbing Capacity of Global Systemically Important Banks in Resolution*. http://www.financialstabilityboard.org/wp-content/uploads/TLAC-Condoc-6-Nov-2014-FINAL.pdf

Fleming, S. 2014. Bank of England Publishes "Stress Test" Scenarios'. *Financial Times*, April 29. http://www.ft.com/cms/s/0/87283344-cf92-11e3-9b2b-00144feabdc0.html#axzz313P449RO

Foot, R., and A. Walter. 2011. *China, the United States, and Global Order*. Cambridge: Cambridge University Press.

Foucault, M. 1978. *History of Sexuality Vol. 1: Translated by Robert Hurley*. New York: Pantheon Books.

———. 1980. The Confession of the Flesh. In Gordon, ed. 1980, 194–228.

———. 2003. *Society Must Be Defended: Lectures at the College de France, 1975–6*. New York: Picador.

———. 2007. *Security, Territory, Population: Lectures at the College de France 1977–78*. Basingstoke: Palgrave Macmillan.

———. 2008. *The Birth of Biopolitics: Lectures at the College de France, 1978–79*. Basingstoke: Palgrave Macmillan.

Freshfields, Bruckhaus & Deringer. 2010. *The New Structure for UK Financial Regulation*. http://www.freshfields.com/publications/pdfs/2010 /July10/28528.pdf

G20. 2012. *Communiqué of Meeting of G20 Finance Ministers and Central Bank Governors*. http://www.g20.utoronto.ca/2012/2012-121105-finance-en.html

Giles, C., and D. Pimlott. 2009. Bank Urges Restraint in Boom Times. *The Financial Times*, November 21. http://www.FinancialTimes.com

Gordon, C. 1980. *Power/Knowledge: Selected Interviews and Other Writings 1972–1977*. New York: Pantheon Books.

Gordon, C. 1991. Governmental Rationality: An Introduction. In Burchell, Gordon and Miller, eds. 1991, 1–52.

Haldane, A. 2009. Why Banks Failed the Stress Test. Marcus-Evans Conference on Stress-Testing, February 13, pp. 1–23.

Haldane, A., and T. May. 2011. Systemic Risk in Banking Ecosystems. *Nature* 469: 371–355.

Helleiner. 2010. What Role for the New Financial Stability Board? The Politics of International Standards after the Crisis. *Global Policy* 1 (3): 282–290.

Helleiner, E., and S. Pagliari. 2009. Towards a New Bretton Woods? The First G20 Leaders Summit and the Regulation of Global Finance. *New Political Economy* 14 (2): 275–287.

Helleiner, E., S. Pagliari, and H. Zimmermann, eds. 2010. *Global Finance in Crisis: The Politics of International Regulatory Change*. London: Routledge.

IMF. 2004. *Biennial Review of the Fund's Surveillance*, August. www.imf.org/external/np/pdr/surv/2004/082404.htm

———. 2009. *IMF Annual Report 2009: Fighting the Global Crisis*. Washington, DC: IMF.

———. 2010. *The IMF-FSB Early Warning Exercise: Design and Methodological Toolkit*, September. http://www.imf.org/external/np/pp/eng/2010/090110.pdf

———. 2011a. *IMF Introduces Framework for Low-Income Country Vulnerability Exercise to Assess Impact of External Shocks*, March. http://www.imf.org/external/np/sec/pr/2011/pr11102.htm

———. 2012b. *Modernizing the Legal Framework for Surveillance—An Integrated Surveillance Decision*, June. www.imf.org/external /np/pp/eng/2012/062612.pdf

———. 2012c. *The IMF's Financial Surveillance Strategy*, August. Available at www.imf.org/external/np/pp/eng/2012/082812.pdf

Independent Evaluation Office. 2011. IMF *Performance in the Run-Up the Financial and Economic Crisis: IMF Surveillance in 2004–07*. Washington, DC: IMF, January.

Konings, M. 2016. Governing the System: Risk, Finance and Neoliberal Reason. *European Journal of International Relations* 22 (2): 268–288.

Krippner, G. 2011. *Capitalizing on Crisis: The Political Origins of the Rise of Finance*. Harvard: Harvard University Press.

Langley. 2013. Anticipating Uncertainty, Reviving Risk? On the Stress Testing of Finance in Crisis. *Economy and Society* 42 (1): 51–73.

Lehmann, M. 2014. Civil Liability of Rating Agencies: An Insipid Sprout from Brussels. LSE Working Paper 15/2014, pp. 1–26. https://www.lse.ac.uk/collections/law/projects/lef/Rating%20Agencies%20Civil%20Liability%20-%20Part%201.pdf

Lenztos, F., and N. Rose. 2009. Governing Insecurity: Contingency Planning, Protection, Resistance. *Economy and Society* 38 (2): 230–254.

Lombardi, D. 2011. The Governance of the Financial Stability Board, Brookings Institution Issues Paper, September. http://www.brookings.edu/~/media/research/files/papers/2011/9/23%20financial%20stability%20board%20lombardi/fsb_issues_paper_lombardi

Lupton, D., ed. 1999. *Risk and Sociocultural Theory: New Directions and Perspectives*. Cambridge: Cambridge University Press.

Mckinsey and Company. 2017. *Basel "IV": What's Next for Banks? Implications of Intermediate Results of New Regulatory Rules for European Banks*, April. https://www.mckinsey.com/~/media/mckinsey/business%20functions/risk/our%20insights/basel%20iv%20whats%20next%20for%20european%20banks/basel-iv-whats-next-for-banks.ashx

McPhilemy, S., and J. Roche. 2013. *Part II: The Work of the European Systemic Risk Board*. Brussels: European Union.

O'Malley, P., ed. 2005. *Governing Risks*. Aldershot: Ashgate.

———. 2010. Resilient Subjects: Uncertainty, Warfare and Liberalism. *Economy and Society* 39 (4): 488–509.

———. 2013. Uncertain Governance and Resilient Subjects in the Risk Society. *Oñati Socio-Legal Series* 3 (2): 180–195.

Pisani-Ferry, J. 2014. *The Euro Crisis and Its Aftermath*. Oxford: Oxford University Press.

Rasmussen, M.V. 2006. *The Risk Society at War: Terror, Technology and Strategy in the Twenty-First Century*. Cambridge: Cambridge University Press.

Ravoet, G. 2014. Banking Union Helps Restore Confidence. *Bankar*, March.

Rose, N., and P. Miller. 2008. *Governing the Present*. Cambridge: Polity Press.

Schultz, P. 2014. Conclusions. In *Perspectives on Dodd–Frank and Finance*, ed. P. Schultz, 227–232. Cambridge, MA: MIT Press.

Securities and Exchange Commission. 2013. *Report to Congress: Credit Rating Agency Independence Study*. Washington, DC: Securities and Exchange Commission, November.

Singapore Risk Management Institute. 2013. *Global Credit Review*. Vol. 2. Singapore: World Scientific Publishing.

Tarullo, D. 2008. *Banking on Basel: The Future of International Financial Regulation*. Washington, DC: Peter G. Peterson Institute for International Economics.

Tett, G. 2009. *Fool's Gold: How Unrestrained Greed Corrupted a Dream, Shattered Global Markets and Unleashed a Catastrophe*. London: Little Brown.

The Economist. 2009d. Financial Reform in America: New Foundation, Walls Intact, June 20–26, p. 29.

———. 2009e. Reforming Finances: The EU's Proposal – Divided by a Common Market, July 4–10, p. 67.

The Economist 29 March – 4 April 2014. American Banks: A Harsh Light – A Handful of Banks Are Caught Short by the Fed's Annual Stress Test, p. 77.

The Financial Times. 2009. Bernanke's Remarks to the Federal Reserve Bank of Boston, October 23. http://www.FinancialTimes.com

Tysiac, K. 2013. Bill Prohibiting Mandatory Audit Firm Rotation Passes U.S. House. *Journal of Accountancy*, July. http://www.journalofaccountancy.com/news/20138294.htm

Vestergaard, J. 2009. *Discipline in the Global Economy?: International Finance and the End of Liberalism New Political Economy*. New York: Routledge.

Zebrowski, C. 2009. Governing the Network Society: A Bio-political Critique of Resilience. *Political Perspectives* 3 (1): 1–36.

———. 2016. *The Value of Resilience: Securing Life in the Twenty-First Century*. London: Routledge.

6

Disciplining the Sovereign Periphery of Europe

Introduction

As was highlighted in the introduction of the book, despite the fact that many of the highly indebted European countries were fiscally prudent prior to the financial crisis, a binary discourse has emerged of profligate peripheral sovereigns (tellingly labelled the PIIGS) and a financially prudent North. This depiction of an economically bifurcated Europe masks the fact that many of the peripheral states actually did not have high levels of debt prior to the crisis. In addition, although most countries succeeded in producing productivity gains, they still struggled to match the competitiveness of Germany as a result of its domestic policies. This portrayal of the sovereign periphery as profligate has served as an enabling device preventing a deeper analysis of the economic issues—not least, the uniform interest rate across the Eurozone despite the different stages of development and attendant differential growth rates (and therefore inflation rates) of each country (Lapavitsas et al. 2012). Problems also issued from Germany's suppression of wage demands since the nineties in order to continue its positive trade surplus. This policy led to low domestic growth, improved German competitiveness through productivity gains

J. G. Glenn, *Foucault and Post-Financial Crises*, International Political Economy Series, https://doi.org/10.1007/978-3-319-77188-5_6

and suppressed wages and high levels of financial flows from the core to the periphery as investors sought returns outside of Germany, prompting property and consumer booms as households took on ever-increasing levels of debt (Lapavitsas et al. 2012).

This binary discourse has also enabled a shift from a consensual economic regime to one in which the emphasis has been on disciplinary mechanisms. As this chapter argues, this shift towards a disciplinary regime has also involved a shift in neo-liberal governmentality at the European level. In contrast to the post-modern version of resilience thinking that predicts a shift from neo-liberalism to a new form of politics, the European experience has been quite the opposite. Europe has actually shifted from a less rigid and more consensual form of neo-liberalism to one where discipline and punishment dominate. Since the crisis, we have witnessed the promotion of IMF-style structural adjustment policies in the sovereign periphery of Europe by the more industrialized core in the North—something that would have been unimaginable just a decade before.

Foucault's work on governmentality brings to our attention the rationalities of government, the technologies of government and the constitution of subjects. We can understand the rationalities of governing as 'styles of thinking, ways of rendering reality thinkable in such a way that it [is] amenable to calculation and programming' (Rose and Miller 2008, p. 16).[1] The technologies or *techne* of government refers to the practical rationalities (expertise and know-how) together with the 'means, mechanisms, instruments, tactics, techniques and vocabularies' through which authority is constituted and rule accomplished' (Dean 2010, p. 33 and 42). Lastly, the governmental approach brings to our attention the forms of subjectivity associated with certain rationalities of government and the 'practices and programmes of government' that attempt to inculcate these subjectivities (Dean 2010, p. 43).

With regard to the latter, Dean has pointed out, a liberal regime of government seeks to 'operate on the conduct of the governed' but 'seeks a direction of conduct rather than a violent or gross form of corporeal domination' because it 'assumes a "free subject"…one whose subjection is consistent with forms of choice' (Dean 1994, p. 178). As such, liberal regimes of government 'do not *determine* forms of subjectivity. They elicit, promote, facilitate foster and attribute various capacities, qualities and statuses to particular agents' (Dean 2010, pp. 43–44). Yet, although this 'non-coercive' socialization process is the usual *modus* operandi, as others have pointed out, disciplinary mechanisms are subsumed within liberal regimes of government and may come to the fore when less direct attempts at inculcating certain norms, values, forms of behaviour and so on fail (Merlingen 2003).

This chapter argues that the post financial crisis, Eurozone is experiencing a transformation away from the more consensual and indirect methods of inculcating neo-liberal norms towards a regime based on surveillance, discipline and punishment. In other words, since the financial crisis, the subjectification process involving self-identification with the European Union (EU) and its economic regime has moved to the background. At the same time, the process of 'othering' through scientific classification and dividing practices (financially delinquent indebted states vs. the rectitude of financially prudent states) has come to the fore, identifying certain countries as profligate and in need of reform—a process that requires discipline and punishment to ensure compliance with neo-liberal practices.[2]

As Jonathan Joseph has detailed, governmentality in the EU tended to emphasize an intergovernmental approach that worked through consensus building (Joseph 2012, p. 202). Of course, the governmental regime employed scientific technical apparatuses in assessing whether countries were being fiscally prudent or not—but the assessments were frequently ignored. For example, when France and Germany ran budget deficits of over 3% GDP in 2003, they avoided sanctions. There were, of course, associated surveillance techniques, such as, the submission of detailed economic and social data to Eurostats. But just how loosely these techniques of control were employed became rather obvious when, in October 2009, the new Greek Prime Minister George Papandreou announced that the budget deficit had been under-recorded for over a decade (Djankov 2014, p. 63). The level of surveillance and nature of disciplinary mechanisms therefore changed radically as the Euro crisis took hold. Eurozone states are now subjected to hierarchical observation, examination and normalizing judgements and, of course, punitive mechanisms in the form of market reactions and fines (Vestergaard 2009, p. 126).

This chapter therefore examines this further deepening of neo-liberal governmentality in the Eurozone and the concomitant shift towards disciplinary mechanisms to ensure this transformation. The first section examines the neo-liberal form of governmentality associated with the open method of coordination (OMC) initially favoured by the EU. Because of this emphasis on learning through coordination, cooperation and consensus, the disciplinary mechanisms built into the Stability and Growth Pact (SGP) from its very inception, by and large, lay in abeyance. Yet, as the second section outlines, as the consequences of the financial crisis ramified out through Europe, the discipline, surveillance and punishment measures associated with the SGP were fundamentally strengthened. Moreover, these disciplinary mechanisms eventually moved to the forefront of Europe's response to the crisis. The third section argues that this is most clearly seen in the bail-out/bail-in programmes administered by the Troika with their regime of economic discipline, intensive surveillance monitoring compliance and punishment in the form of withdrawal of funds if states fail to comply with the financial rectitude required of them.

Whether it is through the 'lighter' Economic Partnership Programmes (EPP) associated with the SGP or the more severe Economic Adjustment Programmes (EAP) associated with the bail-outs, these sovereigns are subjected to structural adjustment policies and funding is subject to compliance with these neo-liberal policies. We are therefore witnessing not only the maintenance of neo-liberal conditionality in the Eurozone, but also its deepening. Conditionality is being used to further promote the marketization of the social sphere, the European crisis has thus been marked by further interventions so that 'competitive mechanisms can play a regulatory role at every moment and every point in society' attempting to ensure the 'general regulation of society by the market' (Foucault 2008, p. 45). This has entailed further commodification, labour market deregulation, privatization and state retrenchment.

Building a Neo-Liberal Consensus in Pre-crisis Europe

As Joseph has previously detailed, governmentality in pre-crisis Europe involved a long-term socialization process of economic reform that states had formally agreed to. EU governance with regard to improving economic competitiveness has tended to be relatively indirect by establishing a general agenda of principles, mobilizing and responsibilizing political elites and other actors in carrying out this agenda and establishing standards in various fields of activity. In particular, the Lisbon Strategy of 2000 which set the EU the objective of becoming 'the most competitive and dynamic knowledge-based economy in the world capable of sustainable economic growth with more and better jobs and greater social cohesion' adopted an open method of peer review and mutual learning as the way forward in terms of introducing best practice for its members (European Council 2000a). States were to compare their policies and share experiences and reflect upon how best to introduce reforms in order to enhance their competitiveness. Crucial to this process was the need for states to take ownership of this reform process. As the New Start for the Lisbon Strategy in 2005 emphasized, in order for the European project to work, it is vital to 'mobilise support for change. Establishing broad and effective ownership of the Lisbon goals is the best way to ensure words are turned into results. Everyone with a stake in Lisbon's success and at every level must be involved in delivering these reforms' (European Commission 2005a, p. 5).

In order to enhance learning between member states, the EU embraced the OMC. As Claudio Radaelli has pointed out, this method differed from previous models of European governance on a number of fronts. It moved away from a reliance on top down regulation and 'courts do not provide the main mechanisms of accountability' (2003, p. 24). It also introduced a new approach to problem-solving, with a method based on 'iteration, mutual cooperation (across levels of government and between public and private actors), and standard-settings'. Power sharing and participation are also key to the OMC with 'different levels of government and the civil society' participating, thus reaping benefits 'of local knowledge and local experimentation' (Radaelli 2003, p. 24). The acceptance of a diversity of approaches and recognition that there are many varieties of capitalism also features as a core element of this method. Indeed, the OMC is 'supposed to work like a network looking for usable knowledge at all levels…learning from local knowledge and by generating trans-national diffusion, policy-makers can improve at their own pace' (Radaelli 2003, pp. 24–25).

The OMC was actually being used throughout the nineties in various policy areas, such as the Broad Economic Policy Guidelines, European Employment Strategy, social inclusion and pensions but was expanded to the information society, research policy, enterprise, educational and vocational training, immigration policy and sustainable development (Chalmers and Lodge 2003, p. 4). The OMC is 'designed to support learning. It builds on, and encourages, mutual co-operation and exchange of knowledge and experiences. It also entails an element of mutual correction, through peer governance or "collective self co-ordination", exerted in various types of peer group review bodies and in media. Yet, rather than operating by sanction, the method seeks to foster incentives to learning and consensus-making' (Borras and Jacobsson 2014, p. 189). The hope was to produce 'some degree of voluntary policy convergence', whilst maintaining a relatively high degree of state autonomy. States 'agree on a set of policy objectives but remain free to pursue these objectives in ways that make sense within their national contexts and at differing tempos' (Scott and Trubek 2002, p. 5).

However, the OMC was only formally adopted as a method of coordination after Lisbon in 2000 as a 'means of spreading best practice and achieving greater convergence towards the main EU goals' (European Council 2000a; Radaelli 2003, p. 14). The presidency conclusions of Lisbon 2000 set out in some detail what the OMC would entail:

1. fixing guidelines for the Union combined with specific timetables for achieving the goals which they set in the short, medium and long terms;
2. establishing, where appropriate, quantitative and qualitative indicators and benchmarks against the best in the world and tailored to the needs of different Member States and sectors as a means of comparing best practice;

3. translating these European guidelines into national and regional policies by setting specific targets and adopting measures, taking into account national and regional differences;
4. periodic monitoring, evaluation and peer review organized as mutual learning processes. (European Council 2000a)

As Joseph points out, OMC can be understood as a form of liberal governmentality, given that it 'works through consensus-building' enabling the European Commission to operate from a distance, 'making suggestions, recommendations and promptings, but also operating through establishing the correct procedures, methods, aims and objectives with progress and performance measured through a set of targets, or through peer review and benchmarking' (Joseph 2012, p. 202 and 211). The method developed 'a shared vision of social challenges, fostered a willingness to cooperate and learn from each other's practices, created a new dynamism in furthering and implementing reforms and promoted more knowledge-based policy making, geared towards openness, transparency and participation'.[3] As such, it has been a key instrument in the socialization of national elites, inculcating 'ideas, concepts, norms defining good and bad practice, and ultimately policy discourse' (Radaelli 2003, pp. 27–8; Borras and Radaelli 2014).

However, the overall agenda promoted through OMC has been of a neo-liberal nature, involving a 'dual strategy of extending competition into all aspects of social life and shifting responsibility to the individual to take care of their own life chances'; ...it... 'is quite clearly a neoliberal project that combines strategies of capital accumulation with the political project to dismantle the institutions of the postwar welfare system' (Joseph 2012, p. 188). This can clearly be seen in the aforementioned 2000–2010 Lisbon Strategy for jobs and growth, which, amongst other things, recommended the further liberalization of 'gas, electricity, postal services and transport', 'promote competition and reduce the general level of State aids' and 'redirect public expenditure towards increasing the relative importance of capital accumulation—both physical and human' (European Council 2000a). Great emphasis has also been placed on developing a 'dynamic welfare state' which ensures that 'work pays' and that state spending should be targeted towards life-long learning enabling individuals to respond to the vagaries of the market, producing a mobile and flexible work force (Ibid.). In order to deal with the issue of burgeoning pension commitments, states are encouraged to develop 'active ageing policies to discourage people from leaving the workforce too early' (European Commission 2005a, p. 9).

These recommendations are thus directed towards developing responsible subjects, equipping them 'with the right skills to give them a better chance in the modern economy as workers, entrepreneurs and consumers'.[4] However, as Joseph has argued, in practice this has meant 'putting more pressure on the trade unions and workers' organisations to accept more flexible conditions' (Joseph 2012, p. 199). These documents often couch the overall agenda in terms of freedom and equality, but the actual policies that are implemented more often than not 'attack things like full-time employment, standardised working hours, collective wage agreements, job security and other gains made by working people' (Joseph 2012, p. 198).

In line with a liberal governmental approach, the reforms are presented in terms of choice:

> Europeans have made choices about how to express the values they hold in common: a commitment to the social contract that underwrites the risk of unemployment, ill-health and old age, and provides opportunity for all through high-quality education, a commitment to public institutions, the public realm and the public interest, and that a market economy should be run fairly and with respect for the environment. These values are expressed in systems of welfare, public institutions and regulation that are expensive in a world where low cost and highly efficient producers are challenging the old order. If Europe cannot adapt, cannot modernise its systems and cannot increase its growth and employment fast enough then it will be impossible to sustain these choices. (Joseph 2012, p. 193; European Commission 2004, p. 16)[5]

However, more often than not, the key European bodies have presented globalization as an external apolitical pressure requiring states to reform, rather than viewing it as an inherently political process shaped by the very states that are said to be at its mercy (European Council 2000b). The 'choices' presented were therefore inherently limited and neo-liberal in direction emphasizing workforce mobility and flexibility, the need for individuals to engage in life-long learning to equip themselves for employment in dynamic market conditions and a restructuring of social security so that it does not act as a disincentive to work.

This neo-liberal agenda continues to dominate in post-crisis Europe—probably more than ever. But since the financial crisis it has become more overt and the indirect subjectification process through gradual socialization has been replaced more and more by direct disciplinary procedures. This chapter details these changes. First, it does so through an analysis of the SGP and the introduction of more intrusive surveillance and sanctions for aberrant states. Second, it does so through an investigation of the structural adjustment programmes that Portugal, Ireland and Greece were subjected to.

Discipline and Punishment: Reform of the SGP

It was hoped that the Stability and Growth Pact of 1997 would encourage state elites to internalize a certain degree of fiscal responsibility through the setting of benchmarks. This was supposed to be supported by the regular establishment of the Broad Economic Policy Guideline, such as, growth-oriented and stability-oriented macro-economic policies, maintaining sound public finances and improving the quality and sustainability of public finances (European Commission 2000, p. 17). However, it also encompassed certain disciplinary measures from its inception. Indeed, many of its stipulations were already included after the Maastricht Treaty, such as, the budget deficit ceiling of 3% GDP, the debt ceiling of 60% GDP (stipulated in protocol 12) as well as economic sanctions if the member state ignored recommendations with regard to their excessive deficit (European Union 1992; European Union 2012, Arts 121, 126, 136; European Union 2008).

How to deal with excessive deficits of member states was given a more concrete form in the SGP.[6] The Pact consisted of one resolution and two regulations. The former represented the political commitment by all Eurozone members to abide by the objectives and implementation of the Pact (European Council, 1997). The first regulation, the so-called preventative arm obliges states to set out their budgetary and other economic policies for meeting the medium-term objective of a 'budgetary position of close to balance or in surplus' (Council of the European Union 1997a, Art 3). These stability programmes (convergence programmes for non-Eurozone members) are subsequently assessed by the Council to ascertain whether the measures taken are sufficient and may be subject to recommendations.[7] Moreover, the regulation established an early warning procedure in an attempt at avoiding excessive deficits. As such, the Commission was tasked with monitoring the implementation of each member state's stability programme and passing that information to Council 'with a view to identifying actual or expected significant divergence' and for Council to recommend adjustments accordingly (Council of the European Union 1997a, Art 6).

The second regulation, the so-called corrective arm sets out the actions to be taken when a state is deemed to have an excessive deficit which is not deemed to be exceptional and temporary. The European Commission is charged with the responsibility of forming an opinion and recommendation with regard to the excessive deficit, which is passed to the Council. The Council then issues a recommendation and deadline for correcting the deficit (Council of the European Union 1997b, Art 3). If the state fails to take corrective action the Council also has the power to apply sanctions in the form of a non-interest bearing deposit (Council of the European Union 1997b, Art 11). Initially, this deposit was to be equal to '0.2% of GDP, and a variable component equal to one tenth of the difference between the deficit as a percentage of GDP in the preceding year and the reference value of 3% of GDP' (Council of the European Union 1997b, Art 12). However, if the state failed to rectify the overspending, then further sanctions could be applied every year equal to 'one tenth of the difference between the deficit as a percentage of GDP in the preceding year and the reference value of 3% of GDP' up to a maximum value of 0.5% GDP (Council of the European Union 1997b, Art 12). Moreover, after two years the non-interest paying deposit was supposed to be converted into a fine (Council of the European Union 1997b, Art 13).

Despite the SGP including disciplinary measures in its constitution, in de *facto* terms the emphasis was on sovereign members taking responsibility to restore a fiscal balance—subscribing to 'a self-commitment to apply the EDP' (Heipertz and Verdun 2010, p. 7). Indeed, when the European Commission attempted to launch an excessive deficit procedure (EDP) against France and Germany because of budgetary overspends (around the same period eight other countries were subject to the procedure), the Council decided that the procedure should be held in abeyance. Despite many countries being in excessive deficit and failing to meet the fiscal objectives set out under the procedure, the EU—before the financial crisis of 2007/2008—had declined to apply the sanctions available to it.

Of equal import was the decision to reform the SGP's methodology for assessing whether a country had an excessive deficit or not. The 2005 reforms meant that country-specific circumstances were to be taken into account with regard to assessing if a country had an excessive deficit, such as, the business cycle, potential growth and debt sustainability—'The report shall appropriately reflect developments in the medium-term economic position (in particular potential growth, prevailing cyclical conditions, the implementation of policies in the context of the Lisbon agenda and policies to foster research and development and innovation)...debt sustainability, public investment and the overall quality of public finances' (Council of the European Union 2005b, Art 2) However, the excessive deficit reference value of 3% GDP and 60% debt/GDP ceilings remained in place (European Commission 2005b).

The medium-term objectives were strengthened by amending the preventative arm so that for Eurozone members the annual structural deficit 'shall be specified within a defined range between—1 % of GDP and balance or surplus, in cyclically adjusted terms, net of one-off and temporary measures' (Council of the European Union 2005a, Art 2a). Moreover, the reforms meant that the Council would assess a member state's adjustment path towards its medium-term objective, using a benchmark of 0.5% GDP per year improvement in its budgetary position ('net of one-off and other temporary measures') (Council of the European Union 2005a, Art 5a). The corrective arm of the Pact was also strengthened so that the Commission's analysis of whether a country has taken sufficient corrective action shall be made public (Council of the European Union 2005b, Art 9).

Yet, the Council and Commission failed to accede to the European Statistical Office's (Eurostat) request for audit-like powers over national public accounts as a result of its growing concerns regarding Greece's statistical reporting after it announced in 2004 significant revisions for 2000–2003 (Pisani-Ferry 2014, p. 54). Instead, although the Commission put forward a recommendation for in-depth monitoring visits, the Council decided upon weaker provisions with Eurostat relying upon dialogue visits and exceptional methodological visits (rather than the regular visits that were sought) (Council of the European Union 2005c, Article 8). Most significantly, the Council Regulation that was finally agreed upon limited the methodological visits solely to the 'statistical domain' thus ruling out a deeper investigation into the quality of data provided, for example investigating actual balance sheets (European Commission January 2010a, p. 9).

So, even though it was hoped that states would engage in best practice and abide by the agreed benchmarks, there were disciplinary elements within the original version of the SGP. The Pact places economies 'in a field of surveillance, situate(s) them in a network of registration, and engage(s) them in a whole mass of assessments that capture and fix them' (Vestergaard 2009, p. 126). The potential for the Council to publish its recommendations, the publication of the Commission's analysis of a country's efforts in reducing its excessive deficit and the requirement for states to make public their stability programmes provides a backlight on their performance placing them in a 'continuous field of visibility' (Council of the European Union 1997a, Art 4; Vestergaard 2009, p. 125). Such transparency provides the Council and Commission with leverage that goes beyond the sanctions outlined. Making the stability programmes public alongside Council recommendations and the analyses of the Commission make visible the health assessment of an economy and the effectiveness of corrective policies, which financial markets will react to in a positive or negative manner. Punishment for non-compliance is not therefore simply limited to EU sanctions; states need to take into account the reactions of the financial markets and the potential increased costs in borrowing.

At the same time, the Pact established the norm of a budgetary balance/surplus and the upper limits of deviation from this norm, beyond which behaviour is deemed aberrant and subject to punishment. As such, the process involves a 'normalizing gaze, a surveillance that makes it possible to qualify, to classify and to punish' (Foucault 1995, p. 184). As Foucault argues, this normalizing judgement is both individualizing and homogenizing at one and the same time. It does so by establishing classificatory grids that are distributive in nature. This classification of behaviour not only produces a ranking but also establishes the gaps between individuals enabling micro-punishments to be implemented—thus establishing a 'classificatory, penal distribution' (Foucault 1995, p. 181). The surveillance enables a judgement to be made as to how well countries are implementing the established fiscal standards, they establish 'a comparative system—measuring, comparing, hierarchizing and determining gaps and distributions, in and among different groups of economies' (Vestergaard 2009, p. 126). It therefore embodies the central elements outlined by Foucault—'hierarchical observation, normalizing judgement and their combination in a procedure that is specific to it, the examination' (Vestergaard 2009, p. 126; Foucault 1995, p. 170).[8]

The normalizing judgement of the Pact was therefore supposed to individualize by placing the state within a distributive classification, but it also homogenizes by applying micro-punishments that increase in severity according to the degree of transgression from the norm. This 'perpetual penalty' is clearly evident in the original Pact—the greater the fiscal overspend, the greater the level of monetary deposit (and fine if the aberrant behaviour continues) (Foucault 1995, p. 182). The normalizing judgement thus has 'the function of reducing gaps. It must therefore be essentially corrective' (Foucault 1995, p. 179). Countries were supposed to increasingly abide by these European standards because they recognize that there is an escalating cost to non-conformance.

Yet, despite these mechanisms being in place at a very early stage of monetary union, the emphasis was overwhelmingly on a gradual socializing process. The OMC sought to promote mutual cooperation, exchange of knowledge and mutual learning through peer review as part of the move towards a more unified Europe. Although at the heart of the SGP there lay certain disciplinary mechanisms, there was clearly a reluctance to employ them, preferring the procedures associated with the OMC. However, as is detailed below, this changed dramatically after the financial crisis.

Post-crisis SGP: The Domination of Discipline

Following the announcement by the Greek Prime Minister George Papandreou in October 2009 that the budget deficit would be twice (12.5% GDP) that predicted by the previous government, financial panic ensued accompanied by an abrupt increase in borrowing costs as several countries' credit ratings reached junk status. The ramifications of the crisis and the rapid introduction of various mechanisms by the EU to try and manage events has been well documented elsewhere (Djankov 2014; Lapavitsas et al. 2012; Pisani-Ferry 2014; Marsh 2013; Soros 2014). But, the subsequent need for the EU, ECB and the IMF to bail-out Greece, Ireland, Portugal and Cyprus raised serious questions about the effectiveness of the SGP.[9] As one commentator put it, the 'assumption that it would have been possible to govern the common currency through the logic of voluntary policy coordination has been dramatically unmasked by the euro crisis' (Fabbrini 2015, p. 11).

Such revision was primarily associated with the so-called six pack (September 2011) and two pack (May 2013) legislation alongside the intergovernmental Fiscal Compact of January 2012. The six pack, which consists of five regulations and one directive, not only strengthened the disciplinary and surveillance aspects of the SGP in several ways, it introduced a certain degree of automaticity to the procedures and increased the breadth of surveillance going beyond fiscal matters to encompass a range of macro-economic indicators. The surveillance procedures are now integrated into the newly devised cycle of surveillance (European Semester) with all member states required to submit three reports every year on their National Reform Programme, Stability/Convergence Programme and macro-economic balance. The Commission and Council assess these reports and recommend changes in policy, particularly to those states that are deemed to have deviated from the norms established.

The annual National Reform Programme reports are associated with the objectives set out in the European Strategy 2020 and the Annual Growth Survey set out by the European Commission in January of each year. The main thrust of this strategy is to produce growth and employment, but in a sustainable and inclusive manner. Each member state translates these objectives into national targets that take into account the development paths of the state in question. There are currently five main objectives associated with the European Strategy. The first is to ensure that 75% of those between 20 and 64 years old are in employment. The second is to ensure 3% of GDP is invested in research and development. The third is to lower greenhouse gas emissions by 20–30% and to provide 20% of energy needs from renewables whilst also increasing energy efficiency by 20% (these three targets are in relation to 1990 levels). The fourth is to lower school dropout rates to less than 10% and to ensure at least 40% of 30–34 year olds complete tertiary education. Finally, there is an overall aim of reducing the number of poor and socially excluded by 20 million compared to levels in 1990.[10]

Every year in April, each member state produces its National Reform Programme with regard to the Annual Growth Survey and how it is tackling outstanding recommendations and fiscal concerns of the European Commission. Although it is called the Annual Growth Survey, it would be better named strategy because it actually incorporates a variety of aims promoting convergence and further integration. The Commission also publishes its own country-specific reports in February. In reaction to each national programme, the country-specific reports, the Stability and Convergence Programmes (see below) and the Annual Growth Survey, the Commission issues recommendations to each country (country-specific recommendations) which are formally adopted a month later in July by the Council of the EU.

In addition, thematic summaries complement the country-specific reports and help form the Commission's recommendations. Such 'summaries' are, in fact, highly detailed comparisons of each country's performance in a given area with other member states and represent a classic example of micro-surveillance. Thematic fiches are used within each summary to indicate each state's performance on a scoreboard with regard to a quite exhaustive list of behaviours. The themes include aspects related to the 2020 strategy, such as labour market policies, health and health systems, resource efficiency, tertiary education attainment, undeclared work, transport and skills for the labour market. This surveillance is then further broken down into micro-surveillance through the use of scoreboards that identify deviance from the average, for example, for the theme effective justice systems, each state is compared against all other members with regard to time needed to resolve litigious cases, rate of resolving cases, number of pending cases, ICT use for case management, benchmarking of small claims cases online, perceived independence of courts and judges, perceived judicial independence and so on.

On the fiscal side, the Stability/Convergence Programme (convergence for non-Eurozone members) involves submitting budgetary plans and forecasts in reaction to the Annual Growth Survey presented by the European Commission (refer to the Two Pack below). For example, national budgets are compared with the Commission's own independent assessment and the onus is on the member state to explain 'significant differences between the chosen macro-fiscal scenario and the Commission's forecast' (Council of the European Union 2011b, Art 4). In addition, the Commission and Council will continually monitor the implementation of the stability programmes set out by each member.

Significant deviations from the agreed medium-term objectives (these are country-specific but the overall aim is to produce a balanced budget in structural terms) and from adjustment paths towards these objectives have been quantified, making the assessment procedure more straightforward (European Parliament 2011a, Art 6).[11] In such cases where states have deviated from their budgetary path, recommendations are issued to the relevant state by the Commission and Council. The deficit should be reduced by at least 0.5% per annum (more should be done by states with a debt greater than 60%) (Richardson and Mazey 2015, p. 341). If a Eurozone member fails to follow such recommendations, then the recommendations are made public and sanctions can now be applied in the form of an interest bearing deposit of 0.2% GDP for failing to comply with its budgetary obligations, that is, even before a member state has an excessive deficit (European Parliament and Commission 2011b, Art 4). Debt is also taken into account with regard to the EDP. If a member's debt exceeds the norm (60% GDP mark), then it must reduce the excess beyond this level by an average rate of 5% per year over three years to avoid an EDP (Council of the European Union 2011a, Art 2). For Eurozone members, a degree of automaticity has also been introduced for the excessive deficit/debt sanction under a reverse qualified majority voting mechanism. The Council will adopt recommendations by the

Commission with regard to sanctions unless a qualified majority rejects them (European Parliament and Commission 2011b, Art 4 and 5).

The quality of surveillance has also been deepened with member states obliged to 'ensure the professional independence of national statistical authorities' (European Parliament and Commission 2011a, Art 10).[12] At the same time, fines of up to 0.2% GDP can now be applied to those member states that 'intentionally or by serious negligence misrepresent deficit and debt data' (European Parliament and Commission 2011b, Art 8). Moreover, during enhanced surveillance missions, member states 'shall provide all necessary information for the preparation and the conduct of those missions' (European Parliament and Commission 2011a, Art 11).

In addition to the fiscal balance, the six pack introduces surveillance and sanctions with regard to macro-economic balances. The EU's annual cycle of surveillance now includes the monitoring of macro-economic imbalances. The so-called Macroeconomic Imbalance Procedure (MIP) involves the production of an alert mechanism report (ARM) centred on a scoreboard of balances/imbalances for each member state with alert thresholds.[13] The scoreboard includes both internal and external imbalances with 13 indicators in total and, once again, each state is placed in a comparative classificatory grid against other member states.[14] The internal imbalances include 'public and private indebtedness; financial and asset market developments, including housing; the evolution of private sector credit flow; the evolution of unemployment' and also includes the balance between a country's productivity improvements in relation to wage increases (European Parliament and Council 2011b, Art 4; European Commission 2014b). External imbalances include 'current account and net investment positions; real effective exchange rates; export market shares; changes in price and cost developments; and non-price competitiveness' (European Parliament and Council 2011b, Art 4). Based on the multilateral surveillance and the alert mechanism, the Commission can initiate an in-depth review of a member state. These reports create a classificatory grid establishing degrees of deviance with states grouped into one table based on four categorical characteristics: no imbalances, imbalances, excessive imbalances or excessive imbalances with corrective action.

This micro-surveillance of deviance has associated with it corresponding degrees of punishment. Country-specific recommendations are made to those deemed to have imbalances and excessive imbalances and their progress is monitored through what is called 'specific monitoring'. But, those deemed to be in the 'excessive imbalances with corrective action' category become subject to an excessive imbalance procedure (EIP) through which it is requested to take corrective measures (European Parliament and Council 2011b, Art 7). The scoreboard, recommendations and report by the Council with regard to the excessive imbalance, and the member state's corrective action plan plus progress reports of the member's policy implementation are all made public (Novotny 2013, p. 465). Punishment for non-compliance in the Eurozone comes in two forms. If the council makes two recommendations and the corrective plan submitted by the member state continues to be inadequate, then a fine can be imposed (0.1% GDP). If the member state fails to take corrective action, then an interest bearing deposit (again 0.1% GDP) will be levied (European Parliament and Council 2011c, Art 3).

For both the corrective action plans in the EIP and the lighter touch country-specific recommendations, the overriding emphasis is on restoring competitiveness vis-à-vis other EU members and extra-regional trading states. Given that the single currency rules out currency devaluations, the reforms fall back on well-rehearsed neo-liberal policies. The EU now assesses a swathe of policies, for example, current account balance (savings and investments); debt levels (particularly with regard to mortgages and potential housing bubbles) and capital adequacy of banks, 'efficient labour markets', that is, wage setting (urging wage restraint), reduction in collective bargaining (reducing the influence of trade unions) and even policies on education/workforce skills; social protection provisions—unemployment and social housing policies, developing a more business-friendly environment—reducing regulatory barriers; ensuring corporate competitiveness—promoting competition and transparency and so on.

The Fiscal Compact and two pack further increase the surveillance and sanctions outlined above. The Fiscal Compact is part of an intergovernmental treaty (i.e. the fiscal part of the Treaty on Stability, Coordination and Governance) and in many ways overlaps with and reflects the principles underpinning the SGP and the reforms to it (six pack and two pack) that are enshrined in EU law.[15] Member states that are signatories to the treaty are committed to embedding the budget rules (which are, by and large those set out in the SGP) in national law through 'provisions of binding force and permanent character, preferably constitutional' one year after the treaty comes into force (TSCG 2012, Art 3,2). The commitment includes the establishment of a national automatic mechanism to correct deviations from a country's medium-term budgetary objectives. If a signatory fails to adequately implement these rules into national law, then the European Commission or a signatory state can bring a case to the European Court of Justice. If a member state fails to comply with the Court's judgement, then the Court can impose a fine of up to 0.1% GDP to be paid in to the European Stability Mechanism (ESM) if it's a Eurozone member or to the general budget if it's a non-Eurozone member (TSCG 2012, Art 8). As with the SGP, The treaty differentiates between those countries that have a low debt and those that do not. For those states that have a national debt of 60% GDP or below, their structural deficits should be limited to 1% GDP. But, for those states with debt above this level, structural deficits should not go beyond 0.5% GDP (TSCG 2012, Art 3,1).

The main aspects of the two pack are that, in addition to a stability programme, states now have to submit their draft budget for the next year every October so that the Commission can examine whether it complies with the SGP and can issue an opinion on the budget (European Council and Parliament 2013a, Art 7). Member states must now have independent bodies that assess whether they are abiding by the agreed fiscal rules—the assessments are again made public (European Council and Parliament 2013a, Art 5). The EDP means that actions required of Eurozone members that have an excessive deficit go beyond fiscal consolidation with the requirement that they produce EPPs that include policy measures and structural reforms to rectify the deficit (European Council and Parliament 2013a, Art 9). In order to better coordinate debt issuance, all member states are required to submit their plans for debt issuance in advance (European Council and Parliament 2013a, Art 8).

Largely based on the alert mechanism mentioned above, the Commission may subject a member state to enhanced surveillance if it deems the financial instability or the potential instability within the state may produce adverse spillover effects in the Eurozone (European Parliament and Council 2013, Art 2). Such enhanced surveillance also applies if a member state is receiving financial assistance on a precautionary basis from other countries, the various financial institutions of the EU or an external body such as the IMF (European Parliament and Council 2013, Art 2). Such enhanced surveillance includes regular reporting of macro-economic imbalances and stress tests assessing the resilience of its financial sector (European Parliament and Council 2013, Art 3). Moreover, the Commission 'in liaison with the ECB and with the relevant ESAs and, where appropriate, with the IMF' will carry out frequent review missions and make quarterly assessments of the economic situation (European Parliament and Council 2013, Art 3).

The European Commission describes EPP rather innocuously as 'detailed structural reforms' which are intended 'to put in place to improve competitiveness and boost growth' (European Commission 2013a). In actual fact, they mirror IMF structural adjustment policies in their objectives of diminishing the role of the state in the economy, privatization/part privatization of state companies; and reducing welfare and workers' rights and social transfers. The programmes have a very wide economic remit, encompassing the selling off, wholly or partly, of state utility companies; increasing the pension age, eradicating/reforming rent controls, reducing employment rights to induce labour flexibility, reduction of public sector wages, reduction of social security payments and reduction of health care and so on.

The 'Bail-Outs'

The loans made to Greece and the conditions attached to them were initially in reaction to fast moving events and were therefore ad hoc in nature. Although funding arrangements differed radically for the different countries involved, the conditionality and surveillance attached to the loans were very generic. These general arrangements became ever more institutionalized as the crisis deepened, but the nature of the loan conditionalities and the surveillance of indebted states existed from the start and remained relatively unchanged. At the heart of these arrangements lies a disciplinary mechanism that seeks to instil the norm of fiscal balances and the further marketization of societies.

In terms of funding, the initial loans for Greece came from Eurozone members and the IMF (and since then the IMF has been involved in providing part of the loans); as the crisis deepened with Ireland and Portugal, a special purpose vehicle issuing bonds guaranteed by Eurozone members—the European Financial Stability Fund (EFSF)—was established in May 2010 alongside the European Financial Stabilization Mechanism (EFSM) issuing bonds using the EU budget as collateral to secure emergency funding for members experiencing economic difficulties. With regard to finance, the Long Term Refinancing Operations to prop up European banks was established in December 2011 alongside the Securities Markets Programme created in August 2011 which attempted to stabilize state borrowing costs through intervention in the secondary bond market by the ECB (replaced by the Outright Monetary Transactions mechanism in September 2012). Much of this has been replaced by the European Stability Mechanism (ESM), which was ratified in October 2012. The ESM relies on contributions from Eurozone members and seeks to address the instability the Eurozone has confronted by providing not only loans in support of macro-economic adjustment programmes, but also precautionary loans, bank refinancing (through loans to governments who then pass the funds on) and intervention in primary and secondary bond markets.

The shift towards IMF-style structural adjustment policies became very apparent during the bail-outs of several peripheral states. Indeed, when establishing the EFSF, European leaders stressed that 'Its activation is subject to strong conditionality, in the context of joint EU/IMF support, and will be on terms and conditions similar to the IMF' (Kirkegaard October 2010). So-called Economic Adjustment Programmes are now established through memoranda of understanding between the recipient of the loan and the so-called Troika (European Commission, the ECB and the IMF). The recipient country signs a Memorandum of Understanding on Specific Economic Policy Conditionality addressed to the European authorities, a Memorandum of Economic and Financial Policies (MEFP) and a Technical Memorandum of Understanding (TMU) addressed to the IMF (Pisani-Ferry et al. 2013, p. 22). Moreover, the ESM has institutionalized the coordination activities of the Commission, the ECB and the IMF that began with the Greek bail-out. The treaty establishing the ESM states that the Commission is to liaise with the ECB and 'wherever possible the IMF' with regards to the memorandum of understanding (ESM 2012, Art. 13, 3).

These programmes differ to the EPPs under the EDP in the intensity of policy reforms and degree of surveillance. With the implementation of EAP, we see the full force of neo-liberal disciplinary mechanisms both in the fiscal and more general economic realms alongside IMF surveillance techniques as well as regular (usually quarterly) visits by the Troika to the recipient countries.

Under such reforms we have seen the usual pattern of policy proposals surrounding fiscal balance, financial stability and structural reforms to restore competitiveness. The EAP have therefore focused on recapitalizing banks and frequent stress testing, fiscal consolidation, improved productivity, privatization and the commodification of hitherto public goods. The most obvious example of the latter is the introduction of direct water charges (previously funded through general taxes) and the subsequent privatization of the water utility Irish Water, but it has also occurred through the privatization of utility companies and the subsequent deepening of marketization (eradication of subsidies) and greater profit making. Examples of this abound. In Ireland, the Gas Company Bord Gais was recently sold off alongside the selling of the government's stake in Aer Lingus (25%) and the planned return to full privatization of AIB, Bank of Ireland and PTSB (O'Donovan 26 March 2014; McDonald 31 May 2015; Kelpie 4 October 2014). In Portugal, privatizations included the airport operator ANA, the national airline carrier TAP Portugal, the health care subsidiary CGD and the full privatization of the electricity company EDP (European Commission 2013b, p. 48). Cyprus intends to privatize its utility EAC, its telecoms utility, CYta and the Cyprus ports authority (Hadjipapas and Hope 04 March 2014). As mentioned below, Greece must now transfer assets worth €50 billion to a privatization body (Greek MOU 11 August 2015, p. 25). The many privatizations cancelled by Syriza have been placed back on the agenda. These are likely to include the management and operation of regional airports, the Piraeus and Thessaloniki Port Authorities; the Greek refiner

Hellenic Petroleum, the country's two biggest ports in Piraeus (OLP) and Thessaloniki (OLTH); Thessaloniki Water (EYATH); Larco, one of the world's biggest nickel producers; and its main water utility companies (Kathimerini 16 October 2015). Indeed, in the case of its national electricity network (ADMIE) and the airports, 'irreversible steps' must be taken to privatize these entities (Greek MOU 11 August 2015, p. 23 and 25).[16] And for the ports, the MOU states that binding bid dates must be announced by the end of October 2015 (Greek MOU 11 August 2015, p. 25)

In terms of fiscal discipline, Ireland had already embarked upon a certain degree of austerity before its bail-out with a pension levy averaging 7.5% and a pay cut of 6.5% for public sector workers (Sheahan 09 August 2014). Under the MOU with the IMF and EU, the pension age will be increased in step fashion until it reaches 68 years in 2028 and pensions for public sector workers was reduced by 4%. The minimum wage was reduced by €1 per hour and income tax was increased (Council of the European Union 7 December 2010). A commitment to a reduction in social expenditure was made and consequently the €144 per week job seekers allowance was cut to €100 for under-25 s (McDonald 15 October 2013).

Portugal froze all pensions between 2012 and 2014 and applied a 3.5% levy and attempted to reduce public sector pensions by 10% (but a challenge to this was upheld by the Constitutional Court) (Portugal 17 May 2011). Early retirement was suspended during the emergency period and the pension age increased to 66 years (European Parliament 2015, p. 84). In addition, in 2012, there was an extraordinary solidarity contribution of 25% if the pension income was between €5030.64 and €7545.96—above this figure the surcharge was 50% (EUROMOD 2013). There was also A surtax on incomes of 3.5% alongside a progressive solidarity surcharge starting at 2.5% for incomes over €80,000 and 5% for those over €250,000 (Price Waterhouse and Coopers 2014). The income tax base was increased alongside VAT for certain services (e.g. VAT on restaurant services increased from 10% to 23% in 2012).

Cyprus cut its public sector wages and pensions from 6.5% increasing progressively (once a €1000 per month threshold is reached) to 12.5% from December 2012 to December 2013 and then a flat rate reduction of 3% in 2014. Furthermore, increments and general wage increases are frozen until 2016. A temporary contribution to government revenue ranging from 2.5% (once a €2500 per month threshold is reached) to 3.5% of income for public and private employees as well as pensioners. At the same time, a contribution to the Widows and Orphans Fund of 3% was required of public sector workers and a health care contribution of 1.5% that also applied to public sector pensioners. With regard to the latter, pensions were frozen and the statutory retirement age increased by two years (European Commission 2013c).

Although the Greek bail-out is ongoing, the pattern of reforms is very similar but more intensive. A special solidarity tax has been levied since 2010 on all workers, increasing progressively so that those earning €12,000–20,000 are taxed 1%; €20,0001–50,000, 2%; €50,001–100,000, 3%; above 100,000, 4% (Caruso-Cabrera 20 June 2012). All public sector wages were frozen until 2014 and the two additional supplements to wages—the 13th and 14th 'doro'—have been cut for any public servant that earns more than €3000 a month and for all pensioners receiving more than €2500 a month (Drachma 2015). Although the Troika have interpreted these payments as additional emoluments above the standard salary, traditionally they were part of the salary held back to ensure workers had money during their holiday periods (similar practices exist elsewhere e.g. Japan). Pensions were frozen and the retirement age was raised to 67 (The Economist 18 June 2015). Pension payments above €1400 per month were subject to a solidarity tax that increased progressively from 3% up to 10% if the pension received was €3500 a month or above (EUROMOD 2011, P. 3). Although recently there has been an attempt to reduce this burden on pensions, the new 2015 bail-out will see this reversed given it has targeted pension reform as an area that should produce a 1% of GDP saving in 2015 (Greek MOU 11 August 2015, p, 10). The monthly minimum wage was cut by 22% (it was €750 euros gross) and for those younger than 25, it was cut by 32% (Georgiopoulos 28 February 2012).

Indeed, the negotiations between Greece and the Eurogroup (plus Eurozone leaders) just after the rejection of further austerity measures by the Greek population started to veer towards the 'spectacle of the scaffold' with German sovereign power being fully displayed (mediated through the Eurogroup) (Foucault 1995, p. 49). At the time (13 July 2015), the initial list of conditions for a third bail-out demanded that the Greek body, TAIPED, tasked with privatization of public assets become fully independent; the government transferred €50 billion of public assets to an independent trust in Luxembourg so that they could be privatized over time; and that the bail-out fund would be administered from Luxembourg through the ESM, rather than Athens (Bolton 12 July 2015; 'Schäuble Plan' 11 July 2015). Moreover, the Troika would not only return, they would now 'have a say in all relevant Greek draft legislation before it is presented to parliament. Furthermore, the Greeks had to amend all legislation already passed by the Syriza government this year that had not been agreed with the creditors' (Traynor and Rankin 13 July 2015).

Although several of these proposals were absent from the final agreement, the latter remained. The negotiations were in danger of shifting from disciplinary action aimed at correcting aberrant behaviour and 'an economy of example', towards a 'policy of terror' in order to make 'everyone aware, through the body of the criminal, of the unrestrained presence of the sovereign' (Foucault 1995, p. 49). Many of the above proposals may have simply been threats to ensure Greek compliance. But, the objective of the Euro Summit began to look less like re-establishing neo-liberal economic discipline and more like asserting the paramount power of the German sovereign over subaltern sovereigns, so that 'the punishment is carried out in such a way as to give a spectacle not of measure, but of imbalance and excess … by breaking the law, the offender has touched the very person of the prince; and it is the prince—or at least those to whom he has delegated his force—who seizes upon the body of the condemned man and displays it marked, beaten, broken' (Foucault 1995 p. 49). Indeed, such has been the severity of proposals that the IMF has reminded the key players of the objectives of such reforms (a stable economy) and the need for some form of debt relief/maturity extension if debt sustainability is really going to be achieved (IMF 2015).

In the end, the negotiations climaxed with an agreement with a familiar refrain. In order to restore fiscal discipline, Greece has to make its national statistical body independent (ELSTAT). It must transpose the Bank Recovery and Resolution Directive into Greek law—which means that if a bank is in financial trouble, then depositors may now be involved in a 'bail-in'. A VAT rate of 23% on food and beverage consumption will be extended to restaurants and catering. Taxes will be increased through the levy of a 'solidarity supplement', which progressively increases with the level of income—ranging from 1% to 3% (Inman 23 June 2015). The Greek government must introduce quasi-automatic spending cuts if the fiscal balance deviates from the primary surplus targets agreed (this surplus increases progressively up to 3.5% in 2018) (Greek MOU 11 August 2015, p. 3). The solidarity grant for poorer pensioners will be phased out and health contributions from pensions will increase by applying a 6% levy on main and supplementary pensions (Greek MOU 11 August 2015, p. 10). Labour laws will be reformed with regard to trade unions and industrial action and even protection from collective dismissal is likely to be repealed (Greek MOU 11 August 2015, p. 10). The government must also further reform Sunday trading laws and liberalize various sectors of the economy—'pharmacy ownership, milk and bakeries…as well as for the opening of macro-critical closed professions (e.g. ferry transportation)' (Inman 23 June 2015; Greek MOU 11 August 2015, p. 20).

As with the SGP, conditionality seeks to reinforce the norm of a budgetary balance/surplus insisting that at a minimum, recipient states achieve a primary surplus within a set time limit. But the loan conditionality goes much further in terms of broadening and deepening market relations within a state. The policies foisted upon loan recipients are part of a wider disciplinary mechanism that seeks to instil neo-liberal patterns of behaviour at the state level, entailing a 'policy of coercions that act upon' the state that enters a 'machinery of power that explores it, breaks it down and rearranges it' (Foucault 2007, p. 138). Fiscal balances are produced through the shrinking of state commitments, leading to reductions in pensions, social welfare provision, public sector employment, public sector wages, education and health and so on. Generally, macroeconomic reforms have as their objective the broadening and deepening of market relations with the privatization of state enterprises, attacks on collective bargaining rights and the opening up of hitherto closed professions and protected industries to market forces. Loan recipients must discipline themselves and adhere to these severe structural adjustments and fiscal targets if they are to continue to receive loan disbursements.

Indeed, in the Greek case, the potential for almost immediate punishment is inscribed in the loan conditionalities in the form of *ex-ante* prior actions that the state must enact. In its most recent Third Economic Adjustment Programme, the Memoranda of Understanding stipulates 35 prior actions for the Greek state to take before loans are disbursed (Traynor and Henley 11 August 2015; Greek MOU 11 August 2015).

The Troika not only brings to bear neo-liberal technologies instilling financial, fiscal and market discipline, but it also brings with it a micro-physics of surveillance. Indeed, one of the key constitutive elements of the memoranda of understanding is an array of commitments to provide detailed information concerning the pace of reforms. Moreover, where the surveillance and information systems of the loan recipient state are deemed inadequate, improvements must be made. This includes statistical analysis and information gathering, but also involves the adoption of the Single Supervisory Mechanism's methodologies for assessing the health of the financial sector, for example, bank capitalization, overall risk exposure and so on. It has even involved establishing centralized credit registers producing a breakdown of credit lines, borrower by borrower, through the creation of individual identification numbers and improved electronic monitoring for the delivery of health care to each individual patient. Each loan recipient state must provide highly detailed analysis on the state of affairs concerning fiscal, financial and macro-economic balances as well as reform measures implementation. The information is usually gathered month to month, but in some sectors of special interest, the Troika even demands weekly reporting.

At the same time, the IMF brings with it its own technologies of expertise. These include the Reports on the Observance of Standards and Codes (ROSCs) that use a set of international auditing standards in 12 economic areas ranging from banking to insurance which serve as benchmarks by which the quality of economic governance within a country is measured.[17] In essence the ROSCs have as their object states and their quality of economic governance—its aim is to ensure adherence to standards of economic behaviour within a range of prescribed parameters (Vestergaard, 2009, p. 94).

These provide essential information for the IMF's Financial Sector Assessment Program (FSAP)—a macro-prudential surveillance with the explicit objective of assessing 'soundness and vulnerability of financial systems, encompassing a range of economic, regulatory, and institutional issues pertaining to financial stability' (Vestergaard, 2009, p. 94). The FSAP can include the whole of the ROSCs, but at a minimum will cover monetary and financial policy transparency and then five jointly with the ROSC—banking supervision, securities, insurance, payments and securities settlement systems, and anti-money laundering and combating the financing of terrorism. In essence, FSAPs seek to provide a '"comprehensive health check-up" of a country's financial sector' using an array of financial soundness indicators established by the international financial institutions (IFIs) (Vestergaard, 2009, p. 94).

Indeed, since the crisis, 'risk-based assessments of the standards that apply to the regulation and supervision of banks, securities markets, and insurance have been introduced to better target the assessments of these standards' (Viñals and Brook 2009). This Risk Assessment Matrix (RAM) based on the FSAPs significantly increases each country's visibility by producing a matrix that not only provides a numeric evaluation of the risk associated with each individual country's financial governance, but also provides a means of cross-comparison. The use of such a matrix is designed to 'combine the identified major sources of risks (e.g., over-indebted households, undercapitalized banks), possible triggers (e.g., a severe macro-economic downturn, a failure of a systemically important institution), and transmission mechanisms, with the assessment of regulatory, supervisory, and crisis management frameworks and the results of stress tests to arrive at qualitative assessments of (i) the probability of risk triggers being activated (low, medium, high); and (ii) the potential impact on financial stability and on the broader economy were those events to materialize' (IMF and World Bank, August 2009, p. 36).

This surveillance aspect of the disciplinary mechanism serves to establish a field of visibility, backlighting state behaviour and ensuring that even the slightest deviation from these financial, fiscal and macro-economic adjustments will be readily apparent and checked. These classificatory grids set out the reforms to be achieved, when they should be achieved and current progress towards this achievement, thus producing a 'normalizing gaze, a surveillance that makes it possible to qualify, to classify and to punish' (Foucault 1995, p. 184; Vestergaard

2009). The surveillance enables a comparison of state performance against an array of benchmarks enabling a judgement to be made as to how well countries are implementing the established goals. If a state deviates from the proposed policies, the Troika has the option of punishing it by withholding some or all of the loan which, after the first instalment, is delivered on a quarterly basis—the timing of which coincides with their quarterly examination concerning the reform agenda. As with the SGP, the classificatory grids and quarterly visits by the Troika embody the central elements of a disciplinary mechanism—'hierarchical observation, normalizing judgement and their combination in a procedure that is specific to it, the examination' (Vestergaard 2009, p. 126; Foucault 1995, p. 170).

Conclusion

This chapter has argued that in order to enhance learning and cooperation between member states, the EU embraced an OMC. This method of achieving benchmarks and the adoption of similar neo-liberal policies can be understood as a form of liberal governmentality, given its emphasis on consensus building and its modus operandi of operating at a distance, 'making suggestions, recommendations and promptings, but also operating through establishing the correct procedures, methods, aims and objectives with progress and performance measured through a set of targets, or through peer review and benchmarking' (Joseph 2012, p. 202 and 211). The method helps to 'develop a shared vision of social challenges, fostered a willingness to cooperate and learn from each other's practices, created a new dynamism in furthering and implementing reforms, and promoted more knowledge-based policy making, geared towards openness, transparency and participation'.[18] This indirect subjectification process was seen as a key instrument in the socialization of national elites, attempting to inculcate neo-liberal norms, values and beliefs. As such, the OMC sought to 'operate on the conduct of the governed' but 'seeks a direction of conduct rather than a violent or gross form of corporeal domination' because it 'assumes a "free subject"...one whose subjection is consistent with forms of choice' (Dean 1994, p. 178).

Yet, from the point of its inception, the SGP contained certain disciplinary elements. However, the emphasis on the OMC and the unwillingness of the major economic powers to subject themselves to the strictures of the SGP meant that these disciplinary aspects were held in abeyance. Although the SGP was strengthened somewhat in 2005 because several members had failed to maintain fiscal discipline, the major shift away from a consensual subjectification process towards the imposition of a regime of discipline and punishment came during the Euro crisis. These disciplinary mechanisms are most clearly seen in the highly intrusive procedures for those countries requiring bail-outs in which sovereigns are subjected to macro-economic adjustment policies and lending is dependent on compliance with the conditionalities that attend such reforms. But this chapter has also highlighted the imposition of fiscal discipline through the SGP, the heightened surveillance associated with its post-crisis reform and the punishment meted out to those states that fail to comply. Moreover, the EPP associated with the SGP may differ in degree to the EAP attached to the bail-outs but they do not fundamentally differ in kind.

We are therefore witnessing not only the maintenance of neo-liberal conditionality in the Eurozone, but also its deepening. Conditionality is being used to further promote the marketization of the social sphere, the European crisis has thus been marked by further interventions so that 'competitive mechanisms can play a regulatory role at every moment and every point in society' attempting to ensure the 'general regulation of society by the market' (Foucault 2008, p. 45). The chapter has highlighted how this has entailed state retrenchment, further commodification, labour market deregulation, privatization of national industries and so on. This is a far cry from the post-modernist version of resilience thinking that sees a new paradigm emerging, one that replaces neo-liberalism and interventionism with an emphasis on *post-facto* adaptability of states, communities and individuals.

Given that Germany's earlier adoption of more intensive neo-liberal policies shortly after reunification had a very negative impact on the economic growth of the EU as a whole, then it is unlikely that these policies will provide a long-term solution to Europe's problems (Lapavitsas et al. 2012). There has been no real attempt to address the problem of a uniform interest rate applied to states with very different growth and inflation rates as a result of being at very diverse stages of development. It is also unlikely that there will be strong convergence in competitiveness given the difference in productivity rates between the northern industrial core and the southern periphery and the reduction in real wages in the northern core (thus undermining much of the competitive gains the periphery may have accrued through wage reductions). In addition, if Germany continues its quest of being a net exporter within the EU, then it is difficult to see any alternative scenario than the replay of the economic dynamics that have beset the Eurozone from its inception.

Notes

1. The verb has been changed from the past as it appeared in the original to the present.
2. Foucault identifies three modes of subjectification: dividing practices, scientific classification and the way in which human beings turn themselves into subjects (Foucault 1982, pp. 777–78).
3. Quoted in Joseph (2012, p. 190).
4. Quoted in Joseph (2012, p. 190).
5. Quoted in Joseph (2012, p. 193).
6. The UK was exempt from the excessive deficit procedure under Protocol 15 of the Treaty on the Functioning of the EU, but still receives recommendations and under section 5 of the protocol, it 'shall endeavour to avoid an excessive government deficit' (European Union 2007, Protocol 15).
7. The Council refers to the Council of the European Union throughout this chapter.
8. A similar approach was adopted earlier by Deuchars (2004).
9. Initial bail-outs were in May 2010, November 2010, May 2011, March 2013, respectively. The bail-outs would total five if one included the financial help provided to Spanish banks in July 2012.
10. The list is a paraphrasing of the objectives set out in European Commission (2014b, p. 3).

11. The assessment of whether the deviation is significant shall, in particular, include the following criteria:

    (a) for a member state that has not reached the medium-term budgetary objective, when assessing the change in the structural balance, whether the deviation is at least 0.5% of GDP in a single year or at least 0.25% of GDP on average per year in two consecutive years;
    (b) when assessing expenditure developments net of discretionary revenue measures, whether the deviation has a total impact on the government balance of at least 0.5% of GDP in a single year or cumulatively in two consecutive years.

12. At a minimum, this involves

    (a) transparent recruitment and dismissal processes which must be solely based on professional criteria;
    (b) budgetary allocations which must be made on an annual or a multi-annual basis;
    (c) the date of publication of key statistical information which must be designated significantly in advance.

13. Examples of thresholds include three-year backward moving average of the current account balance as a percent of GDP, with a threshold of +6% of GDP and −4% of GDP; net international investment position as a percent of GDP, with a threshold of −35% of GDP; five-year percentage change of export market shares measured in values, with a threshold of −6%; three-year percentage change in nominal unit labour cost, with thresholds of +9% for euro-area countries and +12% for non-euro-area countries; three-year percentage change of the real effective exchange rates based on HICP/CPI deflators, relative to 35 other industrial countries, with thresholds of −/+5% for euro-area countries and −/+11% for non-euro-area countries; private sector debt in % of GDP with a threshold of 160%; private sector credit flow in % of GDP with a threshold of 15%; year-on-year changes in house prices relative to a Eurostat consumption deflator, with a threshold of 6%; general government sector debt in % of GDP with a threshold of 60%; three-year backward moving average of unemployment rate, with the threshold of 10% (European Commission 2011b).
14. The 11 indicators are current account balance, net international investment position, real effective exchange rate, export market share, nominal unit labour cost, house price index, private sector credit/private sector

debt, general government gross debt, unemployment rate, total financial sector liabilities.

Activity rate (economically active population of 15–64-year olds) which has two sub-indicators—long-term unemployment rate and youth unemployment rate (% of active population aged 15–24).

15. The only member states that are not signatories are the UK and Croatia.
16. For ADMIE, the MOU does state that 'unless an alternative scheme is provided, with equivalent results in terms of competition and prospects for investment'.
17. The ROSCs cover 'data dissemination, fiscal practices, monetary and financial policy transparency, banking supervision, insurance supervision, securities market regulation, payments systems, anti-money laundering, corporate governance, accounting, auditing, insolvency regimes, and creditor rights' (Soederberg 2002, p. 615).
18. Quoted in Joseph (2012, p. 190).

References

Bolton, D. 2015. Greece Debt Crisis Live: The List of Reforms that Greece Must Meet if It Wants Another Bailout from Europe. *The Independent*, July 12. http://www.independent.co.uk/news/business/news/greece-debt-crisis-live-the-list-of-reforms-that-greece-must-meet-if-it-wants-another-bailout-from-europe-10383901.html

Borras, S., and K. Jacobsson. 2014. The Open Method of Co-ordination and New Governance Patterns in the EU. *Journal of European Public Policy* 11 (2): 185–208.

Borras, S., and C. Radaelli. 2014. The Transformation of EU Governance. In *The Eurozone Crisis and the Transformation of EU Governance: Internal and External Implications*, ed. M. Rodrigues and E. Xiarchogiannopoulou, 41–56. Farnham: Ashgate.

Chalmers, D., and M. Lodge. 2003. *The Open Method of Coordination and the European Welfare State: Working Paper 11*. London School of Economics, ESRC Centre for Analysis of Risk and Regulation.

Council of the European Union. 1997a. *Council Regulation No 1466/97 of 7 July 1997 on the Strengthening of the Surveillance of Budgetary Positions and the Surveillance and Coordination of Economic Policies*. http://eur-lex.europa.eu/legal-content/EN/TXT/?uri=celex:31997R1466

———. 1997b. *Council Regulation (EC) No 1467/97 of 7 July 1997 on Speeding up and Clarifying the Implementation of the Excessive Deficit Procedure*. http://eur-lex.europa.eu/legal-content/EN/TXT/?uri=celex:31997R1467

———. 2005a. *Council Regulation (EC) No 1055/2005 of 27 June 2005 Amending Regulation (EC) No 1466/97 on the Strengthening of the Surveillance of Budgetary Positions and the Surveillance and Coordination of Economic Policies*. http://eur-lex.europa.eu/legal-content/EN/TXT/?qid=1412159031745&uri=CELEX:32005R1055

———. 2005b. *Council Regulation (EC) No 1467/97 of 7 July 1997 on Speeding Up and Clarifying the Implementation of the Excessive Deficit Procedure*. http://eur-lex.europa.eu/legal-content/EN/TXT/?qid=1412158400303&uri=%20CELEX:31997R1467

———. 2005c. *Council Regulation (EC) No 2103/2005 of 12 December 2005 Amending Regulation (EC) No 3605/93 as Regards the Quality of Statistical Data in the Context of the Excessive Deficit Procedure*. http://eur-lex.europa.eu/legal-content/EN/TXT/?uri=CELEX: 32005R2103

———. 2010. *Council Implementing Decision of 7 December 2010 on Granting Union Financial Assistance to Ireland (2011/77/EU)*. http://eur-lex.europa.eu/legal-content/EN/TXT/?uri=CELEX:32011D0077. Accessed 20 July 2015.

———. 2011a. *Council Regulation (EU) No 1177/2011 of 8 November 2011 Amending Regulation (EC) No 1467/97 on Speeding Up and Clarifying the Implementation of the Excessive Deficit Procedure*. http://eur-lex.europa.eu/legal-content/EN/TXT/?uri=uriserv:OJ.L_.2011. 306.01.0033.01.ENG

———. 2011b. *Council Directive 2011/85/EU of 8 November 2011 on Requirements for Budgetary Frameworks of the Member States*. http://eur-lex.europa.eu/legal-content/EN/TXT/?uri=uriserv:OJ.L_.2011.306.01.0041.01.ENG

Dean, M. 1994. *Critical and Effective Histories: Foucault's Methods and Historical Sociology*. London: Routledge.

———. 2010. *Governmentality: Power and Rule in Modern Society*. Los Angeles: Sage.

Deuchars, R. 2004. *The International Political Economy of Risk: Rationalism, Calculation and Power*. Aldershot: Ashgate.

Djankov, S. 2014. *Inside the Euro Crisis: An Eyewitness Account*. Washington, DC: Institute for International Economics.

Drachma. 2015. Full list of Greek Austerity/Bailout Measures/Conditions Up to 2015. http://www.δραχμή.gr/docs/Full-list-of-Greek-austerity-measures-bailout-conditions-until-Feb-2015.pdf. Accessed 14 Jan 2015.

ESM. 2012. *Treat Establishing the European Stability Mechanism*. Online at http://ec.europa.eu/economy_finance/articles/financial_operations/2011-07-11-esm-treaty_en.htm

EUROMOD. 2011. EUROMOD Working Paper No. EM3/11: The Distributional Impact of the Crisis in Greece. https://www.iser.essex.ac.uk/research/publications/working-papers/euromod/em3-11.pdf

———. 2013. Country Report Portugal. https://www.iser.essex.ac.uk/files/euromod/country-reports/Year5/CR_PT_Y5_Jan2014_final_12032014.pdf

European Commission. 2000. *Broad Economic Policy Guidelines Convergence Report 2000*. http://ec.europa.eu/economy_finance/publications/publication7572_en.pdf

———. 2004. *Facing the Challenge: The Lisbon Strategy for Growth and Employment*. Luxembourg: Office for Official Publications of the European Communities.

———. 2005a. *Communication to the Spring European Council: Working Together for Growth and Jobs: A New Start for the Lisbon Strategy*. http://eur-lex.europa.eu/legal-content/EN/TXT/PDF/?uri=CELEX:52005DC0024&from=EN

———. 2005b. *Communication from the Commission to the Council and the European Parliament – Public Finances in EMU {SEC(2005) 723}*. http://eur-lex.europa.eu/legal-content/EN/TXT/?uri=CELEX:52005DC0231

———. 2010a. *Report on Greek Government Deficit and Debt Statistics*, January. http://ec.europa.eu/eurostat/documents/4187653/6404656/COM_2010_reportgreek/c8523cfa-d3c1-4954-8ea1-64bb11e59b3a

———. 2011b. *EU Economic Governance "Six-Pack" Enters into Force*. http://europa.eu/rapid/press-release_MEMO-11-898_en.htm

———. 2013a. *The EU's Economic Governance Explained*. http://europa.eu/rapid/press-release_MEMO-13-318_en.htm

———. 2013b. The Economic Adjustment Programme for Portugal Seventh Review – Winter 2012/2013, *Occasional Papers 153*. http://ec.europa.eueconomy_finance/publications/occasional_paper/2013/pdf/ocp153_en.pdf. Accessed 16 July 2015.

———. 2013c. The Economic Adjustment Programme for Cyprus Second Review – Autumn 2013, *Occasional Papers 169*. http://ec.europa.eu/economy_finance/publications/occasional_paper/2013/pdf/ocp169_en.pdf. Accessed 17 July 2015.

———. 2014a. *European Parliament Backs Commission Proposals on New Rules to Improve the Quality of Statutory Audit*, April 3. http://europa.eu/rapid/press-release_STATEMENT-14-104_en.htm

———. 2014b. *The European Union Explained: Europe 2020: Europe's Growth Strategy*. Luxembourg: Publications Office of the European Union.

European Council. 1997. Resolution of the European Council on the Stability and Growth Pact Amsterdam (97/C 236/01).

European Council. 2000a. *Lisbon European Council 23 and 24 March 2000: Presidency Conclusions*. http://www.aedh.eu/plugins/fckeditor/userfiles/file/DESC/2000%20LISBON%20EUROPEAN%20COUNCIL%2023%20AND%2024%20MARCH.pdf

———. 2000b. *Resolution of the Amsterdam European Council on the Stability and Growth Pact*. http://eur-lex.europa.eu/legal-content/EN/TXT/?qid=1412156825485&uri=URISERV:l25021

European Parliament and Council. 2011a. *Regulation (EU) No 1175/2011 of the European Parliament and of the Council of 16 November 2011 Amending Council Regulation (EC) No 1466/97 on the Strengthening of the Surveillance of Budgetary Positions and the Surveillance and Coordination of Economic Policies*. http://eur-lex.europa.eu/legal-content/EN/TXT/?uri=uriserv:OJ.L_.2011.306.01.0012.01.ENG

———. 2011b. *Regulation (EU) No 1176/2011 of the European Parliament and of the Council of 16 November 2011 on the Prevention and Correction of Macroeconomic Imbalances*. http://old.eur-lex.europa.eu/LexUriServ/LexUriServ.do?uri=OJ:L:2011:306:0025:0025: EN:PDF

———. 2011c. *Regulation (EU) No 1174/2011 of the European Parliament and of the Council of 16 November 2011 on Enforcement Measures to Correct Excessive Macroeconomic Imbalances in the Euro Area*. http://eur-lex.europa.eu/LexUriServ/LexUriServ.do?uri=OJ:L:2011:306:0008:0011:EN:PDF

———. 2013. *Regulation (EU) No 472/2013 of the European Parliament and of the Council of 21 May 2013 on the Strengthening of Economic and Budgetary Surveillance of Member States in the Euro Area Experiencing or Threatened with Serious Difficulties with Respect to Their Financial Stability*. http://old.eur-lex.europa.eu/LexUriServ/LexUriServ.do?uri=OJ:L:2013:140:0001:0001:EN:PDF

European Parliament. 2015. *The Impact of the Crisis on Fundamental Rights Across Member States of the EU Country Report on Portugal*. Brussels: European Union.

European Union. 1992. *The Maastricht Treaty: Provisions Amending the Treaty Establishing the European Economic Community with a View to Establishing the European Community*. http://www.eurotreaties.com/maastrichtec.pdf

———. 2007. *Consolidated Version of the Treaty on the Functioning of the European Union*. http://eur-lex.europa.eu/legal-content/EN/TXT/?uri=celex:12012E/TXT

———. 2008. *Consolidated Version of the Treaty on European Union – PROTOCOLS – Protocol (No 12) on the Excessive Deficit Procedure*. http://eur-lex.europa.eu/legal-content/EN/ALL/?uri=CELEX:12008M/PRO/12

———. 2012. *Consolidated Versions of the Treaty on European Union and the Treaty on the Functioning of the European Union*. http://eur-lex.europa.eu/legal-content/EN/TXT/PDF/?uri=OJ:C:2010:083:FULL&from=EN

Fabbrini, S. 2015. The Euro Crisis and Its Constitutional Implications. In *The Future of Europe: Democracy, Legitimacy and Justice After the Euro Crisis (Future Perfect: Images of the Time to Come in Philosophy, Politics and Cultural Studies)*, ed. S. Champeau, C. Closa, D. Innerarity, and M. Maduro, 19–36. London: Rowman & Littlefield International.

Foucault, M. 1982. The Subject and Power. *Critical Inquiry* 8 (4): 777–795.

———. 1995. *Discipline and Punish: The Birth of the Prison*. 2nd ed. New York: Vintage Books.

———. 2007. *Security, Territory, Population: Lectures at the College de France 1977–78*. Basingstoke: Palgrave Macmillan.

———. 2008. *The Birth of Biopolitics: Lectures at the College de France, 1978–79*. Basingstoke: Palgrave Macmillan.

Georgiopoulos, G. 2012. Greece Cuts Minimum Wage as Austerity Drive Begins. *Reuters,* February 28. Online at https://www.reuters.com/article/us-greece/greece-cuts-minimum-wage-as-austerity-drive-begins-idUSTRE81R1KR20120228

Greek MOU. 2015. *Greece: Memorandum of Understanding for a Three-Year ESM Programme,* August 11. http://online.wsj.com/public/resources/documents/greecedoc.pdf

Hadjipapas, A., and K. Hope. 2014. Cyprus Passes Bill to Privatise Utilities. *Financial Times,* March 04. http://www.ft.com/cms/s/0/4c00c91c-a3c2-11e3-88b0-00144feab7de.html#axzz3gEeo5Obw

Heipertz, M., and A. Verdun. 2010. *Ruling Europe: The Politics of the Stability and Growth Pact*. Cambridge: CUP.

IMF. 2015. Greece: An Update of IMF Staff's Preliminary Public Debt Sustainability Analysis. *IMF Country* (Rep No. 15/186). http://www.imf.org/external/pubs/ft/scr/2015/cr15186.pdf

IMF and World Bank. 2009. *The Financial Sector Assessment Program After Ten Years: Experience and Reforms for the Next Decade*, August. http://www.imf.org/external/ np/pp/eng/2009/082809b.pdf

Inman, P. 2015. Greek Reform Proposals. *The Guardian,* June 23. http://www.theguardian.com/business/2015/jun/23/greece-debt-crisis%2D%2Doffer-athens-details

Joseph, J. 2012. *The Social in the Global: Social Theory, Governmentality and Global Politics.* Cambridge: Cambridge University Press.

Kirkegaard, J. 2010. Will It Be Brussels, Berlin, or Financial Markets that Check Moral Hazard in Europe's Bailout Union? Most Likely the Latter! *Peterson Institute for International Economics: Policy Brief,* October. http://www.iie.com/publications/pb/pb10-25.pdf

Lapavitsas, C., A. Kaltenbrunner, G. Labrinidis, D. Lindo, J. Meadway, J. Michell, J. Paincera, E. Pires, J. Powell, A. Stenfors, N. Teles, and L. Vatikiotis. 2012. *Crisis in the Eurozone.* London: Verso Books.

Marsh, D. 2013. *Europe's Deadlock: How the Euro Crisis Could be Solved – And Why It Won't Happen.* New Haven: Yale University.

McDonald, H. 2013. Ireland Announces More Budget Cuts Despite Recovery. *The Guardian,* October 15, http://www.theguardian.com/world/2013/oct/15/ireland-more-budget-cuts-despite-recovery

———. 2015. Aer Lingus Sell-Off: When Cold Economic Logic Meets Nostalgia. *The Guardian,* May 31. http://www.theguardian.com/business/blog /2015/may/31/aer-lingus-sell-off-when-cold-economic-logic-meets-nostalgia

Merlingen, M. 2003. Governmentality: Towards a Foucauldian Framework for the Study of IGOs. *Cooperation and Conflict* 38 (4): 361–384.

Novotny, V., ed. 2013. *From Reform to Growth: Managing the Economic Crisis in Europe.* Delft: Eburon.

Pisani-Ferry, J. 2014. *The Euro Crisis and Its Aftermath.* Oxford: Oxford University Press.

Pisani-Ferry, J., A. Sapir, and G. Wolff. 2013. *EU-IMF Assistance to Euro-Area Countries: An Early Assessment.* Belgium: Bruegel Blueprint Series.

Portugal. 2011. Memorandum of Understanding on Specific Economic Policy Conditionality, May 17. http://ec.europa.eu/economy_finance/eu_borrower/mou/2011-05-18-mou-portugal_en.pdf

Price Waterhouse and Coopers. 2014. Portugal IRS: Surtax and Additional Solidarity Rate. Online at IRS: Surtax and Additional Solidarity Rate.

Radaelli, C. 2003. *The Open Method of Coordination: A New Governance Architecture for the European Union?* Stockholm: Swedish Institute for European Policy Studies.

Richardson, J., and S. Mazey. 2015. *European Union: Power and Policy-Making.* London: Routledge.

Rose, N., and P. Miller. 2008. *Governing the Present.* Cambridge: Polity Press.

Scott, J., and D. Trubek. 2002. Mind the Gap: Law and New Approaches to Governance in the European Union. *European Law Journal* 8 (1): 1–18.

'Schäuble Plan'. 2015. Comments on the Latest Greek Proposals, July 11. http://www.sven-giegold.de/wp-content/uploads/2015/07/grexit_bundesregierung_non_paper_10_juli_2015.pdf

Sheahan, F. 2014. Public Sector Staff in Line for Reversal of Pay and Pension Cuts. *The Irish Independent,* August 09. http://www.independent.ie/irish-news/politics/public-sector-staff-in-line-for-reversal-of-pay-and-pension-cuts-30494594.html

Soederberg, S. 2002. On the Contradictions of the New International Financial Architecture: Another Procrustean Be for Emerging Markets? *Third World Quarterly* 23 (4): 607–620.

Soros, G. 2014. *Tragedy of the European Union: Disintegration or Revival?* New York: Public Affairs.

The Economist. 2015. Greek Pensions: Why They Are a Flashpoint, June 18. http://www.economist.com/blogs/freeexchange/2015/06/greek-pensions

Traynor, I., and J. Henley. 2015. Greece and Lenders Agree New Bailout Deal, Finance Minister Says. *The Guardian*, August 11. http://www.theguardian.com/world/2015/aug/11/greece-and-lenders-agree-new-bailout-deal-says-finance-ministry-official

Traynor, I., and J. Rankin. 2015. Greek Debt Crisis: Tsipras Resists Key Bailout Measures After 15 Hours of Talks. *The Guardian,* July 13. http://www.theguardian.com/world/2015/jul/13/greek-debt-crisis-tsipras-resists-key-bailout-measures-after-15-hours-of-talks

TSCG. 2012. *Treaty on Stability, Coordination and Governance in the Economic and Monetary Union.* http://www.consilium.europa.eu/en/workarea/downloadAsset.aspx?id=27066

Vestergaard, J. 2009. *Discipline in the Global Economy?: International Finance and the End of Liberalism New Political Economy*. New York: Routledge.

Viñals, J., and P. Brook. 2009. *The Financial Sector Assessment Program After Ten Years: Experience and Reforms for the Next Decade*. Washington, DC: IMF.

7

Conclusion: Resisting Neo-Liberalism

This book has examined the key reforms that have occurred in the aftermath of the dual crisis through a Foucauldian lens. In so doing, it argued that the rise of resilience thinking and its sedimentation as a dominant discourse has much to do with the fact that it resonates strongly with the principles underlying neo-liberalism. It was argued that the regulatory reforms at the global level put in place after 2008 continued to treat finance in a biopolitical manner. Moreover, the book contended that the lack of fundamental reform has led to ever-greater reliance on surveillance, pre-emption and ensuring the resilience of the financial system should another crisis occur. In examining the European crisis that erupted in 2009, the book concentrated on the discipline and surveillance mechanisms that have emerged over time centred on the Stability and Growth Pact (SGP). In so doing, it was argued that the Economic Partnership Programmes and Economic Adjustment Programmes mirror the structural adjustment policies that the IMF and World Bank promote across the industrially developing world.

One of the underlying themes of the book has been that these reforms and emergent discourses represent both a degree of continuity and change. The global financial regulatory reforms have significantly

J. G. Glenn, *Foucault and Post-Financial Crises*, International Political Economy Series, https://doi.org/10.1007/978-3-319-77188-5_7

strengthened the financial regulatory mechanisms, but the changes are one of degree rather than kind. The solution has been to establish a stricter risk framework for financial activity in the hope that these more restrictive parameters create a stable homeostatic system. In addition, the reforms that have followed have led to greater emphasis on surveillance, pre-emption and resilience. However, these changes do not simply reflect attempts to deal with the uncertainty of such events, but also reflect the lack of political will to engage in radical reform of the financial system. In the contemporary phase of capitalism, states are caught between the Scylla of ensuring economic growth partly driven by financialization (through its maintenance of consumption through relatively cheap credit provision) and the Charybdis of systemic vulnerability associated with such activities.[1] This, in large part, explains why fundamental structural reforms that fully address the current imbalances and levels of instability within the global economy have not been introduced.[2] Since the crisis, there have been clear examples of private actors using their financial clout to lobby governments and/or using their functional power (i.e. the power that derives from them providing a critical function for smooth operation of the financial system) to influence various financial reforms.

Reflexive governance has led to efforts to establish a stricter regulatory framework in which these financial entities operate and to endow both the state and international institutions with far greater surveillance capabilities than have hitherto existed. Moreover, the central objective of these increased capabilities is to try to ensure that any similar potential crisis can be nipped in the bud before it leads to another system-wide collapse. As such, we have witnessed not only the strengthening of the various risk mechanisms associated with financial governance, but also the extension of the rationality of risk into the realm of pre-emption to deal with the uncertainty that crises confront us with.

Further restricting the risk parameters in which these financial institutions operate may reduce the probability of another financial crisis, but it does not eliminate the possibility. In response to this extant possibility, there has been an intensification of surveillance and pre-emptive activities as well as improving the resilience of the financial system should a full-scale crisis erupt. The aim is to search 'over the horizon' for activities that may potentially produce systemic risk and to take remedial action, such as, recalibrating risk parameters, increasing capital adequacy and monitoring innovatory financial instruments. One could see the positive effects of such monitoring and coordinated action with regard to Central Bank intervention to ensure dollar liquidity in September 2011 to counter the negative impact of the Euro crisis (Aitken, 15 September 2007).

The regulatory and pre-emptive aspects of reform have the potential to be mutually reinforcing. By establishing a set of bodies that constantly look out for activities that may potentially produce systemic risk, the reforms provide an opportunity for introducing remedial action before they induce a crisis, such as, recalibrating risk parameters, increasing capital adequacy or monitoring innovatory financial instruments. Although the monitoring of systemic threats, nationally, regionally and internationally is to be welcomed, these various committees have not sufficiently addressed the negative role they may themselves play during a period of financial instability. When to actually intervene will be far harder to calculate than policy makers have thus far acknowledged.

Additionally, the reliance on tighter risk parameters may increase the levels of correlation risk throughout the system because it still relies on assessing risk-weighted assets to capital ratios. The herd-like behaviour that occurs during crises may be amplified as each individual institution reassesses its risk exposure upwards with an ensuing credit freeze similar to that experienced in 2007/2008. As Melinda Cooper points out the paradox of pre-emptive policies is that 'catastrophe risk places us in the uncomfortable position of having to take drastic and immediate action in the face of an inescapably elusive, uncertain threat, decisions which may in turn generate their own incalculable dangers' (2006, p. 119). Therefore, although this surveillance combined with pre-emptive policies is designed to complement the regulatory mechanism, it also introduces certain contradictory tendencies into this form of financial governance, the full consequences of which are yet to be seen.

With regard to strengthening the resilience of the financial system, not only have the nodal points been strengthened through increasing their absorptive capacity but also functional differentiation has been re-introduced. As a result, there have been some attempts to increase modular differentiation within the system by both the US and Europe reinstating the distinction between commercial (UK retail) and investment banking thus creating an essential firewall between the two sectors reducing the possibility of contagion.

Such reforms are to be broadly welcomed. However, the frequent stress testing of banks to ensure that each key nodal point within the system can withstand a financial crisis carries with it the possibility of inducing a certain degree of instability thus supporting Beck's argument that new threats pertain to the risk-reducing practices and technologies created in response to crises. One only needs to examine market reactions to the Federal Reserve's stress tests in 2009 and 2014 to see this paradox at work. In a highly volatile environment in the aftermath of the financial crisis, the 2009 stress test had the effect of calming the financial market. Yet, in March 2014, it had precisely the opposite effect. With a greater emphasis on qualitative factors with regard to banks' ability to evaluate their own risks and with Citigroup and the American operations of HSBC, RBS Citizens and Santander having their plans rejected, shares plunged and volatility ensued (The Economist, 29 March 2014, p. 75). It may be for this reason that in an emergency, the recently created ESRB 'will issue a confidential warning to the European Council', rather than make its analysis public (CMS, March 2012).

Finally, with regard to surveillance, pre-emption and improving the resilience of the financial system, each major crisis tends to emerge from a relatively unique concatenation of events. Using the past as an indicator of future crises can only be applied in the abstract, as such, attempts at establishing a macro-prudential regulatory framework with the objective of calculating and controlling systemic risk will always be prone to miscalculation and misjudgements and are unlikely to prevent another crisis occurring in the long run. There is thus a danger that the new regulation will tend to be 'backward-looking to the dirty deeds done…this means the reforms fall prey to the generals' curse of fighting the last war, that is, training their soldiers with scenarios from the last war instead of possible future scenarios of the next' (Braithwaite 2008, p. 42).

In relation to the European debt crisis, the SGP and associated economic partnership and economic adjustment programmes represent a significant deepening of economic disciplinary and surveillance mechanisms. We have therefore experienced a significant shift away from the

European Union's open method of coordination model with regard to further economic integration. This indirect subjectification process was seen as a key instrument in the socialization of national elites, attempting to inculcate neo-liberal norms, values and beliefs. As such, the OMC seeks to 'operate on the conduct of the governed' but 'seeks a direction of conduct rather than a violent or gross form of corporeal domination' because it 'assumes a "free subject"…one whose subjection is consistent with forms of choice' (Dean 1994, p. 178).

However, clearly the OMC did not lead to the requisite degree of cooperation between states and the degree of compliance necessary to ensure a reasonable level of fiscal convergence. The burgeoning debt levels of the sovereign periphery of Europe after the 2008 financial crisis and the need for bail-outs by the European Union and IMF led to a major shift away from the consensual subjectification process of the OMC towards the imposition of a regime of surveillance and discipline centred on the reform of the SGP. These disciplinary mechanisms are most clearly seen in the highly intrusive procedures for those countries requiring bail-outs in which sovereigns are subjected to macro-economic adjustment policies and lending is dependent on compliance with the conditionalities that attend such reforms. But it is also readily apparent in the imposition of fiscal discipline through the SGP, the heightened surveillance associated with its post-crisis reform and the punishment meted out to those states that fail to comply. Conditionality is being used to further promote the marketization of the social sphere. Chapter 6 has highlighted how this has entailed state retrenchment, further commodification, labour market deregulation, privatization of national industries and so on. We are therefore witnessing not only the maintenance of neo-liberal conditionality in the Eurozone, but also its deepening.

This further deepening of neo-liberalism is not unrelated to the rise of resilience thinking which has rapidly gained in popularity since the financial crisis of 2008. As Chap. 4 argued, the emergence of resilience thinking has its own origins that pre-date the financial crisis, but its sedimentation has much to do with the fact that it resonates with the wider discourse of neo-liberalism. There may have been a brief moment just after the crisis where it seemed that the emergence of a 'global financial public sphere' was possible and those voicing resistance to neo-liberalism could reach a wider audience, but this was quickly closed down and instead policies favouring the status quo took hold (Germain 2010, p. 496).

Resilience thinking emerged as a dominant discourse concomitantly with this closure. Instead of an open public sphere developing with regard to the economic sphere, the dominance of social forces favouring neo-liberalism and laissez-faire finance was maintained. The structurally inscribed bias towards the dominant social/economic forces apparent within the state and various other institutions led to the filtering out of discourses emphasizing resistance to neo-liberalism and the need for change, favouring instead the sedimentation of resilience as a dominant discourse. The success of this discourse, in turn, has helped to maintain the balance of power that dominant economic classes hold within society in general and also the structurally inscribed selectivities that favour these forces within the state and other institutions. Indeed, this bias has favoured financiers to such a degree that many have commented that state policies towards finance have suffered from and continue to suffer from, regulatory capture by this class fraction (Underhill et al. 2010; Pagliari, June 2012; Porter 2005; Porter and Ronit 2006).

As a result, instead of fundamental reform it is striking how little has changed since the financial crises. Indeed, the innovatory financial instruments that were blamed for the crisis, such as, CDOs are increasing in popularity once again. We are still overly reliant on consumer credit that compensates for poor wage growth, we have even more highly indebted states than ever before, major trade imbalances continue, asset bubble in housing and shares have returned and so on. Rather than neo-liberalism being challenged, we are witnessing further squeezes on wages, reductions in pensions and social security, cuts to health and education and so on, alongside the marketization of state-provision.

In the shadow of Lehman Brothers' collapse, Beck warned against attempting to establish the impossible—'the perfected surveillance of the administrated world' (Beck 12 November 2008, p. 10). Yet, in part to compensate for the lack of reform in the financial sphere, we have seen that one of the main solutions adopted to prevent a future financial crisis is ever-greater surveillance and pre-emptive policies. At the time, Beck argued that the realization after the financial crisis that the threats confronting us can be 'averted by political action' could lead to 'the fundamental principles of modernity, including the free market principle and the nation-state order itself' becoming 'subject to change, the existence of alternatives, and contingency' (Beck 12 November 2008, p. 4). We should thus focus our attention on the extent to which, 'the threat and shock of world risk society open(s) up the horizon to a historic alternative of political action' (Beck 12 November 2008, p. 8). Yet, as this book has demonstrated, the reforms have not altered the fundamental practices of the financial sector and there seems little chance that radical alternatives will be adopted (Beck 12 November 2008, p. 10). It is thus unlikely that major change is on the horizon. Instead, the rise of the pre-emptive state in the financial sphere heralds just the type of reforms that Beck warns against—an attempt at remedying a systemic weakness through technical surveillance and control.

The Importance of Resistance

Chapter 4 argued that resilience thinking should be seen as part of a wider practice of neo-liberal enframing, one which typically involves a process of responsibilization. In the particular case of catastrophes, the emphasis is on the post hoc adaptability of individuals/communities and the various capacities they possess to enable them to bounce back from such shocks. Several issues arise with regard to the economy from such enframing. First, there is an implicit levelling of responsibility, where individuals and communities are expected to mine their own resources and capacities in order to survive such shocks. Resilience thinking has little to say with regard to social structures/agency concerning positions of power and the benefits that accrue from such positions as well as responsibility for the policies that greatly exacerbate the contradictions inherent within the capitalist system. In practice, this is clearly seen in the current austerity policies implemented across Europe. Those least responsible for the crisis have felt the greatest economic deprivation. The aforementioned 'naturalistic fallacy' with regard to the economic order also promotes such a perspective. By viewing finance as something akin to an organic homeostatic system, a social construction permeated by power relations and agents who have an interest in maintaining the economic order is rendered agentless and self-perpetuating.

Rather than viewing the social world as both infused with different actors/agents that are internally related (and, as a result, embedded in a network of power relations) as well as actors that are in a position of exteriority to one another, Post-modern resilience thinking argues that the world of becoming 'is an ontologically flat world without the traditional hierarchies of existence and a more shared conception of agency' (Chandler 2014, p. 196). Second, with regard to the wider literature, resilience thinking tends to be reactive in nature. Rather than reform orientated, the emphasis is upon survival and the capacities required to do so. Equally, treating finance as analogous to natural systems and attempting to re-instate a homeostatic system is an inherently conservative endeavour—one which restores the previous order, albeit with stricter risk parameters and pre-emptive policies that attempt to shore up such homeostasis. Finally, this book has argued that the continuation of neoliberal policies, such as austerity and increased competition will greatly exacerbate the contradictions of capitalism (greater reliance on credit and personal debt increasing the risk of a crash, further declines in real wages and the further casualization of employment) and it is therefore likely that another crisis will emerge within the near future.

This conclusion therefore argues that a more fruitful avenue is to examine the current period in terms of power and resistance, rather than resilience (although one must be resilient in order to survive crises and resist). For Foucault, although there is a multitude of multifaceted relations of power and resistance, he argues that we can identify three main types of struggles—'either against forms of domination (ethnic, social, and religious); against forms of exploitation which separate individuals from what they produce; or against that which ties the individual to himself and submits him to others in this way (struggles against subjection, against forms of subjectivity and submission)' (Foucault 1982, p. 781).

Foucault provides a useful counter to resilience thinking, because of his emphasis on the relationality of power, on the 'manifold relationships of force that take shape and come into play' between the multitude of actors within society (Foucault 1978, p. 94). Thus, when he speaks of the 'structures or the mechanisms of power, it is only insofar as we suppose that certain persons exercise power over others. The term "power" designates relationships between partners' (Foucault 1982, p. 786). In contradistinction to resilience thinking that places actors in a position of exteriority to one another, Foucault explicitly states that 'relations of power are not in a position of exteriority with respect to other types of relationships (economic processes, knowledge relationships, sexual relations), but are immanent in the latter; they are the immediate effects of the divisions, inequalities, and disequilibriums which occur in the latter, and conversely they are the internal conditions of these differentiations' (Foucault 1978, p. 94).

The advantage of using a Foucauldian perspective is that it emphasizes the way in which society is infused with a multiplicity of power relations and the entwining of resistance within these relations—'It seems to me that power must be understood in the first instance as the multiplicity of force relations immanent in the sphere in which they operate and which constitute their own organization; as the process which, through ceaseless struggles and confrontations, transforms, strengthens, or reverses them; as the support which these force relations find in one another, thus forming a chain or a system, or on the contrary, the disjunctions and contradictions which isolate them from one another' (Foucault 1978, pp. 92–3). Thus, from a Foucauldian perspective, power and resistance are inextricably intertwined so that 'Where there is power, there is resistance, and yet, or rather consequently, this resistance is never in a position of exteriority in relation to power' (Foucault 1978, p. 95). For Foucault, these relations are best understood as agonistic in nature, which are 'at the same time reciprocal incitation and struggle, less of a face-to-face confrontation which paralyzes both sides than a permanent provocation' (Foucault 1982, 791).

Foucault is also clear that such resistance can go beyond the individual/group level, extending out to the wider body politic, so that 'knots, or focuses of resistance are spread over time and space at varying densities, at times mobilizing groups or individuals in a definitive way, inflaming certain points of the body, certain moments in life, certain types of behavior. Are there no great radical ruptures, massive binary divisions, then? Occasionally, yes' (Foucault 1978, p. 96). Indeed, with echoes of the cosmopolitan nature of struggles in Beck's work (although not the state aspect), Foucault argues that such resistance can entail '"transversal" struggles; that is, they are not limited to one country' (Foucault 1982, p. 780).

Just as there is a plurality of power relations, then, there is a 'plurality of resistances, each of them a special case: resistances that are possible, necessary, improbable; others that are spontaneous, savage, solitary, concerted, rampant, or violent; still others that are quick to compromise, interested, or sacrificial; by definition, they can only exist in the strategic field of power relations' (Foucault 1978, p. 96). Indeed, one can append to Foucault's original idea of capillary power, that 'point where power reaches into the very grain of individuals' the idea of capillary resistance that always accompanies power relations and is as varied in terms of its character, duration and sites (Gordon 1980, p. 39). For Foucault, power emanates from the 'the system of differentiations which permits one to act upon the actions of others: differentiations determined by the law or by traditions of status and privilege; economic differences in the appropriation of riches and goods; shifts in the process of production; linguistic or cultural differences; differences in know-how and competence; and so forth' (Foucault 1982, p. 792). Foucault's view of society is thus one in which a network of power issues forth from this multitude of social structures or 'mechanisms of power'—but equally so does resistance (Heller 1996, p. 85).

For the post-financial crisis period, we can see that the regulatory capture associated with the reforms of the financial system and the tactics pursed by individual financial institutions have resulted in a general strategy of limiting reforms. Although each individual/firm's tactic exhibits a degree of variance, they have aligned themselves with this overall strategy. Even though this strategy may result in another financial crisis in the near future, the individual tactics of financiers pursuing their own self-interest by minimizing the reforms appears perfectly rational within their habitus. It is also important to note that the condensation of class forces within the highly industrialized countries is such that the financial class fraction continues to have greater influence than the industrial class fraction, thus ensuring the success of a limited reform strategy. For sure, a degree of path dependency also influenced this state of affairs with state mandarins and politicians favouring incremental solutions that did not challenge the overall framework that they were familiar with. But the policy outcomes were clearly influenced by the fact that most highly industrialized states had become reliant upon revenue generated by the financial sector. Moreover, the use of so-called privatized Keynesianism has clearly become a key economic instrument of the state, boosting the economy in downturns through the provision of cheap credit.

However, we can also see the resistance to both the activities of financiers by the occupy movement and the resistance to various austerity policies has taken a variety of forms with different aims and objectives. This is the counter reaction to the conservatism of neo-liberal govermentality that has continued to enframe finance in a naturalistic manner (with its extension and deepening of risk rationalities) and its deepening of neo-liberal austerity thus further exacerbating the contradictions of capitalism. As Ernesto Laclau and Chantal Mouffe argue, 'All struggles, whether those of workers or other political subjects, left to themselves, have a partial character, and can be articulated to very different discourses. It is this articulation which gives them their character, not the place from which they come' (2001, p. 178). From such articulation, we can see potential transversal struggles and solidarities emerging from the financial crisis. These struggles are likely to combine recognition and redistribution, producing a wider more generalized struggle and strategy against 'sexism, racism, sexual discrimination, and in the defence of the environment'...'articulated with those of the workers in a new left-wing hegemonic project' (Laclau and Mouffe 2001, p. 168). Although there is some evidence of such a counter-hegemonic movement (e.g. Greek resistance to austerity and the occupy movements), we are as yet unable to divine the overall strategy that will emerge because this will depend on how such struggles become articulated with other resistances. We may have to experience other economic crises before a cohesive and effective opposition evolves and with it an alternative to neo-liberalism, but evolve it will.

Notes

1. For example, one of the finance industries lobbying bodies, the Institute of International Finance estimated that the Basel 3 standards could reduce GDP by 3% for the US, the Eurozone and Japan (*The Economist* 2–9 July 2010a, pp. 71–3).
2. Although there have been suggestions concerning the creation of a modern-day Bancor through the use of SDRs rather than the dollar, this has not, as yet, been taken up. Neither has one of the most important policy proposals of John Maynard Keynes—that of charging fines on excessive trade surpluses which would help redress the current trade imbalances that are in many ways at the heart of current instabilities (*The Economist* 6–12 November 2010b, pp. 85–7).

References

Aitken, R. 2007. *Performing Capital: Toward a Cultural Economy of Popular and Global Finance*. Basingstoke: Palgrave Macmillan.

Beck, U. 2008. Risk Society's "Cosmopolitan Moment". *Harvard Lecture*, November 12. http://www.labjor.unicamp.br/comciencia/files/risco/AR-UlrichBeck-Harvard.pdf

Braithwaite, J. 2008. *Regulatory Capitalism: How It Works, Ideas for Making It Work Better*. Cheltenham: Edward Elgar.

Chandler, D. 2014. *Resilience: The Governance of Complexity*. London: Routledge.

CMS. 2012. The New European System of Financial Supervision – Institutional Reform Within the EU, March. http://www.law-now.com/cmck/pdfs/nonsecured/ neweuropean reform.pdf

Cooper, M. 2006. Pre-empting Emergence: The Biological Turn in the War on Terror. *Theory, Culture & Society* 23 (4): 113–135.

Dean, M. 1994. *Critical and Effective Histories: Foucault's Methods and Historical Sociology*. London: Routledge.

Foucault, M. 1978. *History of Sexuality Vol. 1: Translated by Robert Hurley*. New York: Pantheon Books.

———. 1982. The Subject and Power. *Critical Inquiry* 8 (4): 777–795.

Germain, R. 2010. Financial Governance and Deliberative Democracy. *Review of International Studies* 36 (2): 493–509.

Gordon, C. 1980. *Power/Knowledge: Selected Interviews and Other Writings 1972–1977*. New York: Pantheon Books.

Heller, K. 1996. Power, Subjectification and Resistance in Foucault. *Substance* 25 (1): 78–110.

Laclau, E., and C. Mouffe. 2001. *Hegemony and Socialist Strategy Towards a Radical Democratic Politics*. 2nd ed. London: Verso.

Pagliari, S., ed. 2012. *The Making of Good Financial Regulation Towards a Policy Response to Regulatory Capture*, June. http://www.icffr.org/assets/pdfs/June-2012/ICFR-Regulatory-Capture-Book-25-June---The-Making-.aspx

Porter, T. 2005. *Globalization and Finance*. Cambridge: Polity Press.

Porter, T., and K. Ronit. 2006. Self-Regulation as Policy Process: The Multiple and Criss-Crossing Stages of Private Rule-Making. *Policy Sciences* 39: 41–72.

The Economist. 2010a. Not All on the Same Page: America's Congress Nears Agreement on a Financial-Reform Bill, But the Final Shape of the New Regime Is Unclear. The International Picture Is Murkier Still, July 2–9, pp. 71–73.

———. 2010b. Beyond Bretton Woods 2, November 6–12, pp. 85–7.

———. 2014. American Banks: A Harsh Light – A Handful of Banks Are Caught Short by the Fed's Annual Stress Test, 29 March–4 April, p. 77.

Underhill, G., J. Blom, and D. Mügge. 2010. *Global Financial Integration Thirty Years On: From Reform to Crisis*. New York: Cambridge University Press.

Index[1]

[1] Note: Page numbers followed by 'n' refer to notes.

J. G. Glenn, *Foucault and Post-Financial Crises*, International Political Economy Series, https://doi.org/10.1007/978-3-319-77188-5

www.ingramcontent.com/pod-product-compliance
Ingram Content Group UK Ltd.
Pitfield, Milton Keynes, MK11 3LW, UK
UKHW020956050925
462611UK00012B/1010
* 9 7 8 3 0 3 0 0 8 3 9 3 9 *